# Divine Hunger

Peter C. Emberley

# Divine Hunger

Canadians on Spiritual Walkabout

HarperCollins*PublishersLtd*

Canadian Cataloguing in Publication Data

Emberley, Peter C. (Peter Christopher), 1956–
Divine hunger : Canadians on spiritual walkabout

Includes index.
ISBN 0-00-200094-6

1. Baby boom generation – Religious life.
2. Baby boom generation – Conduct of life.
  I. Title

BL624.E466 2002   291.4'4'0844
C2001-902524-6

HC 9 8 7 6 5 4 3 2 1
Set in Minion

For what shall it profit a man, if he shall gain the whole world, and lose his own soul?

Gospel of St. Matthew

It was not man who implanted in himself the taste for the infinite and love of what is immortal. These sublime instincts are not the offspring of some caprice of the will; their foundations are embedded in nature; they exist despite a man's efforts. Man may hinder and distort them, but he cannot destroy them.

Alexis de Tocqueville, Democracy in America

The human story is too grand and awful to be told without reverence for the mystery and the majesty that transcend all human knowledge. Only humble men who recognize this mystery and majesty are able to face both the beauty and terror of life without exulting over its beauty or becoming crushed by its terror.

Reinhold Niebuhr, Faith and Politics

# Contents

Faith and Modernity · 1

Believers at the Crossroad

Traditionalism I · 24

Back to Basics

Traditionalism II · 66

Latins and Greeks

Tweaking Modernity · 99

Widening the Present Moment

Fusion Faith · 148

Renegotiating Modernity

Turning East · 203

The Rejection of the Modern West

Conclusion · 246

Suspending Disbelief and the Growth of Sensibility

Acknowledgements · 267
Endnotes · 269
Permissions · 287
Index · 289

# Faith and Modernity

Believers at the Crossroad

D aylight is barely breaking through the grey-orange haze floating above the Ganges River in Haridwar. At the riverbank stands a proud Rajput warrior from the neighbouring state of Rajasthan, naked, daubed in vermilion paste, his lips around the mouth of the vulva-shaped conch shell. The haunting and primordial sound – reminiscent, it is said, of the primal sound of the cosmos prior to its differentiation into the manifold of daily reality – undulates across the Ganges, hitting successive bathing *ghats* (steps descending into the Ganges), like the lapping waves of the river itself. Small families, performing their morning *pujas* (devotional worship), raise their heads at the sound. It is a holy moment, a moment out of time. The warrior sets down the conch shell and enters the river, fully immersing himself four times. Back on the *ghat* and glistening wet in the now streaming sun, he takes out of his sack a banana leaf shaped into a floatable boat, places two marigolds in it with a ribbon of incense paste between them, ignites the paste, and lets the boat float off down the Ganges. He ends his ablution by turning and bowing in the four cardinal directions, then strews the remaining marigold petals over the water, picks up his discarded *dhoti*, and slips back into the throng of early morning worshippers.

All along the river, at similar *ghats*, the ritual of devotion to the Ganges is repeated. Some pilgrims are sick and suffering, others need consolation, others celebrate the good fortune of health and fertile fields, farm animals, and families. They do not turn to doctors, agricultural engineers, and social workers, but to the river – to the Mother Ganges. On her banks, they sing *bhajans* (devotional hymns), clinking brass cymbals, evoking and engaging the power of the Ganges. The river is alive and redemptive, a divine presence, God. In her, all the cosmic levels of reality intersect. This god, unlike our own, is not impassively transcendent and distanced from daily life, but evident in the earth and water in the pilgrims' hands. Physical nature, the contingencies of the day – singing, praying, washing, even spitting and urinating, at the river edge – all are part of one process of sacred harmony, where the smallest detail of everyday activity is saturated with holiness. When an unassuming family from a village in Kerala – who have endured the hard travel of thousands of miles – releases its banana leaf oil lamp in offering to the river, the Ganges is simultaneously physical and spiritual reality, for she will take the offering, like a Jacob's ladder, directly to the gods. She is the connection, or the threshold, between two worlds, and floods this world with divine reality. As son blesses mother, thus reconsecrating the simple piety of family relations, so the whole family is caught up in a living theology of devotion. The *puja* (worship) ends when the son's hair – the most evident sign of vital, regenerating life in every body – is shaved off and offered to Ma Ganga, signalling the perfect consonance of existence and eternity. For a few hours, this family has lived effortlessly and has experienced the truly *real* at the centre of the world.

The twelve million pilgrims crouching at the riverside are here to re-experience a great battle between the gods and demons over a *kumbh* (pitcher) containing *amrit* (divine nectar). Once upon a time, the myth relates, a sage was visiting Lord Indra, the ruler of heaven and king of the gods. Slighted by Lord Indra's apparent indifference to a garland gift, the sage pronounced a curse on him, depleting him of his divine powers and virtues. Exploiting Lord Indra's weakness, Bali, the king of demons, seized the gods' riches. Lord Vishnu intervened, advising the gods to restore their powers by finding the divine nectar lying in the primordial ocean. The gods enlisted the help of the demons to churn the ocean, using the mountain Mandrachal as the staff of the churn, and a serpent as the rope to turn it. As the ocean foamed, deadly poisons emerged which Lord Shiva had to imbibe before the three worlds could be destroyed. Then, many riches emerged – including a magical moon, Lakshmi (the auspicious goddess of fortune), a wish-giving cow, and a priceless jewel. At last a divine healer emerged holding a pitcher of nectar, the drink that confers immortality. The demons seized the pitcher, but Lord Vishnu retrieved it and handed it over to Jayant, the son of Indra, who used Garuda, Lord Vishnu's winged mount, to flee the pursuing demons. On four occasions, Jayant was forced to repel the demons, and each time, a drop of nectar fell from the *kumbh* to the earth. Jayant's travels took twelve days and, since each day of divine travel is one human year, the battle, the gods' final victory over the demons, and the recovery of the power of immortality, are commemorated every twelve years at the four sites where the immortal nectar fell. Today's pilgrims – some of whom have travelled for more than a year to perform the ceremony of dipping into the Ganges to achieve permanent release from the cycle of death and rebirth – have come to this *mela* (fair) to stand in the Brahma Kund pool, the very spot where the nectar fell, adjacent to the temple where Lord Vishnu's footprints are said to be imprinted, the Kar-ki-Pauri. They will enact mythic time, not merely as historical recollection, but as a process in which for a brief duration they are in *illus tempore*, the original time. The present – with all its worries and disappointments – temporarily slips away.

Not all of this harmony is peaceful and joyous. The holy, as the eminent religious scholar Rudolf Otto observed, is an encounter with the *realissimus* – the *really* real – yet it is, simultaneously, a brush with fearsome power, *mysterium tremendum et fascinans*. While satisfying the human desire to shake off our determined, dependent, and differentiated condition and live effortlessly, the encounter with the sacred Ganges is also ambivalent, with even a hint of the terrifying. The divine manifests itself as a *kratophany* – a manifestation of power – whose potency cuts two ways. The *kratophany* reminds humans of the permanent and inextinguishable boundaries between life and death, human and divine, ignorance and knowledge – while at the same time promising regeneration of life and fleeting abode with the gods.

The Kumbh Mela, the largest pilgrimage in the world, is a concentrated image of the Hindu world of omens and amulets, propritiating songs warding off death and the evil eye, and frightful ecstatic dances inviting the gods to possess the body. Danger and purity cohabit the sacred space, where both suffering and joy are indices of proximity to the sacred, and where a continuous relation of exchange and reciprocity – in birth and death, sexuality and isolation – marks living together with the deities. The sacred is terrible and, to endure its presence, it must be set aside through ritual. All along the river, Hindu families perform their simple *pujas*, while on the streets of Haridwar, ecstatic dancing provokes the divine to appear, like stirring ashes to restart a fire. And this fateful marriage of contraries will be perpetuated when pilgrims go home with Ganga water, carried in brass pots in the shape of India's sacred cow, to fertilize their fields, to sprinkle over their expectant wives, to anoint a sick relative – extending the organic presence of the divine and cosmic fertility in every minutia of daily life, and accepting the complex contradictions of human existence.

We have come to watch this last Kumbh Mela of the millennium, standing outside the circle of immediate contact with gods and goddesses, of awe and fear, yet trying to feel the sanctity of the place. Many of us – we are Germans, Norwegians, Canadians, Americans, Brits – are well-educated, skeptical, occasionally morally outraged, and at the same time enchanted. Here is a moment of eternity snatched out of the relentless, merciless march of time – or at least time as Western history conceives it.

I ask my fellow observers: What are you reading while in Haridwar? They answer: Paulo Coehlo's *Alchemist.* Bruce Chatwin's *Songlines.* Salman Rushdie's *Midnight's Children.* Ben Okri's *Astonishing the Gods.* Naguib Mahfouz's *Palace Walk.* Books of nostalgia, sentimentality, and enchantment. Later that morning, sitting up above one of the bathing *ghats* and sipping *chai* (spiced tea) in clay cups, we speak together of wholeness and roots. There is a sadness and melancholy to our discussions, despite the sentiment we are each expressing that here, on the riverbanks, we are in touch with the living waters of reality and tradition. But, as the scholar Edward Shils once poignantly commented, "An experienced sentiment is not a tradition. It is a state of sensation at a given moment."[1] As much as we are touched by India's magic, by the supreme mystery of the eternal descending into time (the sacred coinciding with the profane), and as beautiful as the brief interlude from the fever of our material and secular lives is, observing, as Mircea Eliade phrases it, "the turning of simple existence into living drama,"[2] we are far removed from this traditional world by hundreds, if not thousands, of years.

And yet, dim recollections of spiritual wholeness and life as a sacred drama intrude in our observations. All of us have experienced water's attraction – its invitation to temporarily lose our determined and differentiated state by being dissolved into its formlessness, as the prelude to being regenerated. As we scoop up some of the ash, sandalwood paste, *kum-kum* powder, and camphor lying in great vats on shop floors, and let it lightly sift through our fingers, we can still sense a world of substances signifying purity and transcendence. In the hot afternoon, roaming through the *akhara* camps – the tent cities temporarily constructed by the thirteen militant spiritual brotherhoods of *nagas*, India's famed naked holy men – we find the *sannyasin*, or renunciants. Theirs are extreme forms of denial: the *saddhu* (sage) who has held his left arm in the air for twenty-five years, his joints now calcified and bonded, his fingers elongated to talons; the young renunciant who for twelve years has forsworn sitting, and is draped over a cushion suspended from the roof of his *akhara*'s tent; the two *nagas* twisting and wrapping their penises around canes, while another burly *naga* clambers up onto the cane so as to exert even greater weight on the rolled-out organ. We recall the stylites, the Encratites, the Cappadocians – the flagellants and hermits of early Christianity – who exhibited such impossible, if enviably supreme, holy lives. Or, as we look upon the tridents, fire tongs, lingams, and water pots – the emblems of Lord Shiva – surrounding the heads of the *akharas*, or the mala beads worn around the *nagas*' necks, we remember our own past of icons and venerated artifacts. And, as we navigate the congested lanes of Haridwar, amid a flowing mass of humanity, linking arms with peasants from tribal villages, we recall a humanity prior to our lives as disconnected, autonomous individuals.

But, however rich and suggestive our own personal experiences, or whatever stalling mechanisms percolate out of our collective unconscious to temporarily arrest the forward march of time, our world – that network of ideas, institutions, and common sense constituting the everyday – is demythologized. The autochthonous spirits of our land, the gods of the Rockies, the spirits of our redwood forests, the moral legacy of those who laboured on our land (*If ye break faith with us who die, we shall not sleep …*) – all these icons of the divine may speak, if they speak at all, only through the prism of modern consciousness.

It is nearly impossible to be a modern human being, and not to have shared in what the philosopher Hannah Arendt once remarked is the hallmark of modernity – the jettisoning of the trinity of tradition, authority, and religion. To be modern is to accept that self-determination, the liberty of private conscience, and personal experience will nearly always trump older ways of knowing and being. To be modern is to believe that humans are essentially rational and autonomous, and have the power to choose their own purposes and destiny. It is to believe in the power of reason and analysis to demystify the unknown. It is to accept the loss of community in favour of individual liberty, or the idea that community exists only to promote the free and rational agent. Being modern means recognizing that modern science and modern rationalism – this-worldly causation as mechanical necessity – have revealed to us that there are no "first" or "final" causes endowing reality with ultimate purposes. There is no knowable dimension of reality beyond the world observed in ordinary sense-perception or revealed by scientific instruments under the controlled conditions of the scientific laboratory. To recall Karl Popper's vivid simile, the modern way of knowing is like a searchlight turned into the dark sky, illuminating only what appears in its beam, and leaving unknown what is beyond it.[3] That same science has burst the bubble of the presumption that humans have a higher origin and destiny. And it has brought us to the recognition that the sacred is no longer a dimension of our consciousness, but an abandoned stage in the history of human consciousness. Recognition of the innate goodness of individuals, and the potential for limitless human perfectibility, renders ideas of human sin and evil, or the need for divine consolation and intervention, unnecessary.

Traditionally, it was our awareness of suffering and affliction – our "creatureliness" – that made us cry out for a creator. But if our distress is social and political, not metaphysical, then it is a misapprehension to conclude that we need a superintending god. We need, instead, to direct our attention away from expectations of a messiah, and toward the source of our distress in relations between humans. Neither obedience nor hope of grace will fix the world. "The philosophers [and theologians] have only interpreted the world," wrote Karl Marx, affirming the modern project. "The point is to change it."

As moderns, we can no longer inhabit a world where mystery, cosmic purpose, and divine manifestations offer evidence of an invisible reality. Skepticism, not to say cynicism, has caused us to lose trust in symbols of transcendence and perfection. The German Protestant theologian and New Testament scholar Rudolf Bultmann stated it summarily: belief in the Resurrection was made impossible by the invention of the lightbulb.[4] Or, as the members of the Jesus Seminar write in their celebrated book *The Five Gospels*, "The Christ of creed and dogma can no longer command the assent of those who have seen the heavens through Galileo's telescope." Centuries of geology, astronomy, physics, and biology – driven by the free exercise of unassisted reason – make any literal belief in creationism, God-made man, the Virgin Birth of Jesus Christ and His physical resurrection – the paradigmatic events comprising the West's religious narrative – a scandal to reason. How could these happen in evident violation of the universal processes revealed by modern biology, physics, and chemistry? The laws of biological life and death, after all, cannot simply be rescinded. How can verification of the Christian facts conform in any conceivable way to the inductive method, or to the laboratory-controlled tests of falsifiability or repeatability? As modern beings, the theological explanation of the "facts" cannot be true for us. No events or persons can be special, as conduits to a different dimension of reality.

Yet, nearly everything else in Christianity – and the most cherished ideals of the secularized world views which were derived from it, and which still largely inform our present lives – follows from the truth of these facts: theologically, the covenant of God with man, the reality of human sin, and the promise of deliverance and salvation; politically and morally, the unconditional goodness and sanctity of simple existence, the dignity of the person, and the equality of all human beings. Disbelief must, of necessity, dislodge belief.

But … nearly all of us know colleagues, friends, and neighbours who quite suddenly are on spiritual walkabout. Whether they seek consolation, spiritual ecstasy, an exit strategy from everyday busyness, or hope, these individuals are seeking in charismatic and evangelical Christianity, Orthodox traditionalism, new religious movements, Eastern religions, and home-churches for truths which have thus far evaded them. And some of these truths have the potential to significantly rock many of the cardinal principles of modern life and consciousness.

•   •   •

"What we really need today is a spiritual version of acidophilus [a herbal purgative]," whispers Helen, a devotee of Salt Spring Island's Ashtanga Yoga Meditation Centre, confiding in me why she is enduring another round of yoga's complex contortions. "There's a lot that has to be scraped off our systems," she explains. "Look at the product

Greens+™. We're just trying to deluge our bodies and minds with more and more, and do we really need any of it?" Meanwhile, as if echoing her opinion, Babi Haridass, a yogi who practices continuous silence, has scribbled on his chalkboard:

> We have to find out what creates pain. It is first the ego, and then the memory. When the mind knows the unreality of all created things, reality starts appearing. When we identify with the body, senses, mind, and intellect as "I am," and the activities performed by them as "mine," we are unable to surrender to the divine within and so become our own enemy.

I learn during the next few days that Helen is a best-selling author and accomplished consultant, yet despite prosperity, influence, and all the conventional signs of success, she admits to being a very unhappy person, profoundly alienated from the world, and seeking. In Buddhism. Vedanta. New Age. Kabbalah. Angels.

The bells toll loud and long at St. Herman's of Alaska, the non-ethnic English-speaking Orthodox church in Edmonton, filled with converts and the curious. Soon, mournful but sublime plainchant fills the room, and the priests begin their circumambulation, from the iconostasis to the sanctuary, their silver thuribles emitting ribbons of incense sanctifying the sacred space, their bowing and prostrations redolent of the earliest Christian liturgy. The threnody is filled with anguish and atonement. The ninety-minute liturgy covers a lot of experiential ground – from sin and confession, to forgiveness, thanksgiving, and love – uniting tradition and pageantry and re-enacting the wonder of creation imbued with grace. "You are here," the Orthodox priest sermonizes, "not because we are your comfort zone, but to feel conscious holy fear before the mystery and majesty of the liturgy, the blast of divine light of the Resurrection." My host explains the attraction. At first, many are drawn by the bells and smells. But, later, the aesthetic pleasure yields to a more powerful recognition that, in the ancient traditions of Orthodoxy, the human search for roots acquires its deepest fulfillment. And, "After centuries of beating the magic out

of religion," Dave, a recent convert, adds, explaining the solemn veneration of icons, "many of us are just looking again for a little enchantment." And so he too seeks. The United Church's Community of
Concern. The Anglican Church's Prayerbook Society. Anglo-Catholi-
cism. Opus Dei and Tridentine Catholicism.

It is a sweltering June evening at the Corel Centre, the venue for Billy
Graham's Ottawa Mission. Ben Heppner's baritone voice rolls like a tide
through the Centre, "The mighty presence of God, worthy of praise, the
Lord of Lords," and a choir of three thousand singers sways in unison.
Around me are middle-aged women and men, eating tuna sandwiches,
popcorn, burgers, and drinking coffee, purposefully eschewing the
mock seriousness of church. "Religion has been messed up for the last
2,000 years," offers Jim, a professional seated next to me. "This is about
a personal relationship with God, not top-down authority. Billy is
simple, practical, down-to-earth, no bullshit. The appeal is there's no
danger, no sell-job." Nonetheless, below the Centre's rafters, festooned
with American and Canadian flags, is a cluster of vast video screens
scanning, like a great eye in the sky, the 27,000-strong audience. Beneath
this is a slick bank of computer terminals set up to facilitate the identification and subsequent tracking of "enquirers," those enticed to witness
to their faith in public. And on the floor below is a flurry of exact, nearly
regimented activity as "captains" and "counsellors" rehearse their
monitoring responsibilities once the altar call is issued.

As Billy Graham preaches – of the hell that men have made, of the
end times drawing near, of the unmerited salvation offered by Christ –
Jim intones "Amen," over and over, like most of the men around him.
Before disappearing into the dusk, he sums up: "I shopped around, I'm
still shopping around – the men's movement, tribal drumming,
Promise Keepers. But Billy's really got today's pulse. I'm glowing again
with new life, with all the rat-shit around."

In a farmhouse in Ontario, a candle burns at the centre of a makeshift altar draped with an embroidered tablecloth. Surrounding it are

crystals, gems, leather pouches, a feather, a knife, tiny ivory skulls. Each item has been placed carefully to evoke the four cardinal directions, each representing, in turn, the four elements and the four humours of the body. The assembled women sit in companionable silence, trying to expand their awareness by working with occult spirit guides – angels and fairies – in the hopes of achieving "synchronicity." The healer explains that during her own dark night of the soul, she realized that the human world was torn and afflicted, the result of patriarchal authority which for centuries had drastically constricted the range of human experience. Now, "We have to ground our energy in the earth, and restore primary, nurturing communities." And she too seeks. In Shiatsu and Reike. The human potential movement. Celtic spirituality. Goddess worship. Wicca. Pathfinders.

Four seekers, exploring distinct expressions of spiritual consolation and sanctification, but linked by one historical accident – the baby-boom generation. Where none of these baby boomers is seeking is in the mainstream. And they are not alone. For many of the baby-boom generation (8.1 million Canadian babies born between 1946 and 1964), "spirituality" is not happening in the churches, synagogues, mosques, or temples. Canada's premier chronicler of religious belief and affiliation, Reginald Bibby, offers incontrovertible data on the decline of weekly attendance and membership in the mainline faiths: in 1945, 60 per cent of Canadians claimed weekly attendance and 82 per cent professed membership; in 1990, only 23 per cent attended regularly and 29 per cent claimed to be members. Since only the Roman Catholic Church mandates weekly attendance, its statistics are particularly revealing. In the mid-1990s, Bibby reported, 40 per cent of Catholics were weekly attenders.[5] By 1998, a Statistics Canada study showed, Catholic Church attendance had dropped to 24 per cent. While Roman Catholic membership, if not attendance, has remained relatively constant, mainline Protestants have fared less well. In the 1970s, 18 per cent of Canadians were United and 12 per cent were Anglican; in 1995, only 12 per cent were United and 8 per cent were Anglican. Looking specifically at the baby boomers, the data shows that currently only 16 per cent are weekly attenders, and their membership is diffuse, at best.

The same Statistics Canada study also revealed that Canadians claiming no religious affiliation had climbed from 1 per cent in 1961, to 13 per cent in 1991, and to 14 per cent by 1996.[6] Church, the baby boomers find, gets in the way of worship.

Even these figures of 23 per cent (all ages) and 16 per cent (baby boomers) for attendance are ambiguous, at least from the perspective of traditional religion. A 1996–97 Angus Reid poll conducted by Andrew Grenville showed that fewer than 10 per cent of Canadians believe that doctrinal adherence defines a good Christian. As many as 75 per cent of Canadians consider their own beliefs more significant than official church teaching.[7]

On the one hand, these numbers are not surprising, since an appeal to private conscience, freedom of expression, creativity, and a snub to authority have become cardinal indices of what we are as a modern people (as Pope Pius XI once lamented, "Today we are all Protestants."[8]). On the other hand, these numbers are very revealing of our times. Traditionally, spiritual disciplines and spiritually formative experiences were underwritten by coherent metaphysical systems. While this is evidently the case for Roman Catholics – whose complex theology, comprehensively articulated by Thomas Aquinas, is intended to define the experience and meaning of faith down to an infinitesimal point – a world view no poorer or less coherent is propounded in Protestantism, Islam, Judaism, Hinduism, and Buddhism, even when these faith traditions appear to abjure systematic theology. Each subscribes, in its own way, to first principles and meaningfully derived inferences and conclusions, and – in times past – expected from its members adherence to these beliefs. Traditionally, none tolerated a perspective which holds that blessedness, sanctity, or holiness is self-determined or self-defined. So, when polls show that more than 90 per cent of Canadians believe it acceptable to pick and choose among the promulgated beliefs of their faiths, departing when convenient from the counsel of sacerdotal authority or the inner coherence of a faith tradition, even the figures of 23 per cent (all age groups) and 16 per cent (baby boomers) of Canadians who are weekly attenders have to be understood with many qualifications.

While many baby boomers who were so quick to divest themselves of church affiliation are poorly informed about their own religious traditions, particularly the diversity they harbour, and are often carriers of a culturally widespread hostility to traditional Christianity, their plaints and hostilities nonetheless are – to some degree – understandable. Many women have lost patience with a church which fails to recognize their full humanity and leaves them only a minor role in liturgy and pastoral work. Gays and lesbians find the intolerance of some churches toward their lives incompatible with religious sentiments of compassion and universality. Allegations and confirmations of many cases, over numerous years, of sexual abuse of children in the care of religious clergy have generated understandable suspicion of some religious practices and institutions. Most recently, many Canadians have accepted the judgment that great historical injustices were perpetrated by the churches when, decades ago, they took native children away from their homes and families, and placed them in residential schools. All these factors, and many more, both real and contrived, have contributed to a staggering erosion of confidence in institutionalized religion.

Still, it is evidently premature to herald the "death of God." At the same time as the exodus from church, synagogue, and temple is occurring, thousands of Canadians are embarking on complex spiritual searches. If only 9 per cent of Canadians are reporting increased interest in attendance at religious services, 22 per cent of Canadians report increased interest in spirituality. In 1995, Bibby reported, 80 per cent of Canadians said they believed in God; 74 per cent believed in miraculous healing; 74 per cent believed in near-death experiences; 72 per cent in the divinity of Jesus; 67 per cent in heaven; 61 per cent in angels; 56 per cent in psychic powers; 55 per cent in extrasensory perception; 49 per cent in hell; 49 per cent experienced precognition; 43 per cent experienced God; 43 per cent experienced spirit world contact; and 25 per cent communicated with the dead.[9] And, while the baby boomers are increasingly not attending church (or, if they are attending, they are doing so anonymously), 65 per cent of baby boomers, according to Bibby, say "spirituality" is important to them.

The manifest signs of the search are well known, and undue attention to them – while entertaining – risks the admonishment that one has been diverted by the sideshow. Nevertheless, no one can miss the fact that whereas a decade ago bookstores carried a single, meagre shelf of books on religion, today many of the major bookstores have row after row of books on spirituality, with such jaunty titles as *Angel Therapy: Healing Messages for Every Area of Your Life; The Power of Miracles;*

*Stories of God in the Everyday; The Essence of Wisdom: Words from the Masters to Illuminate the Spiritual Path; Honest to Jesus: Jesus for a New Millennium; Spiritual Simplicity: Simplify Your Life and Enrich Your Soul.* There is even *The Whole Heaven Catalog: A Resource Guide to Products, Services, Arts, Crafts and Festivals of Religious, Spiritual, and Cooperative Communities* for those baby boomers who adopted the 1960s *Whole Earth Catalog* as their Bible, and can now continue the quest onwards and upwards. Books like Thomas Moore's *Care of the Soul*, M. Scott Peck's *The Road Less Traveled*, and James Redfield's *The Celestine Prophecy* have even become international bestsellers. Each of Canada's major urban centres has monthly publications (like *Tone, Common Ground*, and *Shared Vision Magazine*) advertising a dizzying array of pilgrimages, meditations, yoga practices, spiritual labyrinths, and wellness retreats. New Age visionaries like Deepak Chopra and Starhawk are virtually household names. Madonna's and Roseanne's devotion to mystical Judaism has piqued renewed interest in the kabbalah. The last five years has seen a proliferation of television shows trading on reports of near-death experiences, special powers, and angelic visitations, and even the Muzak of shopping malls has incorporated the enormously popular Gregorian chants of the Benedictine monks of Santa Domingo de Silos. And private and public corporations, from Nortel and AT&T to the Public Service Alliance of Canada, have discovered "spirituality in the workplace," giving their employees time to express and fulfill needs not directly met at the workstation.

While none of this growth is surprising to those cynical enough to believe that capitalism can and will intrude in (and exploit) every facet of human life, or those misanthropic enough to believe that there is no limit to how individuals will allow themselves to be duped by charlatans, a more balanced judgment – in my estimation – is that the popular, in-your-face spirituality growing around us is a harbinger of the more complex challenges of civilization we are facing in this next millennium. For many seekers, however unsophisticated their understanding of past tradition or of the higher forms into which personal experience can be matured, there is a significant dynamic playing itself out, raising questions about modernity's definition of a person, community, and history. Indeed, I will argue that some of the popular expressions of spiritual revival, the *arrivistes*, are like palimpsests, where traces of old religious debates that took place in the early centuries of our history and before the modern era can again be seen in the new. In a general climate of radical reassessment, the margin is moving into the mainstream, as historical fragments believed to have been left behind are suddenly being reassessed and reactivated. Heretics, fortunately, are no longer consumed by the fires of the *auto-da-fé*.

But there are more subtle signs that another "great awakening" is occurring. Across the country, laity – ordinary Christians, Muslims, Jews, Hindus – are meeting weekly in private homes to study their sacred texts ("Where two or three are gathered together, there am I in the midst," Matt. 18:20). On weekends, dozens of groups meet in empty convents and churches, participating in Alpha and Cursillo retreats, Spiritual Direction, Torah instruction, and meditation. Many baby boomers inherited their religion as a tradition of doctrine, dogma, and ritual, and left the churches. Now, with the time and resources to fulfill some of the deepest human needs, they are rediscovering a tradition of prayer and worship, played out in small intimate fellowships. "The celebration of divine worship," Josef Pieper wrote in his acclaimed book *Leisure: The Basis of Culture*, "is the deepest of the springs by which leisure is fed and continues to be vital."[10]

While it is easy to dismiss or lampoon the grim earnestness and extravagant expectations with which these enterprises are sometimes undertaken, it is the genuine human need to drink the living waters of faith that lies at their core. "In church it was all just yadda-yadda-yadda," a lapsed United Church parishioner comments, explaining why he now spends weekends at the charismatic Toronto Blessing. "We were no longer moved and touched by wooden rituals," claim Jewish and Catholic Canadians at an ashram in the Himalayas, explaining their exodus from churches and synagogues, and their devotion to Swami Shyam, in whose presence "We're listening to revelation, to live scripture." "Quite simply, I needed to read the Bible myself, and not, like a child, have it interpreted to me selectively," a Catholic says, defending her initiative of forming a Bible class. An ardent spiritual need is once again being expressed – even though it may not be religious.

The nomenclature is significant. Few baby boomers admit they are "religious" – they say they are "spiritual," a term whose vagueness is one of the main reasons for its popularity. But their use of it is also a signal they are distancing themselves from the authority of creed, dogmatic theology, and clergy, in favour of an unmediated and unpatented God. "Unmediated" signifies that the "spiritual" search is for a lived experience of the sacred, an unmediated god of mystery and power. Baby boomers want a personal, not an institutional, God. "Unpatented" denotes that this God is cross-denominational – not necessarily of the Book, nor a deity sanctioning a division of the human race into "them and us," nor one who has privileged only the human species, nor one who demands a faith based on class distinction, nor one who compels judgments of right versus wrong. Baby boomers want an inclusive, not a discriminating, God. It has become politically correct to say that one is "spiritual," meaning "not exclusive." Regardless of which precise attributes of God the baby boomers are dispensing with, the "spiritual" search testifies to the scriptural adage – "The letter killeth, but the spirit giveth life." In their search for a personal and inclusive God, the majority of baby boomers are hearing the call to sanctity outside of the church. We are seeing in this turn, perhaps, the fading – if not closure – of twentieth-century religion, of institutions no longer vital with the spirit that engendered them.

Why is there a renewed interest in the sacred? An obvious reason is that baby boomers, whose mean age is forty-eight, are brooding on their mortality. Their bodies – objects of so much pampering – are now showing irrepressible signs of decay. Many baby boomers, so long captive to the myth of perpetual youth (Jerry Rubin: "We ain't never gonna grow up. We're gonna be adolescents *forever*."), are for the first time feeling fragile and vulnerable.[11] Spirituality has always been the anodyne of mortality, and the need for God is most discernible during periods of struggle and suffering. Equally likely, with sick and dying parents, teenage children needing moral guidance, ugly custody battles, and careers and family in sudden unanticipated tatters due to severances and "restructuring," many baby boomers are finally confronting primary questions. Who am I? What am I truly striving for? What is the legacy I leave for the next generation? What can I hope for? Deep down, like so many before them, baby boomers are struggling at mid-life to achieve order and meaning for themselves.

The spiritual awakening may also signal a crisis in our culture. Magazines like *Stuff* and *Equip* – showcasing the latest tantalizing and seductive toys for the bored – are directed at baby boomers who believe that "He who dies with the most toys wins." Just as seductive are travel guides like *Wild Planet! 1,001 Extraordinary Events for the Inspired Traveler* – invitations to search the globe for stimulation, reinforcing the idea that life is a spectacle, and that vast disposable income can make the world one's oyster. And, wistfully, some new social movements seek to tap into baby boomers' recollections of the days of grand politics, where revolution would overcome class oppression or psychic repression, and confer wholeness and authenticity. But in all these diversions lies the centuries-old illusion that the human longing for redemption and transcendence could be displaced onto, and fulfilled in, the consumption of material objects, perpetual newness, and a politics of deep meaning. This illusion rests in the confidence, moreover, that human power and organization can master and subdue all the terrors and unknowns of our lives. Cracks in that great modern dream, however, are widening.

An increasing number of baby boomers now recognize that they are sated but unfulfilled, and are calling the modern project of autonomy and prosperity, and the collective destiny of progress, into question. A computer programmer taking the New Age "Course in Miracles" acknowledges, "The greatest insanity is to believe that the world can be managed, controlled and manipulated to avoid suffering." An architect admits that, when tragedy hit his own family, he realized that years of technical adeptness and confidence in human prowess had done nothing to prepare him for the reality of deep, aching pain and loss. And, in opposition to the downgrading of artifacts in modern society to just "stuff," one finds baby boomers milling around cases of sacred tools and artifacts – crystals, oils, smudge pots, dream catchers, pipes, mandalas, soapstone carvings – in stores like Vancouver's Banyan Books or Toronto's Omega Centre, as if seeking contact with sacred reality. Their actions betray that quintessentially modern sentiment of division and tornness, and the quixotic hope for an enchanted recovery of meaning embodied in things – sometimes out of nostalgia for old times, but as often out of a genuine desire to experience resonance with a greater whole.

It should not be surprising that baby boomers may be leading the rush for overcoming modernity. The desire to start anew and initiate new beginnings was imbued with their mothers' milk. Post-war

Canada was populated with a generation of immigrants and political refugees who had endured a world war and the Depression, whose careers and lives were shattered, whose primary world experience was dispossession, and whose sentiments were defined by regret, resignation, and expectation of the worst.

Many had experienced the full atrocities and obscenity of the war and the Holocaust. Their formative experience was one of dispossession and exile from their homeland, and the urgency of acquiring a new name, identity, and life. They arrived with an inherited sense of order – an inner order which had been the last refuge amid Europe's carnage – but also with a sense of adventure. A wholly new life meant combining traditional manners of behaviour with novelty. Nothing could serve better than a baby. Indeed, to overcome the past, but also to transmit an accumulated wisdom through the generations, they procreated. And onto the resultant product – their baby-boom offspring – they foisted all their expectations of redemption, and also their joy of starting anew. But, at the same time, that joy was tainted by things too painful to be spoken or thought about. They had come to Canada running, leaving behind those worldly things which provide a sense of connection and a story. For those directly touched by the villainy of Hitler, there was the often undiscussed but lingering question: How could a putatively benign God have allowed the obscenity of the Holocaust? Indeed, the war seemed to force the conclusion that God was dead, that God had ceased to be present in history, and that if there was a God, he could only be known by His absence. There is a silence in this generation, and in ours, which many baby boomers would try to fill with prolix chatter.

Some of that prolixity was, of course, the result of the new orthodoxy: Dr. Spock's *Baby and Child Care* was a vivid expression of the novelty of the times. Rather than portraying children as little demons – turbulent wills ever inclined to barbarity and evil, and needing the strictest discipline – Spock taught parents to pamper and be gentle with them. And behind Spock, if only to reinforce his advice, lay progressive educators and developmental psychologists, not to say an intellectual tradition defined by books like Johann Huizinga's *Homo Ludens*, disseminating the idea of the innocence, pure spontaneity, and purity of childhood play. Deferred desire was unhealthy and unnatural. Life presents no hindrances nor compromises; it can be easily brought to conform to our tastes, since the world could be reshaped to mirror our desires.[12] Baby boomers could live a life of wishes, and be the vanguard of all things new and redemptive.

For many years, the magic would be sustained. If spiritual longings are frequently awakened by rupture – love crushed by betrayal, the inexplicable intrusion of evil into innocence, the shock of worldly resistance and limits, dreams extinguished by the reality of labour, disease, and death – the baby boomers' indefatigable youthfulness, and the creativity they used to exploit technology to make it a living reality, hid all this from them. Baby boomers had their fantasies and ideals, and because the world was magically transfigured, they never extinguished them. They could change their beliefs, and reality changed with them. Their education taught them that they had many identities, that if one was frustrated, another could take its place. They had only to feel happiness, and real happiness would ensue. Even when political idealism faded – ideals co-opted by the "system," "by the Man" – they still held out the prospect of returning to a more primitive, or primal, pure reality. Some took magic-bus rides to Asian enlightenment, others went back to the land and natural living; some found the elixir in herbal rejuvenation, others left for housing co-ops to find covenantal communities; some found growth in the human potential movement, others found a buzz in the music of Iron Butterfly or Jimi Hendrix. Many confirmed Kris Kristofferson's words that freedom was "just another word for nothing left to lose." What they all had in common was a dream that they could ski without leaving tracks, surf without resistance, be void of weight and gravity.[13] Consumed with a sense of destiny, living amid a seemingly unending proliferation of choices, confident that nothing could go wrong, styling themselves after adventurers, they experimented for four decades – in revolution, in escape, in work and families.

These are the women and men at the cutting edge of today's spiritual searches. Throughout Canada – from ashtanga yoga practitioners on Salt Spring Island, to novitiates in the Benedictine monastery of Mission, New Mormons in Cardston, Shinto-Buddhists returning to Raymond, Cree natives at the Lac Ste. Anne pilgrimage, Promise Keepers in Hamilton, Lubavitcher Hasidics in Montreal, Inayati Sufis in Toronto, and New Age shamans in Calgary – there is a raw hunger for spiritual wholeness, a hunger for what is real, what *is* in the fullest sense. For many, it is a sentiment that the reality recognized by modern science, and permitted in everyday life, is too narrow and restrictive. They are looking for greater and deeper fulfillment, for reality in its totality. For others, the answer has to be "less and simpler," away from the superficial busyness of the world and the infinite pretenses with which its demands are rationalized.

Whether the search is for more or less, there is a growing need among baby boomers to believe in something profoundly. For a generation which has had perhaps a surfeit of opportunities and experiences telescoped into a few short decades, traditional formulas are not sufficient. For many baby boomers, neither the catechisms of their childhoods nor the social and political ideologies which eventually replaced those catechisms, and least of all the mainstream churches today, speak with sufficient breadth and integrity to what Pascal referred to, and what the baby boomers have directly experienced, as "the grandeur and misery" of our humanity.

. . .

This book is a study of the spiritual searches of Canada's baby boomers and, at the same time, a commentary on the complex state of current religious consciousness.[14] The most general question it poses is, What does it mean to be spiritual in the modern age? Conveyed within this question are smaller, though no less complex, questions: i) To what degree do baby boomers exemplify the dynamics of modern society? ii) What is modernity at the end of the twentieth century? and iii) To what extent are the baby boomers' spiritual searches, like Trojan horses, carriers of a critique, or conveyors of a radical new development, of modernity?

The formulation of my questions arose in the following context: Over the last ten years, I met more and more Canadians of my age – baby boomers – who were raised Catholic, Lutheran, United, Anglican, or Reform Jewish, lapsed from active religious practice and belief, and then experienced serious spiritual longing again. These were individuals who, as a result of socialization, schooling, and vocations, were the apotheosis of modernity – who, when asked how they defined themselves, would respond "as free, rational, self-determining persons," meaning they were, in their own minds, not bound by God, nature, or history, and were confident in the human capability to technologically supersede the dogma and superstition of the past. These were women and men whose formative years were inscribed with a commitment to rational deliberation and solving human problems by open, discursive negotiation. They were baby boomers living the dream of modernity – the dream that life is continual self-overcoming, and not obedience to fixed conditions. Yet, rather suddenly, they were enlisting in programs like "A Course in Miracles" or the "Alpha Program," participating in Cursillo retreats and hatha yoga *asanas*, and joining Opus Dei or the charismatic and evangelical movement, which required them to affirm "Lord, you are the potter, and I am the clay," or "Let go, let God, " or "Sitting in silence makes it safe to be together." I could not understand the conjunction of these segments of their lives, and realized that I would have to investigate more systematically.

At the same time, I was struck by the common lexicon these seekers were using to explain their reawakening. It was a language familiar to me from the writers and ideas I too had been exposed to at school – Herman Hesse's *Steppenwolf* and *Siddhartha*, Kurt Vonnegut's *Slaughterhouse Five*, Richard Bach's *Jonathan Livingston Seagull*, Carl Rogers' *On Becoming a Person*, R.D. Laing's *The Divided Self*, Aldous Huxley's *The Doors of Perception*, Carlos Castaneda's *Don Juan*, Charles Reich's *The Greening of America*, Ram Dass's *Be Here Now*, Alan Watts's *Joyous Cosmology*, Joseph Campbell's *The Hero with a Thousand Faces*. This was the revolutionary language of the romantic counterculture – the inauthenticity of society and its rationalizations, the redemptive power of immediate experience and primitive encounter, and the prospect that society was on the threshhold of discovering alternative realities promising unmediated freedom. Although much of it was platitudinous, by the 1980s, it was already firmly enshrined in education, the workplace, and politics.

For most baby boomers, the heady dreams of the 1960s were replaced by the reality of the structured requirements of the workplace, marriage, and social roles. Revolutionary leaders became establishment players, learning to work and exploit the system, often more successfully than their parents. Were the intellectual and social coordinates of the sixties, then, simply extinguished once and for all and seen for what they were – juvenile rebellion, products of overheated imaginations – or were they merely repressed? My encounters with friends and colleagues who had rediscovered religion, and now sought to articulate the meaning of their experiences, suggested the working hypothesis that the spiritual searches of Canada's baby boomers were, to a considerable extent, informed by a return of the repressed, albeit a return where political aspiration is refracted into spiritual hope. The baby boomers are "keeping the faith." The most potent aspect of their spiritual searches today, in my judgment, is not life cycle or ennui, but a quickening of a way of thinking and being which has lain dormant for nearly three decades. And, in that return, I am surmising, lies the next significant wave of modernity's sustained self-critique.

For this book, I interviewed about 350 baby-boomer Canadians – men and women, seekers and converts, mainstream and margin, East and West, rural and urban, white collar and blue collar. While I inquired about their religious backgrounds and their current beliefs, I was particularly attentive to their "narrative theology," the testimony they gave of experiences of a divine ground of being, and its translation into a living reality within everyday existence. I travelled from British Columbia to Nova Scotia, and included a trip to the Himalayas and another to Pennsylvania. En route, I participated in nearly a hundred masses, services, ministries, missions, worships, retreats, *satsangs*, *asanas*, meditations, sweats, and prayers. I spoke to priests, ministers, bishops, rabbis, elders, pastors, monks, gurus, swamis, specialists, and academics. I pored over dozens of church bulletins and newsletters, newspaper clippings, scholarly works, and academic analyses.

Whether I was a participant-observer at events sponsored by the Anglican Alpha and Essentials movements or the Roman Catholic Cursillo movement, attending the Lac Ste. Anne pilgrimage or Poundmaker Lodge's native spirituality centre, or sitting at the feet of Baba Hari Dass at his Salt Spring Island Ashtanga Yoga Meditation Centre or of Swami Shyam with his 200-strong Canadian community in the Himalayas, or speaking to the United Church's Community of Concern or to scholars drawn to the Jesus Seminar, one pattern was nearly universally visible: Baby boomers were explaining their spiritual searches in the context of a critique of modern life. A vastly useful taxonomy proposed in Peter Berger's celebrated 1979 sociological study of the fate of religion in the modern world, *The Heretical Imperative*, supplied me with a scheme for organizing my materials. Today, in the wake of centuries of secularization, demythologization, and disenchantment, Berger writes, if there is to be faith at all, religion can be lived in only three ways: by reaffirming the authority of the tradition in defiance of surrounding challenges; by secularizing the tradition; or by extracting the experiences embodied in the tradition.[15] My fieldwork was an attempt to find examples within all three categories, and the organization of this book follows Berger's taxonomy. I have, however, added one additional category – the escape to the East – because in my estimation it is the option in which the critique of the modern age and baby boomers' distinctive sentiments are consummately fulfilled.

In the last decade, various media in both the United States and Canada have commented on the resurgence of interest in religion among baby boomers. *Time* magazine devoted its August 5, 1998, cover story to the return of the baby boomers to church, temple, and synagogue, and *Maclean's* magazine has run numerous pieces on the new spirituality over the last few years. However, in his book *Unknown Gods*, Reginald Bibby provides compelling evidence that church memberships and attendance figures in Canada do not warrant the conclusion that baby boomers' spiritual searches are particularly consequential. His argument is that while some churches can claim considerable growth, the recruits are already religious believers and are merely shifting allegiances. The swell of religious interest by baby boomers is merely a "circulation of saints." There may be a great deal of talk about religion, but little actual increase in religiosity. Bibby's conclusion is potentially fatal to my entire enterprise.

My experiences travelling across Canada confirmed Bibby's facts, but led me to different conclusions. Because I was less interested in institutional analysis than in the meaning of the attempt to restore a mytho-poetic way of life, what I saw, heard, and experienced was richly portentous. In my estimation, the spiritual searches of baby boomers are highly significant because, while the numbers are small, they involve people with high degrees of self-consciousness and sophistication, who are in positions of vast authority and influence, and who are beginning to articulate a vocabulary and a vision of a very different modernity from that of today.

Clustered around key pressure points and fault lines in existing religious institutions, and throughout the economic, technological, cultural, and political sectors of Canada, the baby boomers are undertaking spiritual searches that challenge the cardinal principles of modern existence and speak to an idea of humanity and community as yet unrealized. The baby boomers' search taps into the powerful dynamics of contemporary history: those pushing for a substantive reassessment and renegotiation of the cultural and intellectual compass points defining modern Western consciousness. There is, in my estimation, a ferment occurring in this country, led by the baby boomers, which policy-makers, both temporal and ecclesiastical, ignore at their peril. Signals of change do not arise out of statistical clusters, but from disruptive marginal anomalies. Not all events are pivotal, but normal aggregation curves never reveal dramatic turning points. Data are not reality. This is why, however important the statistical and survey compilation of religious affiliations and beliefs is, it cannot tell the whole story. Quite simply, many baby boomers undertaking spiritual searches are flying below the radar screen. The generation that is confident above all of the transformative power of the few – consider the success of just a handful who brought us global awareness, environmental consciousness, and women's empowerment – will now revolutionize spiritual worship. The baby boomers' religious reawakening is an event of historic magnitude because, in the final analysis, the lacunae and tensions it exposes in modernity, and the solutions it submits for our consideration, go to the very core of our destiny, of what is real to us.[16]

# Traditionalism I

## Back to Basics

................................................................................................................................

"Things don't have to get much worse, we're already there," Mark
mutters, shaking his head. "We've really messed up." Moments
later, we are standing, clapping our hands, our arms raised in praise
and exclaiming "Amen" with 3,400 other men in the Ottawa Congress
Centre. Billed as "An Exciting Event for Men: Prepare to Win," the
Promise Keepers' pre-Billy Graham Mission rally is packed to the
rafters – with baby boomers.

Tonight's star human attraction is Paul Henderson, an acclaimed
Canadian hockey star who, while playing on the forward line during
the 1972 Canada–Soviet Summit Series, scored the winning goal in the
dying minutes of the last game and gave Canada its 4–3 series edge. He
is now a motivational speaker. Before his appearance, the audience's
attention is riveted on two Jumbotron video screens projecting the
famed hockey game to the rousing beat of a Christian rock band. On
the screens, interspersed between plays, flash expressive words of
inspiration – DETERMINATION, TEAMWORK, WINNING IN THE
GAME, STRUGGLE, FREEDOM – a man's vocabulary, reminding men
to be men.

But the lively atmosphere is actually intended to evoke "a different
kind of player" – the man who "relates to God." Intertwined with
images of masculine camaraderie in sports are testimonials by hockey
players witnessing to how their strong Christian families and their
Bible studies have reinforced their lives. As if to punctuate the point
that the real game is a man's martial honour and self-respect, the lead
singer exclaims, "God is our soldier on high." He lets rip a sliding scale,

whose portentous modulation evokes the sensation of primordial darkness. "We are here this evening," adds the voice-over, "to help God find all the lost children, like a father looking frantically in a mall. God is on a search and rescue mission. And now we will have a prayer for steadfastness, to overcome our inherent wandering."

As if to plumb our self-mortification and insignificance a little further, we stand to sing of "our debt to pay, of honour and serving God." "Make this the night you make your commitment to Jesus forever," huskily beckons the preacher, Ron Hutchcraft. "Tonight, inoculate yourselves against drugs, sex, prostitution, war, luxury, and the occult, and be open to the call to witness." At this call, many men in the audience raise their arms in praise, palms outstretched, identifying with Psalm 28: "To You, O Lord, I call, my rock; do not refuse to hear me, for if you are silent to me, I shall be like those who go down to the pit. Hear the voice of my supplication, as I cry to you for help, as I lift up my hands, toward your most holy sanctuary."

Gerry Organ, a former Ottawa Rough Rider, is now ushered forward and offers evidence of what manly drive can still achieve. He starts by reminding the "guys" of the solidarity they feel in football, but rapidly changes direction, testifying that he "went to the Cross because my life had no meaning." He admits he had "a need as a man that no other man could fulfill." And when a friend prayed for him, "The burden of my heart rolled away." "Were you there?" Organ asks, pointing to the Jumbotron's replay of Henderson's last remarkable game. The crowd stands, stomping their feet, clapping, and shouting, "I was there." "Were you there when they crucified Him on the Cross?" "I was there," they cry in a collective voice. "I have drawn the line in the sand," Organ concludes. "Now, we have to stay the course, to make the choice – serve the Lord." "I was there," roars the crowd – at the game, at the Congress Centre, at the Cross.

David Sweet, another Promise Keeper, addresses the group. "If there's going to be a revival, it's got to start with this … a man keeping his promises." He admits that he was a juvenile delinquent in the 1970s, that he lost at work and marriage. A buddy became a holy roller, but, in his estimation, this was not preparing to win. He began to realize that there were incredible needs in his life. Another man came to his assistance, and activated a desire to return to a biblically based life. "There is a need for a public proclamation of your faith," Sweet announces. "The upcoming

Billy Graham Mission," he concludes, "is the opportunity to prepare to win, if this event is to be the biggest event of Christendom in Canada."

Hockey-playing winner – now evangelical Christian winner – Paul Henderson finally debuts to witness to *his* faith: "When I was here, I wanted to be there. I was filled with restlessness, anger, bitterness, jealousy." The Toronto Maple Leaf players were given Bibles, he discloses, but he personally looked at Christianity as a "cosmic killjoy." In 1995, Billy Graham came to Toronto and Paul's eyes were opened. He moved from inner division to reconciliation, developed "a personal relationship with Christ," and became a "prayer warrior." Paul's appearance is brief and poignant.

There are many wet eyes in the Congress Centre. Near me, men are hugging, pumping hands, slapping one another on the back. Though Mark continues his bleak commentary on the world, he admits that in the dulcet tones of "Trusting Jesus" wafting around the Congress Centre, he finds a ray of hope: "This music makes you think you are part of something older, venerable – it's just the old tunes. It's getting back to basics." Later, Ottawa's newspapers report that 161 men experienced a call to conversion that night.

Six weeks later, I attend the Billy Graham Mission. So, it appears, does half of Ottawa – many are drawn by the sassy and punchy ads designed by the Toronto-based T B W A Chiat/Day and Shakopee advertising agency: "In a town where it's left versus right, let's talk up versus down." "He's in Ottawa to address the real deficit." "Two thousand years ago, Jesus invited a tax collector to join him. History is about to repeat itself." "He may not have all the answers but he knows who does."

When Ben Heppner belts out the stirring words, "Warrior of the ages … a mighty fortress is our Lord/Jesus is the captain of salvation/A battle plan against the forces of darkness … the power at His command/His mighty presence is in you … we are empowered by His holy word," 10,000 men in the Corel Centre arise as one, clapping, cheering, hugging. "There's been a change in men – we're not afraid to be seen crying," the man next to me, Jim, editorializes. "Contrast this with Gary Cooper in the film *High Noon* – he only says fifty-nine words. Men thought they only had two options – to be brutes or saps. Today, we're trying to find an image. Billy is the middle way."

"I'm Billy, a North Carolina hillbilly," confides the unassuming evangelist, easing his way onto the stage in the wake of an orchestral eruption of French horns, timpani, and violins, followed by a standing ovation. He reveals that he received a letter – "Canada is in deep spiritual trouble," it read – and notes that tonight he is "going to tell you what you're looking for." Billy's forty-minute sermon is simple, folksy, homespun, recondite, baffling ("I have always wanted to come back to Ottawa … like the man who always wanted to kiss a donkey in the face of a shotgun") and yet, at the same time, consummately scripted, running the gamut from walking over anthills and bathing in a tin tub, to damnation and salvation.

> I can't understand God, but I believe in Him, and the Bible tells the truth about Him. [And the Bible says] we're all headed to the grave and then judgment, of every secret thing, for all the world to see. We're going to have to pay for our sin. We know there's something wrong with human nature today. Man has a terminal disease. We're seeing a spiritual death – we're dead people walking, we live in hell and we're not aware of it.

Some of the preaching is delivered in sound-bite form – "We ache for transcendence, a timeless touch." "Our souls need to breathe and grow." "It's a hurting, suffering world" – yet there is rapt attention and utter quiet. Sitting beside me, Jim nods and exclaims "Amen" after each pause. "I'm just glowing with new life, with all the rat-shit around. This is just such a fresh and dynamic way of presenting the Gospels – Jesus Christ as the framework and focus of our lives," Jim explains. As Lena Di Paulo sings "No place so deep and dark you'll not be there/Jesus you are the song in my night/Just to be in the presence of your light," he sobs quietly. "He keeps it simple."

Thirty-five minutes into the event, plastic buckets are distributed. "The giving of money is a ministry as great as giving of charity." The Mission, tonight's moderator reminds, consumes a budget of $2.2 million. Collections in participating congregations – even before Billy Graham has arrived in Ottawa – cover 74 per cent of the expense. Tonight's contributions must, however, keep the ball rolling. "The Christian is the man of humility, abasement, nakedness. Remember, the love of God and faith – greater than tongue or pen could tell." The evening's take, as it happens, tops $88,000.

"You may never have another moment in your life to make a commitment here in this public place," Billy comments. "The essence of hell is the separation from God. Tonight God is alive. Just believe, trust, repent of your sins – and you'll be saved. Do something publicly and openly: 'I open up my heart to Jesus and I wish to serve him. I want a change in my life.' Jesus hung on the Cross publicly, meaning, 'If you don't acknowledge me publicly, I'll not acknowledge you before God.'"

When only a few enquirers initially drift to the centre, Billy exhorts, "This whole mission was planned for you, quickly come. You get up and come. Make that commitment right now. We want to help in any way we can. God has to help you repent; surrender your life, your business, your family, your thoughts – to Jesus your saviour." A strain of vibrato warble discharges from the organ as 2,000 people answer the "altar call" and shuffle forward. "Come, and you will be given extra spiritual strength amidst the problems we all have …. I don't have powers to heal you, only the Holy Spirit does. But you must say 'Oh God, I'm a sinner …. I'm willing to change my ways …. Please help me. From this day on, I want to follow you.'"

The second night of the Mission boasts full capacity. The all-black Montreal Jubilation Choir raves with sheer energy and unabashed joy "To change my world, my life/It's not what it used to be." Native singer and two-time Juno Award winner Susan Aglukark entreats, "Find something to believe in, give in to your dreaming. Look to a brand-new start. We must learn to forget race and colour. We are all family, we are all the same, you come here and celebrate life, you celebrate Christ in your life." Each point is greeted with ebullient ovation. It's hard to resist the tide: 462 churches involved; 15,000 men and women trained to participate in the crusade; 225 meetings, a response of 5,500 people to the Gospel, including 1,600 children; the attendance of 72,000 individuals at the Mission, to hear an evangelist who has spent fifty years preaching to 210 million people, in 185 countries. "The Holy Spirit is moving," Jim, with whom I am leaning over a railing, contributes. "D'ya see the synergy – there's forty-two denominations here tonight." Once again, forty-five minutes into the evening, comes the request for money: "Faith works – look at what happened last night," comments tonight's moderator over the PA.

Tonight Billy wants to talk about "The Battle for the Mind: God versus the Devil for Your Mind." Before he does, he asks Franklin, his prodigal but now repentant son, to witness. "I thought I could create my own happiness. I'm a sinner; I looked for my own pleasure and happiness. Nothing could fill the void. I got on my knees and confessed that I am a sinner and asked for forgiveness." Today, Franklin flies missions from Alaska to Russia, from Africa to Latin America, for his father and Jesus. "Because He lives, I can face tomorrow."

"Do you need peace in your life tonight?" Billy asks, averring that most of us have minds of hidden lust and troubled thought. "As a man thinks, so he is. Your mind starts out against God, it is a carnal mind, an enmity to God, won't obey the law of God – remember all the works of flesh Satan inspires. You know, alcohol is the worst drug we have today." At that moment, the Centre erupts into ovation. "Perhaps we have to return to Prohibition" – an even more deafening ovation greets Billy's suggestion. "Tonight, before you leave this arena, repent. Repentance will allow you to change your way of living."

Around me there is a lot of squirming – Billy's observations have evidently struck home in the crowd of men. Perhaps part of the discomfort exists because of where an invitation to tonight's event was placed – among the sex ads of the local dailies ("Jesus will love you for free"). Billy issues the altar call:

> You may have been baptized and confirmed in a church, but deep down you are not sure. You can know tonight by repenting and Christ will transform and remake your mind after His. Many of you know a lot about Christianity, but do you know Christ for yourself? I want you to get up. Turn from your past life and let Christ control your mind; turn it over to Christ. Come say yes to Jesus – you may never have a moment like this in your whole life, in this generation. God is giving you a chance, a moment.

Again, there is initial hesitation. Given pause, Billy, in a final bid for compliance, adduces signs and wonders: "Canada Day is a golden opportunity to proclaim the way to the land of gold. Was it a miracle that the huge storm that hit Ottawa, and actually killed seven people in the eastern United States, bypassed the Corel Centre and the people sitting outside? We must make a personal commitment and establish a personal relationship with God. Come up here, now." The pearly gates of heaven beckon to the honeyed tune of "Just As I Am."

On the third night, Amy Grant sings, "If there's anything that happens tonight, it's Jesus."

She acknowledges an ongoing dialogue with Jesus in which He asks her to lay down her burden, and He will carry her. "I've seen the darker side of hell; every tear I cried … sleepless nights, and He said, 'Call my name, and I'll come.'"

"We're heading towards a catastrophe in our world … and it's going to start from the ground up," Billy pronounces, after a convoluted tale of a Catholic priest giving last rites to a horse. "A judgment of fire is coming to earth, nuclear scientists have moved the doomsday clock five minutes closer to midnight – it's now nine and a half minutes before midnight, a total destruction, the end of the world." These are "the days of Noah – wars, insurrection, violence, sexual corruption, decadent religion, people preoccupied with things, taken up with everyday living, in neglect of God. We can't go on much longer morally, scientifically – our weapons, nuclear, germ, chemical. Prepare to meet thy God, Jesus says." As Billy preaches, the air is rent with the sound of "Amen," meaning "truly spoken."

"As believers," and here Billy pauses – he is nothing if not the master of the pregnant pause – "we have a hope." There is a standing ovation. "We're going to go to the coronation, the Supper of the Lamb," another pause, "as believers." Another rolling ovation. "Our own death – are you ready for that?" he asks, casting his steely blue eyes around the Centre. "In such an hour as you think not," – the most Melchizedek-like tone he's used yet – "prepare to meet thy God." The man next to me has tears streaming down his face. "At my death, there will be an angel who will take me to Christ. I am looking forward to that."

Finally, the last altar call of the Mission: "Be willing to repent of your sins. Make a permanent commitment to Christ tonight. Make a permanent change in your life. Jesus didn't get much out of the Church. Maybe it was over his head. God wants simple faith – put your weight on Him, you must come in childlike faith to the Cross." There is barely a dry eye in the Centre, as the wheelchairs, the invalids on crutches, the sick on stretchers, the afflicted and wounded, the fright-ened and joyous, glide forward to Billy – amid a silence so yawning it evokes a God who can only be met in fear and trembling.

Graham's avowed purpose is "to declare the Christian Gospel, and make it so simple that even children can understand what I'm saying."[1]

His evangelism is predicated on the judgment that what we need is renewal "in the church, the government, the city and throughout the nation to restore the moral absolutes that the world needs to return to justice and civility."[2] That message is highly congenial to many baby boomers, conforming to cardinal features of baby-boom culture and consciousness: My anguish is world anguish, what befalls me has befallen the world. My saviour cannot be a theological construct, nor patented by any church (we will trust "no men in hats"). Salvation is a product of my personal relationship to a divine being, a relationship so intimate and indwelling as to be known only in personal experience. But God must also enjoy the absolute power to destroy creation and create anew. He must answer definitively to the tiresome non-finality of the perplexities and doubt of human life. My spirituality must come with a great sense of drama – its finest moment is when it plays out world destiny. It must give me and my cohort a "Great Commission." Repentance must comprise the challenge beyond all challenges – no pain, no gain. We need to release the child within and get back to a pure, unadulterated beginning. An acceptable religion must cross denominational lines and bring people together – we have to know we are all going to the same mountaintop.

Billy Graham's attraction, and evangelical Christianity's immense recruiting success in North America, must be understood against a backdrop of liberal Christianity and modern secular culture. At the heart of evangelicals' account of themselves resides a judgment against the modern world – including nearly all the mainstream churches – as being corrupted by moral relativism, permissiveness, moral decay. The source of the collapse lies in the false confidence modern men and women exhibit in believing they have a choice in morals and lifestyles. Evangelicalism's opposition to the modern world is focused on the perception of widespread acceptance of abortion, homosexuality, divorce, the collapse of the traditional family, and the separation of the state and church in the schools. Women pursuing careers has emptied the home of authority, they say, and promoted infidelity, divorce, and children "running free." In the schools, evangelicals despair of the value of neutrality and the limitless confidence in human reason. The short form version of this critique is "secular humanism."

Unlike modernity's mistaken belief in human goodness and perfectibility, and its trust that technology and scientific reason will eventually solve all human dilemmas, evangelical Christians subscribe to a picture of a sinful and fallen human nature whose apostasy is displayed in individualism, rationalism, and conviction of freedom. A strong motif in evangelicals' portrait of human beings is that our quotidian, worldly lives are scorched with pain, loss, suffering, and addictions – all our own doing. Without "letting go, letting God" and "walking with the Lord," there can be no redemption from this dark world. The battle for our souls – God versus Satan, heaven versus damnation – cannot cease unless, and until, we are "born again." And though neither the Promise Keepers nor Billy Graham explicitly subscribe to as stark a millenarian perspective as that of the American R.J. Rushdoony – the founder of the Christian reconstructionist movement who subscribes to the view that literal biblical law needs to be imposed on modern society in preparation for the Second Coming – apocalyptic themes inform the assessment of the failed modern project and the hopes for a new, redeemed Adam to come.

One does not need to turn to Rushdoony to find dire warnings about the world and the conclusion that the world is going to hell in a handcart. Just how dramatically the "world" falls out as the site of sanctification can be gauged even by the pamphlet (entitled *Living in Christ: Beginning Your Walk*) Billy Graham hands out to those answering the altar call. There we read that the gulf between God and humans is so vast that no amount of good works, religion, philosophy, or morality will suffice for human happiness. The only remedy, the seeker learns, is to repent and turn to Jesus. "God" – understood as transcendent and wholly other than human – must never mean the human aspiration to attain a higher consciousness, or the desire to realize one's full potential.

Protestant Christianity was always inclined to diminish the importance of worldly activity on behalf of salvation. Martin Luther's renowned ninety-five theses, tacked to the door of Wittenberg's castle church in 1517, were not just a stinging censure of the excessive worldliness of the Roman Church, mired in the corruption of indulgences and simony. They also conveyed the theological reorientation which would become the Protestant hallmark: Not good works, but faith alone prepared the human soul for God's free gift of salvation. Indeed, so as not to compromise God's absolute freedom of action and to maintain the priority of God's initiative in the divine-human encounter, Protestantism has always downplayed worldly reason and human ambition.

No crude human bartering, and no simplistic human expectations of reciprocity or merit, were permitted to limit the absolute freedom of God. Denying the salvific power of sacraments and the authority of priests to mediate the relation between humanity and God, Protestantism strongly reinforced modernity's overall distrust of institutions and tradition. And while one does not have to search far in Roman Catholicism for extreme denunciations of the human body – flagellation as penance, for example – it is really in Protestant writing that Augustine's dismissive view of the body becomes prevalent. To speak of the body as mere "flesh" spurred by concupiscence, and human activity as a saturnalia of carnal lust, as John Calvin would do, implies that the body's longings and its acts in the world lack any order and ultimate purpose. The more the Christian believer takes seriously the grim depiction of humankind's apostasy against God and the direness of the world's fall, the more sympathetic such an individual becomes to the stark antinomian views of the more radical Protestant denominations like the Mennonites, Doukhobors, and Quakers, where little if any hope for sanctification in this world can ever be held.

Arguably, evangelical Christianity, though often represented as a more muscular expression of Christianity *per se,* is only a credible take on the Christian message from within the Protestant spectrum. While there is a "family resemblance" among the forty-two denominations represented at the Billy Graham Mission, and each of these denominations has an "evangelical" wing, the distinct emphasis on the utter fallenness of this world, salvation through private encounter with Jesus alone, and the turn from clerical authority to evangelists' charisma and the priesthood of the believer denotes that Graham's Christianity is a distinctly Protestant one. That same strapping, showy religiosity is also responsible for the more aggressive – for many, distasteful – intolerance exposed in the Christian imperative to convert the Jews and heathens in preparation for the Second Coming. Combined with a literal reading of biblical scripture which denies the possibility of error or contradiction, and a wholesale censure of "liberal drift" and modern scientism, evangelical Christianity has reached a point where it joins company with Christian fundamentalism.

It is fashionable among intellectuals and pundits to be dismissive, even condescending and derisive, of evangelical and conservative Christianity. These days, nearly any cudgel is good enough to beat down Christianity as a way of insisting that the churches accommodate to the liberal and progressive movements of modernity. A perfect illustration was the intense spotlight directed toward Canadian Alliance leader Stockwell Day's Christianity and the reduction of his faith to a belief, for example, that dinosaurs roamed the earth concurrently with human beings.

An antidote to a too-swift dismissal of conservative Christianity is recollecting that a rich and serious tradition of religious faith underlies it, an idea compellingly portrayed by William James in one of the most important studies of religion in the twentieth century, *The Varieties of Religious Experience.*[3] After discussing "a religion of the healthy-minded," which confidently moves through the levels of perfection in the world toward a knowable and loving God, James turns to "the religion of the sick-souled," which he judges to be the more profound spiritual instinct. The religion of the sick-souled, James observes, is centred on crisis, division, and deliverance. Like St. Augustine, who wrote "my inner self [is] a house divided against itself ... have pity on me and heal me [Lord], for you see that I have become a problem to myself and this is the ailment from which I suffer,"[4] the sick-souled individual rejects the arrogant pride, idle curiosity, and feverish agitation associated with human confidence that humans can know God absolutely by participating in the rational, harmonious created order. The sick-souled individual acknowledges the irremediable human proclivity to error and mischief, even evil, which accompany all actions and thoughts. Instead of a joyful participation in all that life offers, the sick-souled individual acknowledges human fallibility and the mystery of divine love, thus questioning the happiness accompanying our self-sufficiency and power to exalt in our virtues. Broken and contrite, we ought to pine at a distance from the Absolute, and recognize how inadequate our own abilities are to the task of transcendence. The everyday world must be convulsed and shaken if the divine is to appear. Instead of the human presumption that our natural abilities suffice to make us happy, our redemption lies in being "nailed on the cross of despair and agony."[5] In chastity, obedience, and poverty, the sick-souled must attain gladness at deprivation and nullity, for it is not in the excess of sound and sight, but in vast and profound silence that God is encountered. As John the Baptist suggested, we must decrease so that God may increase. In opposition to worldly doing, being, and having, the believer acknowledges, "Naked came I into the world."[6] The technical term for the sick-souled religion is *apophatic* – the believer draws closer to God by drawing away from the world.[7]

And from such observations and conclusions flow the dignified virtues held up by conservative, protestant Christianity: humility, a capacity for mercy and forgiveness, charity toward the afflicted, and gratitude. If sixty years ago Pope Pius xi could already conclude that "Today we are all Protestants," it is as if he presaged that, by the end of the century and the beginning of the new millennium, the evangelical and fundamentalist movements would be the single most influential leaven in a sagging, flabby Christianity with neither a robust theology nor humility. On their own, evangelical and fundamentalist Christianity offer alluring alternatives to historical and institutional Christianity: firm moral anchors, individual piety replacing empty tradition, salvation as a personal responsibility, and an apocalypticism before which all human projects, especially those which have the effect of distinguishing the strong from the weak, pale into insignificance.

But the natural fit between conservative Christianity and baby-boom culture and consciousness is the real key to why Pope Pius xi's observation rings so true to our times. Like the "saving remnant," or the prodigal son, baby boomers have been welcomed to evangelical and fundamentalist Christianity with open arms, their needs and expectations finding an endlessly obliging home. Billy Graham's missions and the Promise Keepers' rallies serve up a Christianity which meets baby boomers "where they're at." "Try it, feel it, believe it," says the evangelist. "You are homeless, you can be where there's something really happening, Jesus can be your personal chum."

That baby boomers perceive themselves to be homeless, and that Billy Graham could speak persuasively to the vacuum they experience, was in preparation for all of their lives. They were the generation born with the detonation of the atomic bomb, and the nuclear threat was experienced in weekly bomb-shelter and air-raid drills. With haunting, harrowing books like Walter Miller's *A Canticle for Leibowitz*, and movies like *The Day After*, it is not surprising that they speculated often about life after the Bomb. The American–Soviet standoff at the Bay of Pigs was a tocsin of the abyss they were hanging over – a harbinger not merely of a new war, but of the potential end of the world. The assassinations of John F. and Robert Kennedy, the National Guard shootings at Kent State, the ruthless savagery of the Tet Offensive and the invasion of Cambodia, the 1968 Paris demonstrations, later (in 1973) the oil embargo and the desolate, empty streets – all somehow morphogenetically connected, though no one knew how – left baby boomers both with attenuated anxiety about the fragility of the world and with the frisson that people were on the move, that outworn forms were about to evaporate, that a world transformation was presaged. Predictably, baby boomers grew up thinking they had a mission to save the world, yet, at the same time, knowing that the world would not endure.

Their ambivalence to these dangers was the strange product of their parents' reserve as it pertained to talking about the past. Growing up, many baby boomers were fed "when-I-was-your-age" stories – harrowing accounts of the war and the Depression – to keep them in line. It bred in them, not so much gratitude for what their parents had done for them, as horror of everything which had come before them. Every generation, of course, has used the preceding generation as a whipping boy to prove to itself that it has progressed, but, in the baby boomers' case, it all remained unspoken. Their fathers rarely told them stories of the warrior's honour, of courage and righteousness on the battlefield. Many of their fathers were silent when it came to valour in battle and, in the resultant vacuum, baby boomers had to create their own coordinates.

The intellectual and cultural climate in which baby boomers grew up reinforced homelessness. The three most formative thinkers of darker moments of the modern era are Karl Marx, Sigmund Freud, and Friedrich Nietzsche. In one way or another, most baby boomers were fed a steady diet of heightened awareness of human exploitation, oppression, and illusion, coupled with the insight that the received world of common opinion and tradition was a chimera. Suspicion of progress and optimism, and dread at a world breaking down, became *de rigueur*. After all, most of Canada's baby boomers were highly receptive to the radicalism of their teachers and the books they thought important: Robert Laxer's *(Canada) Ltd*, George Grant's *Lament for a Nation*, John Porter's *The Vertical Mosaic*, Marshall McLuhan's *Understanding Media*, Kari Levitt's *Silent Surrender*, Pierre Vallières's *White Niggers of America*, Dennis Lee's *Civil Elegies*. The political sentiments expressed in these books became an orthodoxy: Canada lacked a national interest, our economy was comprised of a branch-plant industry of American interests, our culture was lost to the homogenizing influence of Hollywood, public policy was massively influenced by the power structure, marginal peoples were oppressed, the cause of national liberation was unconditionally good, consumers were passive dupes of subliminal advertising and the corporate manufacture of false needs, there were systemic barriers to development imposed by central Canada on the margins, America's wars and political interests were the product of militarism and imperialism. The political message conveniently suited many baby boomers' rebellious adolescence.

But the message was a double-edged sword. Baby boomers were a generation with a deep desire for commitment, yet, ironically, many were persuaded that all bonds were distorting and colonizing, and that they should commit to nothing permanently. While a corrective to platitudinous boosterism of the status quo, this teaching was also highly corrosive of civic trust, partisan loyalty, or pride of inheritance. Indeed, the image of a human being it vaunted was that of a drifter: Charles Baudelaire's *flâneur* who is a detached street voyeur, Claude Levi-Strauss's *bricoleur* who deconstructs and sifts ideas, compounding them at will, Jean-Paul Sartre's skier who leaves no tracks. There is neither commitment nor investment required by such lives, which surf above life, where traditional pieties give way to chic cynicism and disassociation. It allowed baby boomers the sophomoric mien of being against "the System" without having to commit to a specific alternative.

Indeed, baby boomers who carried forward the enormous release of potential represented by the 1960s into the world of work had a paradoxical relationship to the workplace. Many baby boomers achieved a level of success and affluence in the 1980s which, to a more frugal generation that had endured the Depression and wartime rationing, bordered on the obscene. Both their real spending power and the senior positions of influence with which they were already flush in their forties represented a new apex of worldly success. Nevertheless, few baby boomers expected fulfillment from work, and their work was rarely conventional. If many baby boomers eschewed corporations, management, and bureaucracy – preferring freelance consultancies and thus sustaining the anti-establishment ethos of their adolescence – even those in more conventional organizations tailored the workplace to their own needs. Work was a means that, like Lotto 649, allowed baby boomers to "imagine the freedom."

In a decade of junk bonds and corporate raiders, extravagant bonuses, quick stock turnover, and immediate financial gains, the drone-like ordeal of ninety-hour workweeks could be tolerated, especially since it made possible a massive consumption of goods and services, extensive and pampered international travel, and a level of luxury once enjoyed only by the upper class. Our desire for novelty could be endlessly titillated. If the workplace brought petty annoyances – it was, after all, also the era of affirmative-action employment quotas, political correctness, and hypersensitivity to subtle forms of discrimination – it also provided the wherewithal to live the great myth of modern secularism (that true happiness is this-worldly). This myth had stipulated that the conditions of existence that produce disappointment and unrest can be overcome, and that transcendence from the world is not necessary to humans.

The stock market collapse of October 19, 1987, was the turning point. Mergers and leveraged buyouts were quickly followed by "redundancies," "restructuring," and the superfluousness of middle management, ending the dream that the world and ourselves were happily one and the same. Acrimonious divorces and custody battles soured marital relationships which had, thanks to our idealism, been idealized as "I-Thou" relationships. If the civil rights movement had once drawn the spiritually hungry, "empowerment" had culminated in the zero-sum games of office politics. Unexpected and unbelievable compromise, betrayal, and ruthlessness in a workplace which we had supposedly created in our own image (free, creative, and inclusive) stunned many idealistic baby boomers.

Baby boomers were ill-prepared for a world of deceit, treachery, and misfortune, where absence of gratitude, reciprocity, or compensation – and the need to pander to others' desires and anxieties – belied the mythology of their youth. The rapid turn of the wheel of fortune, the inscrutable will of destiny, were not part of the original script. It may have been arrogant to believe that the world would remain forever in the same state of innocence, but they were incredulous when the world they created in their own image turned out to be a detestable mixture of wickedness, roguery, and rascality.

But it was mostly the disarray of the institutions inherited by baby boomers, and embodying their ideals and ambitions, that caused a collapse of confidence in the modern project. The signs of corruption and danger first appeared in those institutions charged with ensuring the quality of the primary elements of life. By the early 1990s, after reports of high levels of pathogens in the public water supply, baby boomers began to carry around bottled water. Air filters and ionizers were necessary to purify air contaminated by asbestos and lead. After the Red Cross tainted-blood scandal, many baby boomers put their own blood on deposit, exhibiting high apprehension regarding supplies. In the wake of the Ebola virus, AIDS, flesh-eating disease, superbugs, and toxins, we began hoping against hope, to use anti-bacterial handsoaps to ward off unseen dangers, and to purge our bodies with acidophilus. Drive-by shootings in Vancouver, Montreal, and Ottawa, random killings by schoolchildren in Alberta, and road rage in Toronto called the guarantee of public safety into question and led us to arm ourselves with personal security devices. The Canadian military, never exactly a baby-boomer institution, took a serious blow in the post-Somalia inquiry, confirming many baby boomers' worst suspicions of the military establishment's incapacity to secure peace and order.

The rot could be spied out equally in our "civilizing" institutions. That "Johnny can't read," or do mathematics, was a signal of serious problems in the school system. Canadian universities seemed more often pitched in partisan "culture wars," and the dubious enacting of controversial "zero-tolerance" policies to manage their fitful environ-ments, than in the dissemination of objective knowledge. Adding insult to injury, their degrees no longer guaranteed students an income to pay back crippling debt loads. Allegations of sexual abuse and scan-dal in the churches subverted any residual natural faith we placed in them. As a nation which finds its heroes in its athletes, revelations of drug doping in professional sports diminished our enthusiasm for heroism. Amid revelations of greed and corruption, the "Mulroney era" ended in distrust and suspicion of not only the Progressive Conservative Party of Canada, but of all political parties. The economic sphere fared no better. Pending bank mergers, and a progression of quarterly reports on unprecedented profits – not to mention the Bank of Montreal's controversial use of Bob Dylan's protest song from the sixties, "The Times They Are A-Changin'," in its corporate message of growth, expansion, and profit – focused atten-tion on the banks' power and our powerlessness. Who could trust any corporation and its consumer goods after the scandal of the leaking and health-impairing Dow Corning breast implant, to refer to only one of modern consumer society's egregious errors? A dramatically high national debt, volatile interest rates, and a falling currency did nothing to improve our moods or our loyalty. The baby boomers' cherished ideals of universality and accessibility came under unrelenting fire, and concessions were made which struck at and imperilled the moral core of these ideals.

The apparent breakdown was not restricted to the human world. The thinning of the ozone layer, and the noticeable buildup of the greenhouse effect, offered us daily evidence of how we had poisoned our skies. Deformed sea-life plucked out of our waters revealed how we were destroying our oceans. (What happens to the spirit of a nation whose motto is "from sea to sea," when its seas are irremediably polluted?) Medical research was providing us with a far greater and earlier understanding of the genetic inheritance of degenerative diseases, causing us to recoil in horror from our own bodies. And the recycling movement – the apotheosis of our idea of how we could freely legislate moral duty to ourselves, yet whose directives increasingly micromanaged our daily lives – was hampered by the reality that much of our recyclable garbage was not being processed. So much for saving the planet.

It does not matter that many of these "facts" of pollution, contamination, and corruption were merely vague feelings and exaggerated fears. It was of secondary importance that many good and beneficial things were happening in the world. For baby boomers, accustomed to rising on a crest of inflated confidence that the world could be managed, its signs of degeneracy were unfathomably alarming. Perception can be more volatile than reality, and the perception that "We fucked up," precipitated real consequences. "If there was ever a time that God did not miss one sparrow falling, that time is not now," comments one baby boomer. "There are too many sparrows falling."

One response was a dramatic loss of confidence in worldly forms, manifest as intensified gloom about the world, and a sense of foreboding that we were on the brink of disaster. While the world can appear strange and formidable at any time, its compromises, ambiguities, and imperfections are generally seen, not as signals of disaster, but as opportunities. But untold numbers of baby boomers, having enjoyed a youth where they and the world were one, and then having continually reshaped the world to meet their expectations, were thrown by the reality of decline and imperfection. Appropriate to a generation which thought it could live a life of wishes, baby boomers had not taken evil into account. Intoxication with life and the search for "more and more" turned out to be the sins of lust and greed.

Recoiling in dread at a world breaking down, these baby boomers were receptive to powerful antinomian sentiments – that all talk is cheap, that all institutions and conventions are distorting, that observable facts and distinctions are just perceptions. In some baby boomers, aversion to the world takes the form of "not in my backyard," where the reasonable give and take between individual and public goods degenerates to a zero-sum game. Such a mentality has given us gated communities, parochial schools, breakdowns in consensual democracy, and, in the extreme, survivalist hoarding. Baby-boomer dread also takes the form of withdrawal from public life in vows of silence, celibacy, and simplicity, conceding the futility and absurdity of all human striving, and betraying derision for the actualities of concrete experience. In its acute phase, it can develop into the belief that not only are we living in a hateful age where no one is safe, but that the world has become demonic. Here, deep healing is a dire necessity.

Baby boomers, alienated from the world and desperately searching for healing, are hearing Billy Graham's call. If baby boomers are looking for the last "good man," such a man must also fit their "comfort zone." Billy Graham is an eminently suitable match. As one commentator put it, "He is simply an unabashedly common man who brings gifts of intimacy and connection to what he does."[8] Baby boomers, so fretful over the world they have messed up, so incapable of returning to institutionalized religion, yet yearning for a searing experience of sanctification, see Billy as the answer to their dreams. No mock solemnity, no shopworn pageantry – just good old-fashioned preaching and a call for repentance.

Most important of all, Billy – and Paul Henderson – offer up "tradition." In a world where the only norm is change and no habits of behaviour are ever settled, it is inevitable that a sense of dread and unease will prevail in some quarters, and that a desperate search for anchors will ensue. Over against the widening gyre of perpetual novelty, and the abyss of non-finality it opens up beneath every choice and action, "tradition" is a reminder of a past where there was no ambiguity about authority, and of old-time morality, where the ten commandments were sacrosanct, where scripture was judge, jury, and executioner, where men were men, and women and children were in their proper places. Conservative baby boomers like Jim find in evangelical or fundamentalist Christianity "something really old and venerable." Here are roots, of a kind: a moral code, a social outlook, an intimate fellowship, the infallibility of scripture. All good companions of righteousness. Never mind that "old and venerable" is translated into sentimentality over schmaltzy contemporary tunes like "Trusting Jesus," or that "getting back to basics" equals rending the veil of everyday life with tears and sobs of mortification so as to have a private chat with Jesus. "Tradition," for Jim, is not so much time-tested legacy, or the historical evolution of a living faith being acted out in the world and accommodated to altered circumstances, as a lifesaver to hold onto over against modernity. It matters little that "tradition" is a simplistic simulacrum of the original spiritual discipline, or that its ideas make only minor concessions and compromises to the essential spirit of the modern age. The important thing for Jim is that it is old, that it is dissident, and that it works its healing power.

Others seeking a healing ministry with the more vivid hue of charismatic Christianity prefer to be "slain in the Spirit" at the Toronto Christian Airport Fellowship, or, more colloquially, the Toronto Blessing. It is a steamy summer evening, but over two thousand people have responded to the invitation to "be drunk at the party." For those with somewhat more spartan tastes, the evening has also been advertised as a "convention." Either way, the parking lot is overfilled – a car bumper sticker reads "Honk If You Love Jesus" and nearby everyone is honking – and buses and minivans are disgorging passengers and congesting nearby streets. In the kaleidoscope of faces, one sees hilarity, po-faced solemnity, elation, bliss, despondency, heartache. Hustled along by the mob of people, we eventually stream into the warehouse facility adjacent to Pearson International Airport. Sparsely appointed – a few banners, flags, and streamers; a medley of foldup chairs; a stage with a roughly hewn cross – the warehouse itself is disappointing, giving away nothing of the flamboyance that explains the fame of the Toronto Blessing. One whole wing is under messy construction so that even more participants can be accommodated in what can only be called the nightly "spiritual rave." Though jets are flying overhead, there is far too much tumult within for anyone to notice what is occurring without.

My first sight is of seven middle-aged women hopping up and down, chanting "Let's get close to the Holy Spirit." Another group is clapping, thumping their feet, and dancing in the aisles between the seats. In the middle of the hall, a huddle of men in their forties begins to wriggle and convulse like worms in a St. Vitus dance, their abrupt motions, like a mimetic contagion, catching on with several other groups that also begin to shake and tremble. At the periphery of the room are punk kids with mohawk cuts, carrying their skateboards under their arms, contorting and jerking their bodies to a hidden beat. Free-form dancers swoop around the premises. Someone is barking.

"The energy is on the rug," says Peter, who introduces himself as a businessman, noting my bewildered look at two ladies writhing and jerking on the ground. "Are you a believer?" he asks suspiciously. I prevaricate, inviting a two-minute admonishment that, without fully participating in tonight's revelry, I will never appreciate what is really happening here. His wife is wearing a T-shirt inscribed with "God is my co-pilot." They have been attending "parties" for four years, sometimes three times weekly. "We came here because we heard something was going on. I have a new wife every day; she's drunk every day with the Holy Spirit."

We're invited to join in the singing, accompanied by the band on the stage. "The church is loading up its spiritual gun/The devil is in the phone booth, dialing 9–1–1/The tables are turned and now he's on the run." Many individuals have their arms outstretched, singing with gusto; others are clapping, shouting, "JESUS, JESUS, JESUS." Another in-your-face religious T-shirt slides into the chair in front of us: "Don't Die Wondering." Like the cross on the stage, sundry participants have a bare cross on a leather thong around their necks. The resurrected Christ, not the crucified Christ, is on show tonight.

"Why are you here?" I ask Paula, a late-thirties law clerk. "To be ravished; to be drunk in the Holy Spirit." A pause, during which visible incredulity crosses my face. She adds, "Scripture reads, 'We do not know what we ought to pray for, but the Spirit himself intercedes for us with groans that words cannot express' (Rom. 8:26) and 'Do not get drunk on wine, which leads to debauchery. Instead, be filled with the Spirit' (Eph. 5:18) and 'We, who with unveiled faces all reflect the Lord's glory, are being transformed into His likeness with ever-increasing glory, which comes from the Lord, Who is the Spirit' (2 Cor. 3:18)." At this moment, some of the most ebullient parties have worked their way up in front of the stage, and there, as in a rock concert's mosh pit, they go into wild spasms. Drums, guitars, and horns fill the air with a tumultuous and cacophonous praise of the Lord.

Peter comments on how the evening is affecting him: "God's drawing me out of myself – like a meat grinder." Before I can respond, he falls to his knees and starts praying fervently, "All we ever wanted, Father, was to become close … to gain favour in your eyes." In front of me, people are contorting their bodies, waving their hands toward the crown of their heads as if to admit the Holy Spirit. As we start to sing "Just a closer walk with Jesus, who with me my burden shares," the middle-aged man in front of me sinks his head into his lap, and begins to sob uncontrollably. As the tempo of the evening increases, and spirits rise mercurially, the songs come harder and faster, with lyrics of abasement and surrender. "Empty yourself, let it go." A more forceful body language starts to take over, with emphatic fingering, wide hand sweeps, and bows of submission, amid howling and shrieking. In the background, a busload of travellers from Sudbury – "spiritual tourists"[9] – start drumming as if on a battlefield. A woman behind me is lying prostrate on the ground, moaning "Come and fill me up." All around the hall, bodies are falling backward, "slain in the Spirit." Many of the participants – one is tempted to say "performers" – maintain a constant eye on the projection screens which mirror the crowd back to itself. "Get up and dance," Peter exhorts me. "Jesus turns our sorrow into dance; the river of God sets our feet dancing." I demur, but wander off to seek further clarification. Again, I'm bidden to dance. "Like a child, I'll dance in your presence," the lead singer croons. "I don't ever want to lose that fire."

"Like a drug high, we are getting high on the Holy Spirit," I am repeatedly told. "It's like never-ending intoxication." Watching the surfeit of emotion, the uninhibited laughter, the conspicuous ecstasy, one has to be forgiven if one concludes that, as the night progresses, distinct shades of an orgy are emerging. Yet, at the same time, there is here the long legacy of John Wesley's holiness movement, where fervent prayer and formal ritual were means of purification and sanctification, and where each individual believer could anticipate the immediate presence of God. And maybe, akin to the Ranters, Quakers, Wesleyans, and Shakers – the "holy rollers" – before them during the Great Awakening of the early eighteenth century, tonight's revellers are truly enjoying the direct experience of divine being.[10] Then, too, convulsions, jerks, falling prostrate on the ground, dancing, barking, and hysterical laughter were means of dissolving the self so that one became a channel for the Holy Spirit. Other aspects of the Toronto Blessing are reminiscent of the Baptist and Methodist Revival, too. Watching the families who have hunkered down for the full seven-hour session, with their bologna sandwiches and thermoses of coffee, it is obvious that the Toronto Blessing is like the legendary days-long revivalist camp meetings of old. Or perhaps Woodstock.

It goes nearly without saying that the enthusiasm (literally, "from the god within") has honourable biblical antecedents:

> And when the day of Pentecost was fully come, they were all with one accord in one place. And suddenly there came a sound from heaven as of a rushing mighty wind, and it filled all the house where they were sitting. And there appeared unto them cloven tongues like as of fire, and it sat upon each of them. And they were all filled with the Holy Ghost, and began to speak with other tongues, as the Spirit gave them utterance. (Acts 2:1–5)

Later that night, true to form, one woman erupts into glossolalia. It is midnight, and the atmosphere in the room is charged with raw emotion. When an apparently drunk and rowdy figure cascades out of the mosh pit onto the stage, I pay scant attention, not suspecting that the climax of the evening is about to be reached. Yet, seconds later, either heavenly voices are in our midst, or, like Teresa of Avila, who heard voices of the Devil pretending to be the voice of God, tonight's channel has descended into a personal hell. Gurgling, whinnying, ululating, and yipping, her arms flailing around her, for thirty minutes she sends all the signals of one possessed, and amid the carnage of metaphor and babble seems to be saying that she has died and is reborn, was lost and is re-found, was isolated and is reattached. This she knows because a fire is bursting from her breastbone. Primal speech or staged performance?

While the woman does not exactly inspire the thought that one is in the presence of a prophetic seer, she does excite a battery of confessions from other "witnesses." All dutifully stand, sob on cue, and testify to the challenges in their lives, the disappointments and false paths taken, the epiphany of realization that they had erred, how the spirit now infuses their lives, what salvation has meant to them. The testimonials are often delivered in throaty breathlessness, during which, matching the pathos, fellow believers grimly intone "Alleluia" in a sign of solidarity. I've been there, brother and sister.

The evening winds to a rapid close and, exhausted and racked with a throbbing headache, I slip out into the dank, sultry air of Toronto's suburbs, unclear as to what I have just observed. Inevitably, I run into Peter again, who confides, "I've talked to the Lord."

On a charitable reading, it would be churlish and precipitous to deny that there are baby boomers at the Toronto Blessing who are hearing the call to a life of faith and repentance. It may also be the case that real spiritual transformation, and not mere revelry in religious affectations, is taking place at the Toronto Christian Airport Fellowship. The emotional intensity of the "party" – at times, raw hysteria – should not in itself be seen as compromising such transformation. After all, Rudolf Otto, whose definition of *the holy* we referred to earlier, expressly argued that the essence of religious experience is beyond the sobriety of rationality. The heart has reasons the mind cannot see, wrote Blaise Pascal. So pedestrian and incremental is our ordinary idea of change, that it takes a surfeit of sentiments, ideas, and imagination to even speculate what it might mean to brave the transformative effect of spiritual regeneration. Here, the sober language and prescribed behaviours stipulated by theologians and clerics are simply insufficient to do justice to the intensity of sanctification experienced in dwelling, even if ever so briefly, in proximity to the source of revelation. Speaking in tongues, ecstatic prophesizing, and hearing oracles of the Holy Spirit – so jarring and suspect to minds inclined to the stately solemnity of high-church Protestantism and Roman Catholicism – are often too readily dismissed, their detractors blind to the fact that all religions begin in earth-shaking revelation. In many ways, the Toronto Blessing is as old as the second-century Montanist sect, renowned for religious enthusiasm, which – though denounced as a heresy – still included as august a figure as Tertullian, the Roman theologian and Christian apologist, as a member.

An illustration from India also sheds light on the Toronto Blessing:

In the inner sanctum of a Hindu temple, devotees may be shrieking or wailing, for to enter the superworld of the gods and goddesses, they must ecstatically, nearly violently, remove themselves from the too-orderly world of daily experience. *Darshan* – seeing the god – cannot occur without extraordinary measures. Nor should much be made of the fact that many of those drawn to the Toronto Blessing are the broken and alienated, the also-rans of modern life, the shipwreck of their lives driving them in desperation to seek redemption. To recapitulate, William James wrote that the religion of the "sick-souled" was vastly more profound than a religion which dwelled exclusively on goodness, order, and beauty. Only in the abyss of darkness, in the depth of humiliation, and in the worm of melancholy and affliction, James wrote, do we truly encounter God. Not during the times when we exalt in our achievements and fulfill our natural longings, but instead in the perfidy of our sin and the poverty of our spirit, does God exhibit an interest – "Man's extremity is God's opportunity." And, like the revivalist movements of two centuries ago, the charismatics of the Toronto Blessing want simply to restore to religion the element of being a holy channel for the entry of the Spirit into the world, and of personal responsibility for salvation.

On a more critical reading, however, the Toronto Blessing seems little more than an exercise in vamping up religious affectations. As an observer, one imagines that one is at an event akin to *The Rocky Horror Picture Show* phenomenon. Here is the same kind of scripted and well-rehearsed spectacle, which combines parody, pure make-believe, a raspberry in the face to the establishment, and hamming it up. The histrionic atmosphere of the Toronto Blessing invites a command performance – dress down, farm out the kids, skip the town and head for the warehouse, cry a little, laugh a little, cut loose, and be saved. But do it with drama. It is a spectacle which attracts exhibitionists and voyeurs, and which thrives on upping the ante. I had been watching one young man throughout the evening as he rent the air with barks, tore at his hair, threw himself to the floor, sobbed, and frolicked. He told me that he had heard the call to Jesus that night. I was reminded of Pascal's comment that "Men often mistake their imagination for the prompting of their heart, and believe they are converted the moment they think of conversion."[11] Later, reflecting on why so many of the participants kept glancing over at the Jumbotron to watch themselves "doing it," I concluded that the Toronto Blessing was where the ideas of Christopher Lasch, the author of *The Culture of Narcissism,* meet those of Guy Debord, the author of *The Society of the Spectacle.* Narcissism as spectacle. Here, where genuine sentiment is mediated by technology and by *amour-propre,* there could only be the surface play of ersatz communal intimacy and sanctity. A collectivity of solitudes and feigned passion cannot substitute for real community and true holiness embodied in daily life, however intense and dramatic it may be. If the Toronto Blessing is satisfying baby boomers' craving for belonging, to its discredit, it is doing so without requiring either fidelity or discipline, those ingredients which stabilize and mature the need for community.

Regardless of the reading, the attractions of the Toronto Blessing to baby boomers are formidable. For one, it satisfies their "ecstasy deficit," which propels them from one event to another in search of total satisfaction. There is a palpable high to be felt at the Toronto Blessing – whether it is psychological or spiritual is a matter for debate – and baby boomers are revelling in it. The encounter with God is "the challenge beyond all challenges," and, for many in this cohort, it is the next station in the search for more and more. The Toronto Blessing also taps neatly into the boomers' lifelong habit of surfing, letting go, and enjoying the exhilaration of freefall. Pragmatism – it's true if it works – and opportunity to play with any variety of practices ensure that no customary ways hinder exploration of the spirit. Since virtually anything goes during the "party," baby boomers can happily continue to be *bricoleurs,* adjusting even spirituality to taste. The communal ecstasy and mass catharsis also confirm their desire to be at a primal axis point from which existence can be recreated. The pre-verbal utterances and noises, the archetypal gestures and body movements, are bids to rejoin Adam before the Fall, to "speak" in his original language, to enjoy his pre-lapsarian enchanted state. At the Toronto Blessing, baby boomers can be children at play – divine play. While many are looking for their friend Jesus, the real hope is to attract the Holy Spirit, for it is the Spirit who comes as a "rush of violent wind" (Acts 2:2), sanctifying by radical regeneration rather than by reconciliation. Above all, baby boomers seek an encounter with something primordial, pure, and uncompromised, for therein lies redemption from a world spinning out of control. While "primordialism" is a simulacrum of tradition, and thus empty of enduring significance, it nonetheless serves as a placeholder of the nostalgic desire for the "old and venerable." And, as one Toronto Blessing celebrant confided to me, by going back to roots, to a Christianity that was at play in the original times of Christ's life, baby boomers like herself were being empowered and recovering their true tribe.

.  .  .

The importance of power and tribe, a phenomenon Michael Adams zeroed in on in his book *Sex in the Snow*, may also be the reason for the allure of native spirituality. Here, too, the return to a way of being which is primordial, where proximity to the land and wilderness becomes an engagement with reality – tinged by the self-remorse of colonialism – is expected to provide some deep sense of belonging and empowerment. Across the country, thousands of Canadian baby boomers, both native and non-native, are looking for answers and affirmation in native sweat lodges, sweetgrass ceremonies, vision quests, and at powwows.

In my judgment, "doing a sweat" has to be directly experienced for its ostensible spiritual significance to be understood. Fortunately, Poundmaker Lodge, a native treatment centre for alcohol and drug addiction situated outside of Edmonton which uses the sweat lodge as one of its key tools to recovery, and where native and non-native baby boomers are seeking rehabilitation and identity, was obliging. The road to Poundmaker takes one past the Loyal Order of Moose and the Alberta Gaming and Liquor Commission, to within a stone's throw of the Edmonton Residential School. The ironies could escape no one.

On arrival, I'm waved in the direction of the trees and I wind my way to a clearing below the lodge, where I find six Sioux teenagers fanning a raging bonfire, within which glow the rocks to be used in the sweat. There are fifteen men and ten women, some aboriginal, some not, standing around uncomfortably. Many of their arms bear knife-wound and needle scars, and equally visible is the craggy, dull-eyed look of the drug and alcohol addict. Dave is the Sioux elder who will take us through the sweat, and he arrives armed with drums, rattles, pipes, and pouches of sweetgrass. The sweat lodge itself is a domed tent, intended to represent mother earth's womb, and the willow frame signifies women's ribs. In the centre is an eighteen-inch-deep hole, beneath which is the entrance to mother earth. The whole edifice is covered in tarps, representing the seasonal robes covering the earth, and there are four doors at the four cardinal points that allow the spirit keepers to access the sacred lodge. We sit in a circle, "the connected way." Above us hovers grandfather, below us lies grandmother.

We are barely seated when the first red-hot rock – representing the coming of life, but also endurance, strength, sacrifice – is brought in and deposited in the pit. Dave pours a ladle of water over the rock. Its hissing steam is said to be the creative force of the universe coming into being, and it will, in turn, communicate prayers to the Great Spirit. Once the tarps are lowered, the lodge is reduced to pitch-darkness, the most unrelenting black I have ever experienced: the darkness of ignorance, void, and emptiness. The heat mounts quickly, rising to 120 degrees Fahrenheit, and within seconds our skins glisten and gush sweat. Dave starts to beat the drum, the rocks hiss, the air is thick and cloying. He tosses sweetgrass – three strands braided together to represent mind, body, and spirit – into the pit, and its pungent aroma hits our noses immediately, "smudging," or purifying, our whole being. The whole eerie environment, akin to standing in the pit of a coalmine, is meant to make us brave, and to cry out to the Creator and the rock spirit to help us endure pain and suffering. There are four rounds of sweats, each lasting fifteen minutes, and four times the door is opened, representing the four periods of time and cycles of life – infancy, childhood, adulthood, and old age. The most important door of the lodge is to the east, the source of light and wisdom, and the means by which the vapours escape and illness is expelled from mind and body. Each time the door is opened, there is an audible cathartic release as the fresh, cool air, and Great Spirit's light, burst in. There are four invocations in each round: to the ancestral spirits, to grandmother, to grandfather, and to the here and now. Four fours are sixteen – the sixteen aspects of Wakan Tanka, the great mystery.

With Dave caterwauling, the drum beating its primordially hypnotic rhythms, a chorus of twenty-five individuals muttering prayers, and the intense black rendering it impossible to determine where sound is coming from, it is hard not to spring to the conclusion that the voices are arising from dead spirits. But the oral message emanating from Dave is this-worldly: Be responsible, be free from alcohol and drugs, heal with the earth, ancestors and family. "Let yourself go," Dave keeps repeating, as he relates how we are about to be hit about the ears by the wings of an eagle, sprung from the feather he had inserted into the ceiling at the commencement of the ceremony. When the lodge door is opened for the last time, Dave solicits expressions of good health from everyone, and one celebrant replies that he has experienced "something very spiritual." Later, a pipe is passed around, its rising smoke carrying prayers to the Creator, and each celebrant blows smoke to the earth to honour motherhood and the giving of life, to the sun and Great Spirit's power of creation and generosity, and finally uses his or her hands to sweep smoke over the head to re-sanctify body and soul. The sweat concludes with declarations of gratitude – an evident catharsis, purification, and reconciliation in force. We have been in the crucible, dissolved to pure potential, and now the imbalances of life have been healed. "It's the pageantry, man," admits one middle-aged man wanly. "It's so beautiful and so terrifying, it just feels right."

A few months later, I am at Tyendinaga's Twelfth Annual Traditional Pow Wow, billed as "Honouring Mother Earth" in *Pow Wow '99: 5th Annual Great Lakes Pow Wow Guide*. As I arrive, Chief Donald Maracle, dressed in full native regalia, is ringing the church bell of Christ Church Anglican, the royal chapel of the Mohawks, announcing that the "Grand Entry" is about to begin. The "host" drum is pom-pomming – seven drummers pounding in unison – drawing visitors to the "sacred fire," a small fire burning inside a deeply rooted pine tree trunk, and kept burning for the duration of the powwow. Twelve-hundred strong, native and non-native, we mill around and are invited to place offerings of cedar and pine sprigs, small twigs, and sweetgrass on the fire. Numerous non-native visitors are carrying copies of *Black Elk Speaks*, the "bible" of native spirituality. The importance of the daily morning "pipe ceremony" is explained: Smoking the sacred pipe cleanses and purifies, restoring unity and harmony. It confers the power to speak to Great Spirit. The sacred pipe's elements are themselves important: The rock that makes up the pipe is the earth, tobacco is the plant world, the feathers and fur attached to the pipe are animal life, and a man's breath is the human world. Only when a man breathes into the stem of the pipe does the peace of Great Spirit enter and infuse it, his power of creation and generosity a response to human initiative.

The smoke from the pipe directed to the earth honours motherhood and life-giving. Directed to the sun, it honours Great Spirit. The rising smoke carries prayers to the Creator. There is a hushed sense of awe in the air.

The powwow ceremonial circle itself is seventy-five feet in diameter, centred on a double arbor covered in pine boughs, within which are the drums of all the visiting First Nations, protecting and announcing the symbolic centre of the cosmos. Around the perimeter of the arbor are posted flags of four colours – red, white, yellow, black – representing all the human races. A chant erupts which makes the hair on the back of my neck stand up. The procession moves into the circle from the east and circles clockwise, following the pattern of the sun. The "Veteran Honour Staff" enters, followed by flag-bearers and the dancers. It is like a scene from a Karl May novel. A speaker recites the thanksgiving address, introducing the Creator into the gathering, importuning nothing from the deity, expressing gratitude for everything. The atmosphere is one of respect, honour, and inclusivity. Many of the attendees are visibly emotionally moved. My host whispers:

> You had asked if powwows were always open to non-natives. They have to be. Absolutely. Our symbol is the circle with the colours of the four races. If we said you can't come because you are white, that would break the circle. We'd be going against ourselves. There are a lot of natives who think it shouldn't be open to non-natives – because of everything that happened, residential schools, lots of abuse. Some young people feel that it looks like you broke the circle. "We didn't break the circle. White society broke the circle. Before we let them back in, we need time to be just ourselves and heal. We are the minority," some of them are saying. But no, we cannot go against our own selves. The circle cannot be broken.

A baby boomer standing next to me, overhearing this explanation, nudges me and says earnestly, "You drew a circle that excluded me and I drew a bigger circle that took you in." A stately drumbeat in the background seems to reinforce the lesson.

After the thanksgiving address, the master of ceremonies greets us more informally:

I'd like to thank that drum … that spirit of the Ojibway First Nation that I carry. For all races, red people, yellow people, white people, black people, we are gathered here to celebrate, not in anger, but peace. In the circle all are equally welcome, in the hope that one day the circle will widen into the other countries. If later you see me coming out dancing and touching you with the feathers, I'm inviting you to come in to dance, to celebrate the circle of life and the health that is in Mother Earth, that you come in and dance to the wellness of your family. I hope you have a really good day, that you might find that vision of wellness.

The dances and singing continue all day, pausing only briefly to allow participants to browse through the stalls of dream catchers and leather pouches stuffed with sage. At one table are seated two native baby boomers. She identifies herself as a Mohawk, belonging to the Wolf clan; he is of the Turtle clan. "I never knew my mother," Susan divulges. "She was Indian. My father raised me, off and on, but I was shuffled around, mostly in white society in foster homes. I have no real record of my background." Matt nods in agreement. "It's very common. It happened to me, too. That's why it's so important to come together to seek and get this connection. Here I can meet these total strangers, other natives, and I can go through the whole book with them. I can talk to them about anything. It's like I've known them all my life." Susan adds, "We come together at these powwows, we get a sense of belonging, a sense of where we are, where we're from, what our history is, and we build on that and it strengthens us, reassures us. It's an identification that is empowering for us." Hurting and in need of healing, these native baby boomers find in the powwow the ancient pact between deity, people, and land.

In one hand, Matt is holding a book entitled *Sacred Path Cards: The Discovery of Self Through Native Teachings*. In his other hand is a deck of fifty large cards. Each numbered card corresponds with a page of the same number in the book. At his urging, I pick a card randomly and he opens the book and begins to read me the corresponding entry. It is about giving and releasing. "It's really a book of wisdom, common sense, tribal wisdom. There's not one negative card or negative [thought] in the book. Our Creator is not punishing but gift-giving."

Matt weaves into his reading an explanation of the bustle of activity happening adjacent to where we are standing. "This is the 'giveaway.' A big blanket is put on the ground inside the circle. This is where people bring and place things they don't need anymore. Maybe give up relationships that are bad for you, or attitudes holding you back, clouding your thinking. Thoughts and ideas that are wrong, hurtful; only by getting rid of these things, only by releasing them do you allow yourself to heal first and make room for good to come in." It's magic, it's mimesis, and it's utterly mystifying.

Before we part, Matt offers his explanation of why so many non-natives are drawn to a powwow:

> I think there'd be a lot of different reasons. But major ones are as tourists. It's a cultural experience. And the spiritual aspect of the powwow can draw non-natives because they crave something spiritual. But they're not getting it in their own world environment. Here, our spirituality is you and the Creator. No elder is going to come between you and the Creator. In the white world you have to have the big cathedrals, rituals, and you've got to dress right. Religion is so over-organized. Here, what works for you between you and the Creator is right. As long as it's peace, love, giving and all that – the basics. How you relate to your Creator is entirely up to you. It's simple. No trappings. People want to see mystery where there is none. There's no mystery. You know in the church there can be mystery. There's no mystery here. By keeping things simple, you can retain the complexity.

Willy, a fortysomething baby boomer of Scottish ancestry and a Vietnam veteran, agrees. Rediscovering his own native roots was a way of releasing and letting go so he could again live in the present. "When I came back from Vietnam, I went to see my mother. I couldn't take care of myself. One day, looking through the big old family Bible genealogy and some photos, I asked, 'How come Nan's picture's not here?' Dead silence. It was Christmastime. Awkward. I persisted and found that my mother's mother was native – Ojibway. The family didn't want to acknowledge this." Not only his family denied its heritage. "When I go to the elders in the native community, they encourage me to find out about the other [Scottish] part of my ancestry. I don't get the same from the Scottish side," Willy cavilled. "By destroying native spirituality, we destroyed an important part of ourselves. We have our feet in a 30,000-year-old tradition and our heads in Europe. As far as my Scottish heritage, it just doesn't answer my questions. There's just nothing for me. But these powwows are like little bright spots which help me get back to the red path." I ask him what had touched him most about the powwow. He liked the thanksgiving address:

> How it mentioned everything in a general sense and yet made it feel very immediate somehow, how everything seemed to be not so much covered as included – everything from the stars to the grass under our feet. But mostly it's the elders, and what they teach you about yourself. You don't really know that they've taught you something until days after. All of a sudden, it will just sink in. Knowledge to them is sacred. The elders are not just going to tell you everything they know. To know things is a privilege. You have to earn it. It's not a right. They want to see if you want it. How much do you want it? Are you ready for it? What can you hear?

Willy's attraction to native spirituality is not hard to comprehend. With a felt immediacy, it achieves what Mircea Eliade described as "the turning of simple existence into a living drama."[12] Participation in organic life is once again sacramental, a kinship with other sentient beings is re-established, the ancestors and tribal wisdom are restored to life, and our land becomes not a mere resource, to be exploited and managed, but a place to be hallowed. Reversing the modern perspective which distinguishes soul from body, human from nature, and life from land – inviting one aspect of life to dominate and control the other – native spirituality restores holism. In opposition to our social world, where anomie and dislocation erode all sentiments of commitment, native spirituality calls for reverence and gratitude. The idea of a sacred pact encompassing people, land, and deity exposes how hollow all modern talk of a "social contract" really is.

Native spirituality conforms consummately to many baby boomers' tastes. Incredulous at the idea of a Hebrew or Christian God who, as potentate, judges and exhibits wrath ("Thou shalt," "Thou shalt not"), baby boomers find only affirmation in the sacred-pipe ceremonies, the powwows, and the sweat lodge. As opposed to a religion that requires one part of the body to war with another, that elevates humans to the apex of all life and thus tolerates arrogance toward nature and other sentient beings, and whose history is a sorry tale of denunciations and excommunications, native spirituality is open-armed and inclusive. In touch with the primal elements – water, earth, wind, and fire – it enchants and is transformational. It contains a great mystery, the Wakan Tanka, revealed to initiates. It holds the key that explains and teaches us how to control human nature: the trickster, the troublemaking twin aspect of our soul that makes us do and be what we do not want; the spider, who lays out webs, springs from a trap door, and drains the spiritual juice out of us. During a vision quest, one discovers that everything is alive and has power, that there are lessons hidden in creation, and ancient truths to be disinterred. By consecrating all life, native spirituality heals the divisions of modernity. There is ritual, but no doctrine. There are no "men with hats," for the "men with feathers" accept and don't condemn. "Magical synchronicity," a psychotherapist who uses native spirituality exclusively in her practice imparts to me, "that's what my clients are looking for. They want a support group where they can be empowered and feel the vibration." In the sweat lodge or around the sacred powwow circle, baby boomers find the covenantal community which has eluded them in family and social life. It offers uncompromised solidarity and affection, without any of the intervening messiness that ordinarily demands accommodation. Finding and then belonging to one's own tribe is empowering.

．　　．　　．

Power and tribe, tribe and power. And tradition. To think of these terms together brings one inevitably to the Latter-day Saints (Mormons) and to Cardston, Alberta. In his book *The American Religion*, Harold Bloom claims, albeit with some hyperbole, that Mormonism is the fastest-growing religion in the world (eleven million worldwide) and that Mormonism and Christian evangelicalism alone now predominate the religious scene in the United States. While Mormons have not had the same phenomenal success rate in Canada, the mytho-poetic world at the centre of Mormon faith has attracted much baby-boomer attention. How could it not? More fantastical than make-believe – just believe it, don't think about it – and more secretive than Freemasonry, the Mormons nonetheless tap perfectly into baby boomers' need for belonging and a return to the source. Searching for lost origins, for tradition as pure as silk? For a nurturing community, the family you never had? For divine empowerment and eternal life? You have come to the right place. Mormonism has it all.

After the Resurrection, scripture relates, Christ spent forty days on earth. Regrettably, scripture offers no information as to what Christ was doing during the time before His Ascension into heaven. The Mormons believe Christ went to America to instruct the aboriginal people. Ancestors of these native people left Jerusalem in 600 BCE with the prophet Lehi, wandered through the wilderness, built a ship and sailed to America. There were, according to the Mormons, two tribes in America – the two lost tribes of Israel. The Lamanites and the Nephites were the descendants of two brothers, Laman and Nephi. Today's First Nations peoples enjoy a direct lineage back to Laman and the ancient Israelites.

Mormons have no doubt about their facts because in 1820 Christ appeared to Joseph Smith to let him know the latest revelation. Smith was also visited by the angel Moroni for four years, between 1823 and 1827, and shown the records of the early inhabitants of America, inscribed on gold plates, and specifically the revelations from God to the prophets. The revelations had been compiled by Moroni's father, Mormon, and Smith set himself the task of translating them into English. The result was The Book of Mormon. Smith was also visited by John the Baptist, who conferred on him the Aaronic priesthood, allowing Smith to baptize and administer the law of Moses. Peter, James, and John also visited Smith and conferred on him the Melchizedek priesthood and the authority to administer all its ordinances. Later, the *Pearl of Great Price*, containing the sayings of Abraham, Moses, and Joseph Smith, as well as the text *Doctrine and Covenants*, would spell out the beliefs of the Church of Jesus Christ of Latter-day Saints. The current LDS president, Gordon B. Hinckley, is a self-appointed prophet who converses with Christ and God, calling the world to repent and prepare for the imminent return of Jesus Christ as messiah and head of an earthly Kingdom of God.

The temple in Cardston, L D s's first in Canada, towers above the small town of 3,500 inhabitants. Completed in 1923, it recently had a $20 million make-over. While Cardston's streets are narrow and congested, sweeping boulevards surround the temple, and not without reason. As my host, Alan (a baby-boomer convert), explains, this is the place of the Lord's return in the last days of time. As a non-Mormon, I am not permitted beyond the vestibule of the temple, but even that offers a revealing glimpse. Like monumental cathedrals and mosques, the interior – wide staircases and breezy balconies, imposing columns, halcyon pools – evokes grandeur, majesty, celestial expanse. It is also decorous. A vase with a fringe of braided twenty-four-karat gold strands resides in a panelled alcove. Wall hangings depict scenes of revelation and prophecy. Unfortunately, they verge on the precious and sentimental – especially when captured in profile with the bank of humming computers lining the entranceway. Here, day after day, data are collected worldwide and input to compile genealogies that provide intelligence for one of the major ceremonies of the temple – the baptism of the dead. Mormons perform this investigation and ensuing rite, Alan explains, as a proxy baptism for those ancestors of Mormons who died before the Mormon revelations were known. Five times a day, ceremonies for the salvation of one's ancestors are held in the temple: The name of the deceased is entered on a bar-coded card, his or her proxy enters the pool, and with the audible beep of the bar-code reader, the deceased is entered on the eternal register. Outside Salt Lake City, the New Jerusalem of the Latter-day Saints, the Mountain of Names contains two billion names of the dead welcomed into the Mormon fold.

Alan remembers with relish his "endowment ceremony," or initiation, to the Latter-day Saints. Though he will not divulge all the details, little imagination – or knowledge of Masonic or other hermetic initiation rites – is required to speculate what these rites involved, given what Alan learned: what really happened in the garden of Eden; that he emerged from an unborn state, where a god and his wife made love and created his spirit; how there is a plurality of gods, and how humans may become gods; that he is part of other worlds, and how he may evolve into the headship of stars all over the universe; that sexual intercourse is sanctified and theurgical; that after his death and resurrection, he will perform the task of begetting spirit-children. During his endowment ceremony, Alan was honoured to be permitted to go through the "Veil" to the celestial room where God and Jesus live, to be shown the "Eternity Mirrors" facing one another and evoking celestial infinitude, and to be given his New Skin, or "Skin of Adam" – a set of underwear embellished with Masonic symbols, which he is obliged to wear for two years and may not remove, even while washing or during sex, and which he may elect to wear for life. A few years later, he was also married in the temple, a "sealing ceremony" involving a vow not merely "until death do us part," but of eternal marriage worthy of celestial divinities. In short, Alan learned what every Gnostic has always wanted in hand: the final definitive answer to, what is above? What is beneath? What was before time? And what will be hereafter?[13] "God," Alan confides, "is just a glorified man."

Theo, who has just completed a two-year stint as the United Church minister in Cardston, offers a credible explanation for these vivid beliefs and ceremonies: "The bizarre exterior serves as the armour to define them as a community." Alan, my host, leaves me with no doubt as to how vigorous the temple's community life is. A full social calendar of activities in the church make it nearly impossible to meet with him at all. Then, complicating the leisure we need to converse, his son is about to depart for his mandatory two-year missionary work. Another son, though only fifteen, has just been asked to assume the office of bishop. Later that afternoon, there is a meeting of Alan's ward (a community unit consisting of about 200 people) and, after dinner – tonight happening to be "family home evening" – they are expecting a home visit by a committee from the stake (a larger unit of about 1,000 people). Obliged to tithe 10 per cent of gross salary, all LDS members are provided with an extensive welfare system, the Relief Society, and these visits ensure that everything is running smoothly. Since there is no pontifex, and priesthood is rotated around the church membership, every individual and family has an investment and a visibility in the community, and most nights are filled with meetings. Organized sports events, scripture readings, work bees, and social clubs take up any remaining evenings. "We keep them so busy, they have no choice," Alan laughs, when I ask if any Mormons eventually just give up and leave Cardston. And, indeed, Cardston is a frighteningly "pan-optical" society, to use Michel Foucault's term for a community in which every behaviour is monitored and gently adjusted.[14] No one in Cardston should ever be troubled by solitude or privacy. Or apostasy.

Maintaining the image of "good, clean living" pervades life in Cardston. The ban on alcohol, tobacco, and coffee minimizes social transgressions and explains Mormon health and longevity (moreover, "the Resurrected Body has to endure the rigours of eternal worship"). Dating and marriage are closely regulated. Young women wear a ring engraved with the letters CTR – Choose the Right – or sport "I am Reverent" pins on their lapels, identifying themselves as Mormons to potential suitors. Many young men wear T-shirts boldly commanding, "Repent." Their fathers protectively watch every move. The occasional out-of-wedlock pregnancy is sent abroad on missionary duty. If marital fidelity or familial duty flags, there are kitschy pictures of happy couples, with fawning smiles and exuding homely domesticity, that keep everyone on the straight and narrow. Yet, for all this appearance of meddling intrusiveness, Mormonism inculcates sage wisdom – in the pamphlet "The Purpose of Life," one reads, "People who encourage us to lower our moral standards are not true friends," and "The most important of the Lord's work that you will ever do will be within the walls of your own home." Safety, sobriety, and family values greet the visitor to Cardston, rich assets at any time and, for some anxious seekers, a haven, particularly now in our turbulent times.

With a membership of eleven million worldwide and a growth rate of 6 per cent per year, with $30 billion in assets and nearly $6 billion in annual gross income, with 525 new meeting houses being built every year and fifteen new temples under construction, and inner loyalty and self-discipline demonstrably unwavering, the LDS is obviously doing something right.[15] Its charities and missions are spread worldwide, from Armenia and Romania, to Brazil and Ecuador, and where there are famines and earthquakes, LDS relief is not far behind.

Why are baby boomers so attracted? One possible line of speculation is the following: Baby boomers are gravely disappointed that the world has not shown itself amenable to an idealistic reformation. Indeed, despite early signs that the world could be remade, what was fresh and promising has staled or soured. Guiltless for decades about the pleasures and power they enjoyed, now, in a dramatic reversal brought about by satiety and disappointment, baby boomers exhibit a desperate need to purge and atone. And shunning the world they designed, where nothing was finally worthy of being believed in, baby boomers long to believe in something – anything. When Creation is discovered to be irremediably flawed, and the world is perceived to be filled with senseless stuff, only a supernatural mysticism will redeem. Baby boomers are building castles in the air because they no longer believe there is ground beneath them. Best of all is a spiritual search which dwells in the occult, with secret truths, promises of divine enlightenment, and ritual – but no doctrine. And, being homeless, baby boomers console themselves with self-righteousness, even or especially when censoriousness is exercised about merely formal trappings. But baby boomers, being baby boomers, will only adopt a religion which fulfills their sense of destiny ("If I am in despair, the world must be suffering spiritual impoverishment") and which fits their "comfort zone" – it must be egalitarian and democratic, affective and sincere. And, for some baby boomers, it must "smell" of authenticity, of the old days when we were children, when humankind was in its infancy, when everything was whole and everyone belonged, when things were not messed up – a coziness like that evoked by Aretha Franklin, who said in a television interview that when she visited her childhood Bethel Baptist Church, it had the comforting smell of fried chicken and hot rolls. Her interviewer confided that she had had a similar experience in a United Church, which had the reassuring smell of old books.[16]

How elegantly Mormonism satisfies these requirements is impressed upon me by Alan as we take a walk down the main street of Cardston. "It's living prophecy, it's a lost heritage recovered, a tradition with the twist that there's none of the corruption of the historical churches," he muses. "The Christian churches have been distorted, the true Church stems from Adam. Ours is the restored church." Our conversation shifts back to the duty of missionary work. We discuss his daughter's imminent departure and the LDS's progressive mindset in giving women an active role in ministry and rotating ecclesiastical office regardless of gender or age. Then we talk about Alan's neighbour, whose pregnant daughter has been sent abroad. "Won't her current condition interfere with her missionary service to others?" I naively ask. "But, Peter," Alan smiles, "our missions don't have the purpose of helping people or evangelizing *per se*, but of inoculating our young people against the world." Indeed, a comment Theo, the United Church minister, had made a few days earlier now made sense. He suggested:

Mormons live in a social world which makes no spiritual demands.
The bipolarity of fallen creation and celestial salvation creates a
bland, unmediated world. Mormons are not expected to do
anything of a civil nature, they have no capacity to think about the
world, the world does not exist for them, its modalities of conduct
can be accepted or declined. It's a virtual community. Their imaginations are not directed to this world. That's why the aesthetic in
their art is just kitsch.

Whether Theo's comments are entirely fair or not, what is not in
dispute is how cozily sociable the Cardston community is. Greetings
on the street as "brother" or "sister," earnest inquiries about health and
business, streams of invitations to tea or lunch, all leave an impression
of homey, intimate fellowship – the cinnamony smell of warm apple
pie and Mom's Chanel Nº 5, the "all-Canadian" happy family. And
maybe they *are* all just one happy family. Our walk happens to coincide
with the arrival of the "Great Trek." In 1887, a group of ten families led
by Charles Ora Card, Brigham Young's son-in-law, left Utah in search
of a state that did not outlaw polygamy. Months later, they arrived in
Cardston, Alberta, and today's parade marks the arrival of ten families
who have re-enacted the whole long trek. "Mom, he looks just like
Uncle Frank," "Isn't she like Aunt Thelma?" I overhear in the excited
young crowd around me, fingers pointing at the Utah caravanners.
Polygamy, of course, is illegal in the United States and Canada, though
it may still be rife in backwater Utah. Some spiritual seekers can have
their cake and eat it too, it seems. The latchkey kids, abandoned by
their families in childhood due to jobs and divorces, have found their
revenge: marriages sealed everlastingly, the dead and resurrected still
begetting spirit-children endlessly, polygamous and theurgical sexual
unions, all adding up to families that will *never* slip away, even unto
eternity.

Finally, there is both "something happening" in Cardston and something to do. Midway between Cardston and Raymond, as the crow
flies, is the town of Stand Off, the native reserve of the Blood tribe.
Here, family names like Bruised Head, Catface, Hindbull, Melting
Tallow, Crying Head, Heavyhead, and Holy Singer leave no doubt that
despite decades of Christian missionaries, tribe pride remains dominant. Until the 1960s, neither the Bloods nor blacks could be Mormons

– they bore the mark of Cain. Today, Mormons see natives as descendants of Israel's lost tribes, as sacerdotal bearers of the revelation of the New World. They are a special people, a chosen people, set apart. In them lies the potential to redeem the Christian churches of the Old World, fallen into apostasy. Yet, they loll around tidy Cardston indigent and drunk, hardly embodiments of celestial wisdom. There is a Blood ward, but much more remains to be done. Perhaps the conversion of the Bloods has some urgency to it.

As the Great Trek caravans reach a bend in the street, I notice for the first time a store plunk in the centre of Cardston called "In Case of Emergency," its windows laden with generators, huge sacks of rice and flour, and industrial-size tins of fruit, fish, and peanut butter, all bearing the L D S label, "Deseret" [the golden nectar of the honeybee]. Mormon families are obliged to keep one year's food supply on hand. "Many people wonder about all the current troubles – political things, floods, deaths," Alan explains. "Duh, of course they're happening, we're in the last days. The end is near because the 6,000-year cycle is coming to a close." From the volume of food leaving the store, I see that apprehensive stockpiling for the Second Coming, and the imminent return to ground zero, is uppermost in many Cardston residents' minds.[17]

Cardston, and the beliefs of Mormons generally, are in many ways incredible to me. But they are not simply beyond belief. The whole organization and atmosphere of Cardston has achieved a level of systematized simulation, of manufactured make-believe, which nearly makes the true suspension of disbelief seem frighteningly feasible. A religion of restitution and restoration (all the way back to Adam), which unites apocalyptic anxiety and an extravagant mythical fantasy with an elaborate unworldly busyness and the promise of total regeneration, cannot fail to be congenial to baby boomers' new traditionalist sentiments. Perhaps not surprisingly, 4,000 Canadians a year – many of them highly educated, thoughtful baby boomers – are joining the L D S church.

•   •   •

It is time, perhaps, to give a name to that family resemblance of wistful remembrance of something "old and venerable," pure and primordial, which links the baby boomers' searches in evangelical Christianity, the

Toronto Blessing, native spirituality, and Mormonism, and which points beyond these religious movements to the examples of the next chapter – conservative Roman Catholicism and Orthodoxy.

Jaroslav Pelikan writes, "Tradition is the living faith of the dead, traditionalism is the dead faith of the living."[18] A wealth of ideas and discerning insights can be unpacked from Pelikan's epigrammatic observation. Consider the following situations: There are baby boomers who return to Roman Catholic and Anglican parishes and complain bitterly that there is neither incense nor chanting. A secular, Muslim woman goes to her traditionalist baby-boom doctor for an annual physical. While he conducts a thorough examination, including a Pap smear, and she is naked in front of him, he asks her to observe the requirements of the *burka* and cover her face. A United Church minister is approached by a young couple who wish their children to be baptized. "To wipe away original sin?" he asks. "No, because it's tradition." A devotee of Baba Haridass on Salt Spring Island phones his mother – he's so happy to be with Babaji, but he feels the group still needs some good hymns and rattles off a few titles. His mother tells him that the hymnal has been changed. Angrily, he phones the United minister to see if he can find some good 1950s hymn books. Fortunately, one is found. A group of feminists at the University of Victoria importunes a United Church minister for "old" spiritual teaching, but it wants no male writers. The group is willing to recognize ancient authority, "the tradition," but on its own terms.

The invocations of "tradition" evidently take many shapes. But they are nearly all expressions of nostalgia – ersatz memories of a church, a religion, or a faith that never was. "Traditionalism" is bells and smells, signs and wonders, gargoyles and angels – all forms of tradition but all without substance, except as a critique of our times. Religion for the traditionalist is not an ordering of the human soul, nor truth and significance, but a precious heirloom, a sacred grotto, an artful performance whose value lies in stimulating the feeling that something old and pure has been restored. It is almost always pretty, and therefore false and anaemic. Since religion is spiritual, and not aesthetic, traditionalism may result in grand effects, but never in real transformation. It is also nearly always reactionary and hence sentimental, a patina which is merely antiquarian but not classical. As mere "heritage," what may be falsely remembered is in fact dead, for it does not point beyond itself to a living reality. A tradition is only truly a living tradition if, as Edmund Burke says, it constitutes "a partnership between those who are dead, those who are living, and those who are yet to be born."[19] That means it lives and breathes, adjusts to new circumstances, and accommodates to change. "Traditionalism" is an idolatrous relation to tradition, for it is an attempt to arrest evolution and submit everything that is living to dead authority. As a token, it is just used to reach somewhere else, such as a state of self-righteous smugness. Traditionalism is magic and theurgy, using received formulae to transform reality by turning back the clock to an imagined time of purity.

# Traditionalism II

## Latins and Greeks

I n the entertainment industry, the Catholic Church is often depicted in Gothic drag, virginal innocence in a landscape rife with the supernatural and grotesque: gloomy, imposing chapels, scowling nuns, and priests wrapped in starched habits and surplices and wearing heavy iron crosses, sacristies full of votive candles and bleak statues of lugubrious saints. Such a church is a horrible caricature of a faith that is actually formidable in its intellectual and spiritual discernment, and of a church that went through the dramatically liberalizing processes of Vatican II in the mid-1960s. But, ironically, in an age where, as Jean Baudrillard says, the simulacrum becomes the touchstone for the real, there are baby boomers who would have the church of St. Peter return to Gothic casting.[1]

St. Clement's Church is obscured beneath Ottawa's furious Queensway Express. Its richly resonant church bell beckons like a flickering storm lamp in a fog. When I arrive one early Sunday morning, the church service is in full swing – well, stately procession – in the chapel clouded with incense. The priest's back is turned to the congregation, but his mellow lilt, intoning the solemn majesty of the Latin Mass, brightens the dark gloom. The church's architectural style is "unfinished Gothic." Unadorned and muted, there is an uninterrupted simplicity to the interior. Whitewashed walls rise steeply to an open cathedral ceiling, where intensely red oxblood-painted planks supply a startling contrast against the pure white marble of the altar and communion railing. The narrow windows are without tracery, in the early English Gothic style. Christ's travail on the road to Golgotha is vividly etched in the bronze Stations of the Cross flanking the pews in the nave. The tabernacle is topped by a statue of St. Clement, the first-century pope who used the clout of the Church of Rome to quell Corinthian licentiousness and unorthodoxy. The substantial crucifix above the tabernacle depicts a wretched crucified Christ and leaves no part of His agony to imagination. Winged angels reside on both sides of the altar. On the altar are assembled a chalice and a ciborium in traditional Gothic design. The sole ornate embellishment is the sanctuary lamp, suspended from the centre of the ceiling by a long brass chain. It is lit and burning olive oil. Apart from a few blue-haired patricians, and a few Gen-Xers, the majority of the 300 parishioners are baby boomers.

The mass is celebrated by Father Louis J. Campbell, a man in his early sixties, whose deep sonorous voice fills the words "*Kyrie, eleison, Christe, eleison, Kyrie, eleison*" ("Lord have mercy, Christ have mercy, Lord have mercy") with terrifying depth. Six altar boys, busily ringing chimes, topping up the censor, and parading around with immense candles during processionals through the congregation, facilitate the tightly scripted march through the Agnus Dei, Anamnesis, Collect, Credo, Epiclesis, Eucharist, Oblation, Offertory, and Ordo. There are no faltering steps in the parishioners' facility in mouthing the Latin responses. Yet despite – and perhaps because of – the regimentation, a spirit of sustained and reverent wonder is palpable, especially in the controlled passion of the choir. The homily is an exegesis of Mary's last recorded words in the New Testament at the wedding at Cana: "The hosts have run short of wine. Mary, pointing to Christ, says, 'Whatever he asks, do it.'" The congregation – the faithful remnant – appears up to the task of following Christ in the re-sanctification of the Church. St. Clement was also the first Christian writer to imaginatively adapt the image of a phoenix rising from its own ashes to Christ's Resurrection. Welcome to the baby-boomer Tridentine Mass.

The 400-year-old Tridentine Mass, although approved by the Council of Trent during the sixteenth-century Counter-Reformation, was replaced in 1969 by Pope Paul VI with the *Novus Ordo Missae*. In 1971, he went one step further and banned the Tridentine Mass entirely. His actions followed credibly from the root-and-branch reforms initiated by Vatican II – the twenty-first ecumenical council, which met between 1962 and 1965. His predecessor, Pope John XXIII, initially presided over the council and assumed its leadership in 1963. These reforms were intended not only to repeal antiquated customs and enhance laypeople's participation in liturgy, but also to reverse centuries of inflexibility – toward other religious denominations, with respect to religious freedom, and in defining the role of religious orders and missionary activity. Lightening up on solemnity and chastisement by restoring emphasis on joy, healing, and reconciliation meant more of a role for diversity and freedom. The Tridentine Mass was a lightning rod for progressive forces within the council. For them, it epitomized the archaism and reactionary tendencies that Vatican II sought to quell. It was unduly wed to a dismal teaching of sin and penitence, instead of the liberating teaching of glory and transfiguration.

Along with the disappearance of the Tridentine Mass, high-profile devotional practices like novenas, the Stations of the Cross, benediction of the blessed sacrament, perpetual adoration, and recitation of the rosary also slipped into oblivion. The church was modernizing. Around the world, altars were reversed so the priest's liturgical actions were open to plain view, congregations were invited to play a more active role, and Mass was said in the vernacular. Guitars took the place of organs, folk music replaced Gregorian chant, council meetings at church rather than clerical home visits became the forum for feedback, incense and communion wine vanished. No one was obliged to practise weekly confession. The faithful could handle the sacred host (and holy body of Christ) and place it into their mouths themselves. Pastoral healing and work on behalf of social causes became as important as (or the equivalent of) saving souls. Ecumenicism, and specifically a search for common ground, meant both openness to other faiths' interpretation of revelation, and a reinforcement of Catholicism's practice of reading scripture not literally, but allegorically.

In some Catholic quarters, the reforms did not stop at the merely cosmetic. North American bishops broke rank publicly with the Pope over such documents as the 1968 encyclical *Humanae Vitae*, which reaffirmed the position against contraception.[2] Most North American Catholics used the Pill without guilt. Creation and liberation theologies were tolerated – after all, Catholicism took seriously the celebration of life and the moral challenge implied by God's judgment in Genesis, observing His creation, that "It was good." Catechism classes, marriage encounters, and seminary training absorbed the techniques, and maybe even the philosophies, of the new psychology of life. Two decades of adaptation to the liberal forces of progress – though never altering the Catholic prohibition on women clergy, abortion, homosexuality, or displacing the Pope's authority – sent strong signals that the church was dynamic and responsive.

In 1984, Pope John Paul II issued an "indult" granting Catholics permission to attend Tridentine Mass, in part reflecting his own conservatism, in part as a response to neo-conservatives on a rampage in the Church. But neo-conservatives are rarely content with conciliatory gestures. The *New Oxford Review*, a conservative Catholic magazine, bills itself as a group of concerned Catholics "fed up with fuzzy-wuzzy Catholicism." Reacting to ongoing ecumenical initiatives, its ads read, "The Church doesn't need any common ground yak-sessions, for, as Cardinal Law said: The Church already has 'common ground.' It is found in sacred scripture and tradition, and it is mediated to us through the authoritative and binding teaching of the Magisterium."[3] Similar voices are heard throughout the Canadian Catholic community. Their plaint? The Church places too much attention on relevance, is too populist, conducts insufficient ritual, has lost its central control. What must be reversed is the drift to liberal theology and ecumenism. And, imitating the Protestant fundamentalist recourse to the infallibility of the Bible, many conservative Catholics want the Bible, rather than scholastic doctrine and living tradition, to be placed at the centre of the faith. While there is a wide spectrum of Catholic grumbling – in his fine book *The Smoke of Satan*, Michael Cuneo canvasses the major groups – what they share is the traditionalist longing to "go back to the basics."[4]

Opus Dei, by contrast to some highly visible dissident Roman Catholic movements, is never crude, outspoken, or lacking in subtlety. Perhaps because of this, it has become a major spokesman for the conservative cause of traditionalism, scourging liberal drift in the Church in particular. *La Obra*, "the Work," was formed in Spain in 1928 by Escrivá de Balaguer, "To form select minorities of apostolic men to exercise various professions without taking religious vows." It demands from its members devotion and obedience to the point of celibacy and self-sacrifice – even, it is rumoured, self-flagellation as "mortification of the flesh." *El Camino*, a members' guide book to living charity practically, is rich in militaristic metaphors and demands for radical obedience and martyrdom. It sets out the ranks of Opus Dei's membership: *cooperadores,* or associates, the rank and file, who must not necessarily even be Catholic but must live an exemplary life and tithe; *supernumeraries,* who must adhere rigidly to Catholic teachings on marital relations and actively practise the apostolate; *oblates,* who must never marry, but must remain with their families; and *numerarios* who, as an élite, must take vows of poverty, chastity, and obedience.[5] It sets out a complete plan of spiritual life, a how-to to reach the summit of holiness. The general idea is that priests alone cannot bear responsibility for maintaining the faith – laymen must take up the apostolate. Since 1982, Opus Dei has had juridical status as a personal prelature of the Pope. And it serves, if you will, as another version of the men's movement, in this case, men meeting in quiet dignity and reasoned faith, aware of the duties and obligations for which they bear responsibility.

Philippe, an officer in the Canadian military, meets me in his office in the Department of National Defence. He has just come from a meeting of lawyers who spent the noon hour discussing the Pope's encyclical *Dies Domini* ("The Day of the Lord"). Philippe's tone is casual, controlled, and circumspect:

> We are never told to carry on the apostolate [spread the Gospel by urging friends, relatives, and workmates to strive for sanctity, particularly by offering their daily work to God]. Vocation was the work of the first Christians. Members of the first Work lived like the first Christians. But we have the Church as it is, with all its heresies, like the many heresies of the early Church. The Work reminds people they have to do their apostolate, that it's not just the responsibility of the clergy. There are many sleeping Catholics.

Philippe refuses to second-guess why baby boomers are drawn to Opus Dei. "It is the work of God. There are no human reasons, God calls and says follow me." But Philippe does admit, "They come to the Work because they want to become saints. We learn together how to undertake apostolate to other people, to bring people back to the Church. Sanctity is not just for a few. Only a few will be canonized, but many more can be saints." To be a cut above, to rise above the "sleeping Catholics," and to turn from mere modern "sensation-seeking" to joy – that is what the Father bids us do, Philippe volunteers. I think for a

moment he is talking about God or the Pope, but no, he is affection-
ately referring to Escrivá de Balaguer himself.

I invite Philippe to comment on the Work's detractors, those who
impugn Opus Dei for its élitism, reactionary conservatism, and extensive wealth and power. A few days earlier, Mike Kropfeld – director of
InfoCult, a Montreal agency tracking religious cults – had remarked:
"For its members, they are the true Church, keeping the Church on the
straight and narrow. The attraction is it's an élite; they target key
people. They own lots of property and include many people in the
media. They even tried last year to get financial exemptions, until Senator Jacques Hébert blew the whistle on that." But Philippe refuses to be
drawn into finger-pointing or denouncing liberal drift. "The Father
used to say the Work has no enemies; we are not against anything, we
are for everything. Holy purity is not about being against something, it
is loving." But even love is exclusive, proceeding by preferences and
discrimination. On the question of the ordination of women, and the
pressure women's groups like WomanChurch and Catholics of Vision
are exerting on the Church, Philippe is adamant: "Having ordination of
women is a matter of faith – it is against the faith. The Church is not a
democratic institution – it is an ecclesiastical hierarchy. It is willed by
God." He is also troubled by the Catholics drawn to the Tridentine
Mass: "They are people who suffered the excesses of Vatican II in its
effects, but don't understand the gains made by Vatican II." Nonetheless, he can appreciate the conservative grievance: "People are upset
when the Church doesn't look like a church."

The *New Oxford Review* is just one of many organizations swept up
in the conservative backlash against Vatican II and liberal theology.
Most of these groups appeal to the now-deceased archbishop
Monsignor Marcel Lefebvre, the ecclesiastic who refused to sign the
Vatican II documents on "Religious Liberty and the Church in the
Modern World," opposing what he saw to be the momentum of
modernism and secularism, and "insipid ecumenicism." Instead, he
created the traditionalist Swiss Ecône seminary, and the Priestly Society of St. Pius X, committed "to the wise norms and customs of the
Church of previous days."[6] His Internet Web site is a popular destination, and its tone is sharp, accusatory, nearly vituperative. There he
makes explicit that the Pope – by having attached to his indult the
condition that priests acknowledge the doctrinal and juridical value of

the *Novus Ordo,* even if for pastoral reasons they prefer the Tridentine Mass – courts evil. And, indulging a little paranoia, he opines that the papal indult was merely a ploy to keep Catholics away from his Society. In 1988, Lefebvre's whole organization was excommunicated for refusing to accept Rome, and a further splinter within the organization – an occasion for plenty of finger-pointing as to who was and who was not still cozying up to Rome – created the Society of St. Pius v, whose followers believe that Lefebvre has capitulated to the papacy.

Anger, bitterness, anxiety, and mutual denunciation bolster the self-righteousness of those conservatives not at home in today's world. While Catholicism has always had its traditionalist literary voices – G.K. Chesterton, Hilaire Belloc, Evelyn Waugh – these were writers whose intellectual engagement was erudite, witty, and charitable. But among traditionalist Catholic baby boomers, "tradition" has not merely a vote, but a veto. The tone is often angry and bitter. The appeal to tradition is used in a jeremiad against all things modern. And some go vastly further than the *New Oxford Review,* subscribing to that censure of the papacy called *sedevacantism* ("the chair is vacant"). Since Vatican ii, they claim, no legitimate pope has presided over the Magisterium, for the Papacy has sold out to modernity.

One of those groups is the Apostles of Infinite Love, who boast an extensive landholding and an impressive monastic hideaway in Saint-Jovite, north of Montreal. For them, Pope Paul vi was planted in the Vatican by Freemasons for the purpose of destroying the Church. Brother André, decked out in a brown cassock emblazoned with the "immaculate heart of Mary," and with burning eyes so manic that he ought to have won a part hands-down in the film version of the medieval *The Name of the Rose,* explains how Paul vi exposed his association with them. "Paul vi, John Paul i, and John Paul ii – they are all Freemasons. But Paul vi was the worst – he took the ordinance against Freemasons out of canon law. He personally arranged much of the persecution of our Apostles. Since 1958, there has been no pope and no legitimate cardinals."

Brother André's indictment, and the long litany of grievances which fill the next hour of our discussion, are divulged with lots of "nudge, nudge, wink, wink, if only you knew … but then you must." If perceived persecution is sufficient for martyrdom, then the Apostles of Infinite Love should be rewarded in spades. They have endured fires, custody suits, criminal investigations into sexual abuse, arrests, denials of visas to visit their ministries abroad, and – putatively – countless subtle forms of mistreatment by the locals. Living in the end times, and having the responsibilities of the persecuted remnant, Brother André confides, was hell. "Steeped in the bitterness of tribulation, scorn is our only protection."

"We are going through a great paroxysm," Brother André continues, "We are going through a funnel, we're going through a childbirth. Look at the chastisements – Rwanda, Bosnia, suicide cults. But God writes straight as well as crooked lines. There is also a new Pentecost coming."

Fortunately for the Apostles of Infinite Love, there is some assurance that they are on the righteous path. Brother John and I bolt down a thick, glutinous gravy of beef chunks and vegetables, washed down with lemonade and followed by a heavy-crusted berry pie – hardy sustenance for the demanding road ahead – as he recounts the evidence.

In their midst, it turns out, lives the true pope, Gregory xvii, who has known since 1967 that he was destined for great things. Born Gaston Tremblay, and a sometime Hospitaller, "Brother John" had a mystical vision in 1952 and founded his first religious community of mendicants. In 1961, he linked up with another Catholic mystic, Father Collin, also head of a new group, but who in one respect was bettering his new acquaintance – he realized that he was already fulfilling prophecy, and specifically the request of the Virgin Mary directed to two children at La Salette, France, in 1846. Rome will lose the Faith and become the seat of the Antichrist, she is said to have revealed, so be attentive during the looming world catastrophe, and assemble a beach-head that will endure the imminent tribulation.

Father Collin and Brother John merged their two organizations, agreeing that there was strength in numbers. But, after an altercation over which one of them was the true pope – one claiming to be Clement xv, the other Gregory xvii, both the recipients of divine revelation – Father Collin disappeared from the picture, and Pope Gregory xvii was left to take on the role of Great Pontiff, chosen by God, to take on what comes – and there is plenty – in the last days. He and his followers are convinced they have their part in the world's destiny down pat. In 1917, the Virgin Mary had, after all, appeared on six occasions to three peasant children in Fatima, Portugal, and confided a three-part secret: a vivid depiction of the terrors of hell, a call for the consecration of Russia, and … a third secret which has not been revealed. In 1982, and again in 1984, Pope John Paul II consecrated the world to Mary's Immaculate Heart, the Apostles note, bar one: He failed to have the bishops consecrate Russia and begin her conversion, so that the errors of communism would cease spreading around the world. This was proof the Vatican was working with Moscow. And the third secret? Expect, in the context of great world disasters, the imminent emergence of a Great Monarch to come to the aid of the Great Pontiff and restore the equivalent of "caesaropapism," the rule of a man who wields the power of both emperor and pope.

Gregory XVII's proof that this is how things stand today is interesting, to say the least, but why should his followers have such faith in the man? Apart from "his faultless teaching of the Gospel for 25 years," the single most important confirmation comes from "the portion of countless humiliations and persecutions that have been heaped on Gregory XVII and his followers, through which they have grown and been strengthened interiorly."[7] While the skeptical may have a few residual questions, and the Apostles themselves might want to second-guess why so many accusations, arrests, and imprisonments have come their way, the answer is quite simple: Pope Gregory was asked by God to be "thwarted and humiliated" and so, because this has happened, he must in truth be what he says.[8] And if doubt is still not quelled, there are other accessible means of being sure – everywhere around the monastery are "eucharistic stations" allowing the brothers and sisters to enjoy the Eucharist over and over, and live every moment in the white heat of sanctification. There is nothing like experience to confirm prophecy.

It all fits, and it is almost logical. Yet nothing fits, and, in most ways, they are all as mad as hatters. The whole enterprise is of a piece: "You lie to me, I lie to you, in time we end up believing the lie." But however far-fetched, and at the risk of committing the error of *reductio ad absurdum*, might one ask how far the Apostles really are from many conservative (especially dissident) Roman Catholics? Consider the relevant terms of analysis: an acutely fallen world, a faithful remnant, the need for the world to be chastised, one big secret truth, the impossibility of trusting the "men with hats" (who are all corrupt), a return to the purity of the early Church, an intimate community with whom God speaks directly, and the link between personal tribulation and the world's destiny. These are building blocks of the baby boomers' culture and consciousness that we will encounter frequently in their spiritual searches. For balanced minds, they are innocuous enough; in the hands of those who have lost touch with reality, they become something fantastic, positively embarrassing to observe. The Apostles live out the chimera, while more timid dissenters limit themselves to the romance of beautiful liturgies and decorous rituals.

If it seems a stretch to equate lovers of the Tridentine Mass with the Apostles of Infinite Love, and overstated to imply that many baby boomers looking for "tradition" are buying little more than a precious aesthetic with a corrosive Gnosticism mixed in, consider the case of one of Canada's most renowned Catholics, Jean Vanier, a man vastly admired by baby boomers seeking consolation in Roman Catholicism. Though Canada does not have the equivalents of America's public Catholic intellectuals like Richard John Neuhaus and Michael Novak, or commentators like William F. Buckley and Patrick Buchanan, Jean Vanier is deemed by many baby boomers to be Canada's most prominent Catholic thinker.

In 1999, Vanier presented the Massey Lecture "Becoming Human." A decade earlier, he had published, to wide acclaim, *The Broken Body: Journey to Wholeness*, a more transparent statement of his core beliefs, and still widely read and cited ten years later. There he writes of contemporary man's brokenness, the world's loss of communion, and a "way" to be saved by walking the path with Jesus. "Let me tell you about this plan and the beginning of it all," is how Vanier starts off his personal search for the secret of humanity and its history, in a heart filled with light and darkness.[9]

The "beginning of it all" is our private hurt and brokenness:

We are seeing the birth of a new fragile humanity, lonely,
bewildered, lacking references and a sense of belonging; feeling
empty, but finding nothing to fill the emptiness .... The quiet grace
of communion has disappeared – was it only an illusion? – and is
now replaced by an overwhelming inner turmoil and pain.[10]

We can no longer have recourse to talking out our hurt with others because the "dynamics of fear" separate us and language divides us:

> Some people can only talk with their bodies; only from there do true words flow. Sometimes it is because they cannot speak, but also it may be because they have lost trust in words. They have heard too often words that have been only empty promises, words that have been lies, words that condemn or despise, words that hurt.

Nor can we look to the world at large to redeem our internal pain and brokenness. "We are no longer in a world filled with optimism," Vanier writes. "Now we are approaching the year 2000 – optimism has given way to hopelessness and illusions are fading. We are confronted with the stark reality of a broken humanity." Our loss of communion with God has arisen with the introduction of "rigid laws, traditions and customs" constituting a surrogate unity of survival. Force, law, authority, and culture are just cheap plaster over the cracks, severing us from the source. And "The sin of brokenness is visited upon us from generation to generation." There can be no redemption in "theories and doctrines ... so often permeated by ... pride and jealousy." Dreams, theories, projects, and rational intellect all betray us.

In our own times, the danger is particularly acute. With shades of Jerzy Kosinski's *Being There* – a tale of humankind's fall into the world of distractions and surrogate happiness, popularized in the film starring Peter Sellers – Vanier writes:

> Television can show us other pictures: flashing, changing, thrilling, colourful pictures, pictures that are seductive, exciting wild, passionate emotions. But they are only pictures on a screen. As we look at them, we cannot be really present to people as one person to another, sharing or listening to one another. For there is no relationship, compassion or communion – they are only pictures that tend to isolate us even more in a world of dreams.[11]

But there is still a faint "light," if only among the outcasts, the "abnormal," the poor, weak, and oppressed. In them Jesus is "hidden" but "pointing to a world of truth which transcends their experience of normality."

Go down the ladder of your own being until you discover – like a seed buried in the broken, ploughed earth of your own vulnerability – the presence of Jesus, the light shining in the darkness.[12]

The weak, he proposes, are the true teachers. We have focused misplaced attention on those who have power and strength, and need instead to look to the lonely, poor, disabled, and old. They reveal:

> Our own terrible brokenness, hidden under our capacity to do
> things, hidden under our knowledge and intelligence, hidden under
> our casualness, security and good humour, hidden even under our
> works of piety and times of prayer. In that fleeting moment, we
> touch our own darkness – so deep and terrible .... Beneath the
> appearance of cheerful generosity, under that image of goodness we
> have allowed others to have of us and have perhaps even fostered,
> we are really no more than a broken person in need of healing. This
> moment can be a moment of salvation, a turning point of growth
> towards wholeness.[13]

To succour our "inner turmoil and pain," a Paraclete (meaning literally "the one who answers the cry or the call") will come and "draw the whole body of humanity into its true oneness."[14] Not in the manifold and differentiated world of creation, not in the historical unfolding of revelation in tradition and the Church, nor in the "broken and fragmented" human world of "different languages and customs, different philosophies and religions," where humans are "fighting, polluting, exploiting," and have been taught to "dominate and enslave," will our salvation ever be found. Instead, we will find redemption only in the deepest recesses of pain, or at a subhuman grade of creation ("what a discrepancy between the joyful winging of birds and the fear in men and women").[15] "We will never win the olympics of humanity, racing for perfection," Vanier insists, "but we can walk together in hope, celebrating that we are loved in our brokenness."[16]

In Vanier, baby-boom Catholics find a congenial fellow-traveller, one who confirms their darkest anxieties and feeds their greatest hopes. The combination of sincerity and beguiling poetry is nearly irresistible, for it masterfully evokes the pathos of the essential predicaments baby boomers face: The world has lost its revelatory power;

since personal anxiety equals civilizational crisis, in private feeling (pain) and sensibility (shared apprehension) alone is diagnosis and cure of what ails us to be found; by retrieving some primordial purity, perhaps present in the (mythical) primitive Church, millennia of error shall be overcome. His thought is antinomian, anti-establishment, anti-history, and – though it is not evident on the surface – anti-creation, for what he dispenses with is the central mystery of Roman Catholicism: that through the incarnation of Christ, God became active in history, expressing His justice and love in the manifold aspects of creation.

At the risk of sounding churlish in detracting from such an admired thinker, in my judgment, if Vanier's discourse passes as enlightened contemporary Catholicism, then Roman Catholicism is clearly in grave peril of losing its characteristic identity. If Vanier appears to be in communion with theological Catholicism, then this artifice, like the Trojan horse that concealed Greek warriors, contains the ammunition capable of destroying Rome. Papal and magisterial authority, apostolic succession, salvation in history, the scholastic tradition, the concept of the "person," the collaborative relation between grace and nature: All are quietly glossed over by Vanier. Christ, the Logos who held together all the gradations and ranks of the created order, is replaced by Jesus, the secret seed hidden in the heart, akin to the subatomic particles physicists believe resonate with one another at a level beneath their worldly appearance.

To illustrate the magnitude of Vanier's revisionism, consider Catholic teaching on the Holy Spirit. The Church teaches that the "indwelling of the Holy Spirit" is the spiritual transformation of personality in the world, and grace is a gift making it possible to act with a heightened agency toward the contingencies of life in the world. In Vanier's writing, by contrast, there is a "call" away from worldly enterprise, a "hidden" Jesus who rebukes our complex being, striving, and longings for "wholeness" and "oneness," that are flights from time and the plurality of humankind. Moreover, reversing the Church's doctrine that the "millennium" is already instituted in the mystical body of Christ – the Church, warts and all – Vanier appeals to the year 2000 as a benchmark occasion to "go down the ladder" to the hidden seed, and to hear in the deepest recesses of personal brokenness the call of the Paraclete. The Church, in contrast, has recognized the greater

objectivity and moderation ensuing from the public exercise of delib-
erative intellect in discussion aiming at consensus, fulfilling St. Paul's
cautionary advice, "The spirits of the prophets are subject to the
prophets" (1 Cor. 14). Private revelations, such as those Vanier points
his readers toward, lack attested meaning, however intensely they may
tap into an invisible undercurrent of oneness in existence.

Now, it is true that a Christian will never be "of" but at best "in" the
world, and that Catholicism has always preached the redemptive value
of suffering. But, in Vanier's characterization, the Christian is never
"leaven" in the world, but always "salt." The solitary individual's naked
encounter of his or her broken self with an utterly transcendent God
opens a crack, and the all-too-human world and the collective struggle
for order and meaning fall into it. In the final analysis, despite the tone
of conciliation, Vanier exposes himself as uncharitable, not because he
lacks sensitivity, but because he fails to see the diverse manifestations
of beauty and being as incarnations of the good. He scorns the varied
gifts given by the catholic God.

And, paradoxically, despite its trendy existentialist language, and its
chic leftist leanings, Vanier's thought in fact reinforces the deepest
traditionalist sentiments. It requires no great leap of anxiety to move
from a desolate account of our utter alienation from the world, and the
hopes of consolation we may find only in our deepest subjectivity, to
the intense aesthetics of authenticity offered by traditionalists. One
finds in the Catholics at the Tridentine Mass, in Opus Dei, and among
the Apostles of Infinite Love, the same needs Vanier voices: to contract
personality to deep sensitivity, to shrink the human family down from
its corrupt complexity in the contemporary world to the faithful
remnant, to find the "last good man," to be bequeathed the key which
will unlock the one big secret, to be sanctified in original purity. And
when they go out sampling different faiths and experiment with which
denomination will fulfill these needs, they all seem to be saying, as
Philippe did, as Aretha Franklin did, that they want the Church "to
look like a church, to smell like a church."

A similar sentiment is expressed by baby-boom members of the
Anglican Prayerbook Society of Canada. Founded in 1985, the Society
"promotes 'The Anglican Way' – the full doctrinal and devotional standard of classical Anglican Christianity, as embodied in the Canadian
Book of Common Prayer." It expresses the strongest opposition to "any

revision of 'the faith which was once delivered to the saints.'" As its mission statement reads, "The Prayer Book is not stuck in the fads and fashions of the latest moment, or dated by the last generation's theological, liturgical, or moral confusion." Together with the Essentials movement, an Anglican movement which fears that reform movements are abandoning the "essentials" – and a magnet for traditionalist baby-boomer Anglicans – the Society opposes ecumenical accommodation. In 1994, at an Essentials conference in Montreal, conservative Anglicans stodgily affirmed that the only way to salvation is through Jesus Christ.

Danielle, a fiftysomething boomer, explains to me over Earl Grey tea how she began to urge somewhat more insistently that the Anglican Church acquit itself. Her story offers a revealing insight into baby boomers' spiritual searches for tradition. Raised Presbyterian, with a mother who was Plymouth Brethren, Danielle grew up accepting the literal truth of the Bible and was cautioned to be strictly honest, even to death and martyrdom. Any display of emotion was frowned upon. Rebelling against the black-and-white moral world she was obliged to inhabit, and personally inclined to want to compromise and to adjust her principles to accommodate gays and premarital sex, she began searching for alternatives. For a while, she fell in with the evangelicals at the Inter-Varsity Christian Fellowship, and later the Campus Crusade for Christ. Her involvement triggered a crisis – she became obsessed with nuclear war, and suffered traumatic nightmares and visions. She went to a Billy Graham Mission and persuaded herself that, since she was expected to have a conversion experience, she would. But later, when she no longer saw the world through the prism of having to save souls, she concluded that the Mission was little more than a big, grand, orchestrated event, intended to be emotionally overwhelming – like falling in love – and deceptively promising something sure and simple. She realized that precisely those attributes that had attracted her had also forced her into a straitjacket and made her an ideologue. She began to doubt she could trust a God who was stern and judgmental, and felt unable to reconcile a loving God and the severity of God's judgment.

Next, she went to a United Church and observed lots of backslapping and handshaking. The thread snapped however when no one engaged her during a coffee klatsch in the church basement. She started to think twice about the attractiveness of the liturgy; it changed weekly, lacked form, was noisy and intellectually demanding, thus tempting human pride. The very set-up of the church accentuated solo performances and showmanship. The minister was a producer, and his sermon was thrust to the front and centre of the worship.

Then she met an Anglican man of great integrity, who would later be appointed a bishop in Newfoundland. She found in the Anglican service – its liturgy, set forms, and beautiful music – a deeply satisfying means of worship. The preacher, the congregation, and the choir were all going in the same direction. There was flow through to the climax of the Eucharist, rather than a spectacle culminating in the sermon. Since individualism was subordinated to liturgy, it was also more democratic, with a greater level of engagement. "It was a real worship thing, we weren't just spectators. It was a quiet church. I thought, 'Gosh, they know how to sit down and shut up.'" In Anglicanism, she realized that a serious engagement with faith was real. It also confirmed her own experience of prayer, and its efficacy. Roman Catholicism was never an option: "Obedience to the Pope sticks in my throat. I don't want a bunch of celibate men telling me what to do."

She joined the Altar Guild and participated as much as possible in the ceremonial aspects of the faith. Today, she campaigns on behalf of the Book of Common Prayer over the Book of Alternative Services. She is involved in the Essentials movement, and is seeking a restoration of the thirty-nine articles – the Articles of Faith drafted during Elizabeth I's reign in reaction to Anglican reform movements. Danielle likes "the roots to medieval times," and wants to ensure they are maintained. "The Anglican Church just feels like a church should," she summed up at the end of our chat.

.  .  .

"To look like a church, to smell like a church" is also drawing baby-boomer Catholics and dispossessed Anglicans to Eastern Orthodoxy. Nowhere, arguably, does the smell and look of traditionalism radiate more strongly than from baby boomers who have turned to the Eastern Orthodox Church. Of course, like the Roman Catholic Church, there is also no church more keenly aware of the importance of tradition's continuity.

But Eastern Orthodoxy beats Roman Catholicism hands-down in going back to the source. From the moment one enters an Eastern Orthodox church, and is hit with the aroma of incense or drawn to its doleful and ethereally glittering icons, is struck by its topography or drawn into the vivid pageantry, one realizes that Orthodoxy – which never went through scholasticism, the Reformation, and the Counter-Reformation – extends an invitation that is a blast to the past, a return to the early days of Christianity. Eastern Orthodoxy is out of step with Roman Catholicism on assorted fronts – including, for many Orthodox communions, the continued use of the Julian calendar, which is fifteen days behind the Gregorian calendar, which, if nothing else, contributes to perpetuating the schism between the Western and Eastern rites (the one significant force to be reckoned with is baby boomers' near-veneration of Orthodoxy's authenticity).

As with most schisms, the differences are ones of degree and emphasis.[17] The key scriptural sources for the Eastern Orthodox Church are: "And God said, let Us make man according to Our image and likeness" (Gen. 1:26), "The Kingdom of God is within you" (Luke 17:21), "The Word became flesh and dwelt among us" (John 1:14), and "Through these promises you may become partakers of the divine nature" (2 Pet. 1:4). The two monumental events from which the Eastern Orthodox derive great meaning are the Transfiguration at Mount Tabor, where the uncreated light of God's divinity shone through Christ's flesh ("And He was transfigured before them, and His face shone like the sun, and His clothes became dazzling white"), and the Resurrection, where, for Orthodox believers, not only Jesus the man suffers, but God suffers and yet manifests His inward glory. What all these cues share is the idea of *deosis* – deification or divinization – which holds that not only may we experience God dwelling in us, and we in Him, but that our whole person (body, soul, and spirit) are sanctified, saved, and restored. And, in the moments of being God, we do not lose even our distinct, individual identity. As Vladimir Lossky, one of Eastern Orthodoxy's most acclaimed writers, explains, "We remain creatures while becoming god by grace, as Christ remained God when becoming man by the Incarnation."[18] "In My Kingdom, said Christ," reads Ode 4, Troparion 3 of the Canon for the Matins of Holy Thursday, "I shall be God with you as gods."

Nearly everything else in Eastern Orthodoxy follows from this emphasis on *deosis*: the layout of the church, the veneration of icons, the centrality of the Divine Liturgy, the sacredness of the human body and the earth, the indwelling of the Holy Spirit, the critical importance of a living continuity with ancient times. And the fateful, even irascible, division from Western Christendom.

An Eastern Orthodox church is laid out, after the image of heaven in the Book of Revelation, to evoke the experience of God dwelling among humans. There is a singular attention paid to the physical beauty of the spiritual world. The church often has a dome to convey the sense of God's encompassing kingdom manifest on earth, rather than a spire which points to a transcendent reality. The majestic dome constitutes the vault of the heavens, so that the faithful may feel that they are in heaven on earth and that God dwells among them. Pews are rare. There is no formal, scripted regimentation of how and when the faithful should sit, kneel, and stand. While the focal point is the Holy Table, the entire church is considered sacramental, thus manifesting the mystery of salvation and integrating the faithful into the life of the Kingdom of God. Parishioners are free to stray around the church, allowing their senses to be stimulated so that the whole person participates in the liturgy in heaven. Many of the faithful are drawn to the iconostasis – the icon screen – which unites the sanctuary, the Holy of Holies, and the place of assembly.

Indeed, the first feature striking a visitor to an Orthodox church is the gallery of icons, their luminous gilding and stylized poses evoking majesty and piety. And the iconoclastic controversy in Constantinople during the eighth and ninth centuries is one of the liveliest moments in the history of Christianity, hardening the once-fluid boundaries between orthodoxy, heresy, denomination, and sect, and contracting each to an either/or spiritual option.[19]

God's incarnation into the historical, material body of Jesus Christ signified that He intended to allow Himself to be represented materially, the Orthodox contend. And, if He intended to signal that matter can be redeemed, then humans have the opportunity to assist in the redemption of creation through beauty and art. Moreover, if religion is a commitment of the whole person, as the Orthodox believe, then the adoration of beautiful icons is a means of using the senses to experience the reality of the Kingdom of God. To deny this conclusion by discounting the physical aspect of God in Jesus is to commit the heresy of docetism – the belief that the human form of Jesus was only an appearance, but not real – or to run the risk of sliding into another heresy, namely Arianism, which accepts only the humanity of Jesus and denies His divinity, conferring that status on the utterly transcendent God the Father alone. In both cases, the Orthodox advance, the full meaning of John's statement "The Word became flesh and dwelt among us" (John 1:14) is misunderstood.

From opponents of Orthodoxy comes the outcry "idolatry," and an invocation of the first commandment:

> You shall not make for yourself an idol, whether in the form of anything that is in heaven above, or that is on the earth beneath, or that is in the water under the earth. You shall not bow down to them or worship them; for I the Lord your God am a jealous God. (Exod. 20:4–5).

At the heart of this difference of interpretation lies one of Orthodoxy's major quarrels with Western Christendom. In Roman Catholicism, an icon is at best a representation, or conveys the form but not the essence of divinity. Thus, admiring an icon is an act of thought comprehending divine mystery. In Protestantism, icons may have some didactic value, serving as a way of honouring the transcendent divinity, but, especially among the "low" denominations, the fear of magic and superstition renders icons indistinguishable from fetishes, and thus icons are deemed idolatrous. St. Augustine may be the source of Western Christendom's reduction of the human-divine encounter to a mental exercise, for in his treatise *De Trinitate* he denigrates the body as "flesh," and stipulates that the human mind alone mirrors the divine trinity. The Cappadocian Gregory of Nyssa and Clement of Alexandria went further by proposing that only human reason encounters the divine. For the Orthodox, this intellectualization is a radical denial of true sacramentality and veers close to doceticism, the heresy that Jesus Christ only appeared to be human. They appeal to Irenaeus, the second-century Greek theologian and Bishop of Lyons, whose concept of "recapitulation" is intended to convey the ongoing, life-giving presence of the risen Christ in the whole person. (To this day, the Syrian Christians of Kerala, India, appeal to Irenaeus in their understanding of worship as the ongoing involvement of the divine in creation.) Finally, for the Orthodox, icons are understood as spiritual witnesses to the unity of the church through history and geography, making the Kingdom of God present in the persons and presence of the saints. Icons are manifestations of direct divine presence and action, conveying the continuing mystery of Christ and His ongoing transformative power.[20] Hence, for the Orthodox, God is neither radically other nor an abstract idea, and Christ is not merely a mediator for the supreme transcendence of God. The sacred, Orthodoxy insists, can never be displaced to a distinct realm away from everyday life. Ironically, in the context of the charge of idolatry and non-Orthodox anxiety about excessive compromise with the world, one of the most distinctive characteristics of Orthodox icons is the purity of the depicted holiness: The saints are depicted without emotion, for emotion is transient and private, whereas saintliness as an image of the divine dwells in the eternal.

Orthodoxy's quibble over icons extends beyond the possibility of sacramental art. It carries over to displeasure with the Roman church's overall theology and its creedal formulations. Roman Catholicism – greatly to its credit, though, for some, equally to its reproach – evolved by incorporating vast doses of Platonic and neo-Platonic thought imported through the Alexandrian school from Clement of Alexandria to Origen. Some of this incorporation entailed using the ideas of the Jewish thinker Philo (20 BCE–50 CE), who had adopted the Greek philosophers' demythologization of the Homeric gods to reinterpret Israel's biblical tradition. It also included Justin the Martyr's Christian appropriation of Platonism, with its intense emphasis on the divinity of Christ. These ideas tended to intellectualize and spiritualize Christianity, for they stipulated, particularly under the neo-Platonic influence, that God was incomprehensible, though from Him emanated the Divine Mind, or Logos, which contains all the forms, or living intelligences, of the finite and visible world, including all individuals and matter. Holiness called for a life of study and prayer through which an individual soul could progressively climb above mere passions and sense impressions to knowledge of divine intelligence, and finally rise to mystical union and absorption with God Himself. The trend of playing down the body, sensuality, and worldly activity was reinforced by St. Augustine in the fifth century, and consolidated into doctrine in the thirteenth century with St. Thomas Aquinas's adoption of Aristotle. Medieval scholasticism, with its intense intellectualism and focus on doctrine – for example, explaining the mystery of the Eucharist by Aristotle's distinction between substance and accidents – consummated the process of abstraction. On the contrary, the Eastern Orthodox take seriously the positive role of the body in redemption and deification. It is possible for the faithful to directly experience the energies of God, though not His essence, and thus, in the words of Gregory of Palamas, make "the flesh an inexhaustible source of sanctification." Christ, he writes, saved the "whole person" and so the "whole person" prays to God.

Running in tandem with Rome's more spiritualized, intellectualized Christianity was Rome's inclination to use the armature of Roman law to surround its rites, and thus insert an inventive formalism at the heart of its mysteries. Henceforth, worship was less a means of sanctification through the direct experience of divine presence, or a spiritual re-experiencing of the reality of Christ's Passion, than a regimented script whose justification was guaranteed by the logical formulations of scholastic theology. Rites like confession became juridical, administered by means of a ledger book of infractions and penalties, and not, as the Orthodox would have it, a *metanoia,* or spiritual conversion. For the Orthodox, not only was Rome's intellectualized and "juridicalized" Christianity a misinterpretation of scripture, it also underscored the increasingly monarchical assertiveness Rome was displaying vis-à-vis other Christian centres. Nowhere did this assertiveness exhibit itself more forcefully than in the dispute over the *filioque* clause.

In the Apostle's Creed, recited during the Roman rite, the faithful profess: "We believe in the Holy Spirit, the Lord, the giver of life, who proceeds from the Father and the Son. With the Father and the Son He is worshipped and glorified." The Orthodox refuse to adopt a procession of the Holy Spirit through Christ and, thus, in the Byzantine rite, during the Great Entrance, the original Nicene–Constantinopolitan Creed is chanted with the words: "[We believe] in the Holy Ghost, The Lord and giver of life, Who proceedeth from the Father, Who with the Father and the Son together is worshipped and glorified."[21] Full stop.

While the challenge has about it the air of the Lilliputian debate between little enders and big enders ("And which side of the egg do *you* slice first?"), it has served to keep Rome and Constantinople apart since 1054. For nearly a millennium, the two churches have decried each other's theology and doctrine, though one is right to suspect that politics had much to do with the Great Schism. The Greeks considered the *ex cathedra* declaration of the inclusion of the clause by Leo III, and his insistence that accepting the doctrine be a condition of reunion, as evidence of Rome's misplaced understanding of the church as a juridical and theological institution whose mission was to dictate the unity of Christendom.

Leaving politics aside, the theological dispute in itself is not a mere splitting of hairs. When the first Council of Nicea was summoned in 325, its task was to combat the Arian heresy – the teaching that denied the divinity of Jesus Christ in an attempt to protect the uncompromised transcendence of God. The resolution of the council was to declare that Jesus was simultaneously human and divine, *homoousios*, a conclusion later doctrinalized further at the Council of Chalcedon in 451 in the formulation that at the Incarnation there was only one *hypostasis*, signifying that Christ was two persons in one – both human and divine – yet of one substance. From 589 onwards, to prevent new flare-ups of Arianism, the *filioque* clause was added to the profession of faith by sundry jurisdictions – the Spanish Church at the Council of Toledo, Frankish monks in their monastery at Jerusalem, the Roman Church shortly after 1000.[22] For, by insisting that the Holy Spirit proceeded from the Father through the Son, the Roman Church emphasized not only the obvious divinity of Christ, but equally the humanity of the divine.[23] From the Orthodox perspective, saying that the Holy Spirit proceeds from the Father and the Son places insufficient emphasis on the persons of the Trinity, directing it instead to the essence or substance which unites them. God is then known by philosophical proofs of the existence of God, not by direct encounter. Moreover, the Orthodox contend the *filioque* clause renders the Holy Spirit subordinate and derivative, of a lower order of procession, and out of keeping with the experience of the Holy Spirit's awesome presence in devotion, prayer, and liturgy.[24]

Orthodoxy's plaint is consistent with its overall concern: The Romans, with their persistent emphasis on reason and intellect, mind and logic, do not fully recognize the true unity of the "person" as body and soul, the redeemable standing of all creation, and the participation of the whole person in the Kingdom of God. And, paradoxically, it allows the Eastern Orthodox Church to maintain that it is the real catholic, universal, and incarnational church, while Roman Catholicism is in persistent danger of veering toward docetism, gnosticism (in this case, of "knowing" the key to salvation), and spiritualism.

And this is why the centrepiece of Eastern Orthodoxy is the Divine Liturgy. "God was made man in order that man might be made God," writes Athanasius, the fourth-century Patriarch of Alexandria. "The glory of God is the human fully alive," observes the third-century theologian Tertullian. Eastern Orthodoxy's doctrine of *deosis,* reaching into every aspect of the Divine Liturgy, ensures that the "whole person" is sanctified. In the "holiness movement" broadly defined, being holy is the ontological reality of increased participation in divine holiness. Rituals and ceremony – and in these Eastern Orthodoxy excels – are the means of hallowing existence, making it possible, if only for a brief time, for humans to participate fully in the divine. In prayer, the faithful have direct access to spiritual reality, to the power of saving grace. The fragrance of incense is a Jacob's ladder, which directly links earth and heaven. Plainchant's modulations comprise a threnody that spans despair to exaltation, glorifying creation in all its dimensions and restoring it to God.

The precise execution of the Divine Liturgy is intended to recapitulate Christ's Passion and enjoin full participation in His reign of universal, eternal divine love. The priest's action of taking the eucharistic bread and cutting out of it a cube imprinted with a cross and letters signifying "Jesus Christ Conquers," then piercing the "Lamb," as soldiers pierced Christ's side, and pouring wine and water into the chalice, just as the blood and water poured from Christ's wound, establishes the immediate presence of the trials and suffering of Golgotha. Worshippers become contemporaneous with the archetypal events of Christianity. In adding particles of bread to the "Lamb" – one representing the Theotokos (Mary, the birth-giver of God), others the saints and hierarchs of the church – the priest signifies that the whole order of the mystical body of Christ, encompassing the Old and New Testament, the living and the dead, is dwelling in the faithfuls' midst. When he covers the chalice and *diskos* with a veil, the expanse of the universe and the image of an infinite vault are evoked, prefiguring the end of time, when the church is fully in communion with God. Antiphonal chanting – the two sides of the church alternate in singing verses – collects diversity into unity. Heaven is not a place, or a future promise, but the experience whenever and wherever God is recognized and manifested. Participation in the Divine Liturgy is participation in the Kingdom of God on earth.

Given mysticism's natural predilection to become private and speculative, and hence the desire to foreclose the pietistic individualism of Protestantism, Orthodoxy labours to ensure mystical experience is tied to the historical revelation of Christ, the corporate life of the church, and its traditional administration of the sacraments. The Divine Liturgy is designed to allow worshippers to directly experience the present reality of the Kingdom of God and the transforming power of the Holy Spirit, within the non-time where everything but the eternal moment of tradition is rescinded.[25]

Every passing moment of the Divine Liturgy assures the faithful that time is cradled in the eternal, that the eternal is not at the end of time but present whenever God is worshipped. Indeed, because Eastern Orthodoxy does not subscribe as heavily as Roman Catholicism to the entwining of history and God's revelation (and its corollary idea of dynamic progress), the importance of a living continuity with ancient times and the changelessness of liturgy is elevated to a state of veneration. Tradition is more than antiquarianism – it is the substance of man's return to God, and salvation. Nothing may compromise tradition.

Or traditionalism? Wanting a religion that has not been weathered by the compromises of history – indeed, whose adoption specifically broadcasts an accusation of modern corruption – and whose "originality" is aesthetically sublime and awesomely purifying, is unquestionably what attracts baby boomers like Leo to St. Herman's of Alaska in Edmonton. After the Divine Liturgy, over coffee, he explains why he converted from Anglicanism to Roman Catholicism to Eastern Orthodoxy. He wanted to burn in the intensity of sanctification. He wanted a church that was not hierarchical and puffed up with the vanity of earthly power and organization, but where the faithful were a "royal priesthood." He wanted fellowship to satisfy his need to belong where he could feel the bondedness of a covenantal community. He was looking for a faith which left room for the freedom of personal devotion (in his case to Theotokos, Mary the Mother of God), whose veneration acknowledges the free choice of choosing God's will, and which reinforces the incarnate aspect of divinity. He was drawn to the doctrine of the redemption of all created life, especially in one of its applications: Orthodoxy's belief in the intrinsic sacredness of the earth and its commitment to environmentalism. He was warmly receptive to Father Philip's intensely emotional and sharply invective sermon, which began, "Do not be too comfortable, before the blast of divine light. Draw near in conscious, holy fear." Father Philip had concluded a half-hour later, with an imitation of Sergeant Schultz on the bygone television series *Hogan's Heroes*: "Nuthing, nuthing, success, career, peer recognition – it's nuthing. We are in moral descent. We are in a demonic trap of our own making. God could have done more [than we have been able to] with a broken broomhandle." Leo resonates with the emphasis on the individual's essential powerlessness, emptiness, nothingness, and brokenness. In firm agreement with Orthodoxy's opposition to modernity's exaggerated attention to history, he now lives for the exalted opportunities for *deosis*.

Leo's virtue has, however, an edge, an irascible quality. At the beginning of our conversation, he questions my right to even sit in his church. Then he makes it clear that, if I don't believe, I can never understand or write anything about Eastern Orthodoxy. He lashes out at the idea that women can become priests. He opposes building bridges to other faiths. He thinks the evangelicals are out to lunch.

This hard-edged, stern, and confident power to judge and dismiss is echoed in my discussion with Vladika Lazar at the Monastery of All Saints (New Ostrog), in Mission, British Columbia. Yet, in all other regards, Lazar is the sort of man whose vast discernment, humour, and generosity of soul easily explain why he is such a sought-after spiritual director. He begins by dismissing baby boomers' spiritual searches: "Spirituality is emotionalism. It is not the same as the Holy Spirit in the soul." Of the baby boomers who look for consolation at monasteries, Lazar advances the opinion that a monastery is a safety valve for Gnosticism, "Where you send people disposed to Gnosticism, so they don't develop a Gnostic theology." He is dubious about most of the baby boomers who descend on New Ostrog: "They are people who come to the monastery for an elder-cult. They want power, not authority. Many people come here to meditate and pray, but they don't realize they have to work. They want visions and want someone to control their lives." Most have failed to discard their whim for instant gratification.

> They come here thinking the Jesus Prayer will give them union with God, but an indwelling of the Holy Spirit requires years of fasting and prayer, and a purification of the intellect. Or they think that by using the Prayer Rope and counting the knots, they will have a mystical experience. There is a *theosis*, but ... only with God's grace.

Evangelicals are met with even greater scorn:

> Moralism is heresy – it is a substitute for life in Christ. The world needs to be healed, not condemned. Moral outrage is a form of confession. What we hate in others, we fear in ourselves – it's a mental and moral perversion. In the evangelicals, you have a legal reduction of redemption to atonement. Christ healed the whole person. Personal atonement and personal suffering are wrong. We have to struggle against fundamentalism and scholasticism, against the moral fascism of evangelicals and Roman Catholics. Church is not a juridical expedition. Everyone forgets the Incarnation.

If stern, there is nothing histrionic or off-the-cuff in Archbishop Lazar's gloss on the world. He speaks nobly, if laconically. There is tumult around us – reports of bears attacking his dogs, a mentally distressed individual arriving on his doorstep, troubles with the upkeep of the facilities – and yet he radiates a quiet dignity. I come to appreciate that Lazar speaks with the authority of tradition, sustaining a rich and subtle conversation on human possibilities and obligations stretching back to Basil the Great, Gregory the Theologian, John Chrysostom, John of Damascus, Gregory Palamas, and Symeon the New Theologian. He is, in a word, in communion with an *inheritance* – and is not a "traditionalist."

The inheritance at New Ostrog is not a precious heirloom, and, despite its difficult unworldly vows and disciplines, it visibly energizes. Before lunch, we join Lazar's fellow brothers in a sublime descant, a Syro-Byzantine "Prayer at Mealtime" which binds self-emptying with gratitude for the manifold of creation. The singing is robust and life-giving. Every aspect of life at New Ostrog is liturgized, and directed to opening up the spiritual sources of religion. Here is not merely the restoration of an established basis for truth, but its living reality. Later, I would find the same talent for spiritual formation in Duchess and Tilly, Alberta's Mennonite communities, and at Prairie Bible Institute in Three Hills, the Protestant fundamentalist missionary school founded in 1922 by L.E. Maxwell. What these enterprises have in common is a remarkable attention to teaching spiritual disciplines while sustaining a great concern for the world – working with mental patients, attending to the dispossessed in Drumheller Prison, serving street people in the food banks. Instead of the fortress mentality that hides away from life, one finds an attempt to live with spiritual depth and to create a civil world with a sense of public responsibility. Here is neither the way of the conservative, nor that of the liberal, but a third way – of tradition, of being in the world with depth. Religious life is not private and speculative, nor simply the adoption of a costume or set of habits. It does not conform to the world, but it has an institutional shape and is in the world. Tradition supplies a language and a web of meaning and significance, binding the fragments of life and existence together. Spiritual formation and spiritual discipline, marshalling life and maintaining focus, are not just disposable and exchangeable tactics in a private quest for personal fulfillment. They are a way of being human, anywhere in the world.[26]

True tradition is not restricted to practices of spiritual discipline. While no religion can suppress the desire for a mystical experience of the divine and continue to have adherents, a prudent faith also makes provision to prevent experience from derailing simplistically into irrationalism and superstition in the hands of the inexperienced and credulous. Nearly all religions attempt a precarious accommodation between mysticism and legalism, or between the prophetic and charismatic wing of the church and its official institutional aspect. Theology, William James suggests, is a way "to reclaim from mystery and paradox, from obscure and wayward personal persuasion, something intelligible and discursive."[27] The voice of prophecy or mystical intuition remains private until its unspoken metaphysic is rendered into principles of belief and credible conclusions are inferred. This is not to say that all theology must be systematic, but rather signifies that a body of beliefs ought to exhibit coherence and be accessible in such a way as to suffer conversion into principles to which one can give or withhold assent.

While no theology could hope to exhaust the field of quite legitimate religious phenomena, and thus we ought always to hold open the possibility of new theologies revealing aspects of the sacred presently outside our grasp, most theologies are products of tradition. The Roman Catholic Church is not, of course, esteemed by those outside the faith, and even by dissidents within, for its decidedly non-modern practice of restraining errant readings of the Bible and – through its Prefect of the Sacred Congregation for the Doctrine of the Faith, Cardinal Ratzinger – insisting on uniform liturgical and ecclesiastical practice. Its doctrine of *proxima regular fidei conscientia est* (the proximate guide for faith is one's conscience) is muted by the protective (some would say paternalistic) measure of constraining a dangerous eruption of personal definitions of God. Upholding a coherent tradition of theological formulations is the means of preventing a runaway proliferation of nonsensical opinions and unverifiable speculations, concocted in antinomian conceit or the heat of present enthusiasms. It is a means of systematizing beliefs into doctrines that are visible to public debate and verification. While longevity does not vouch for the truth of doctrine, traditions of theology have the virtue of having withstood time-tested debate and shown themselves equal to self-reassessment and correction in the interests of coherence.

Take the four rational proofs for the existence of God, elegantly put forward by the medieval philosopher Anselm. The ontological argument is that, from observable and explicable imperfection and transience, we are led to the idea of perfection and eternity. The argument from design stipulates that, because we observe phenomena obeying mathematical natural laws, there must be an intellectual cause and a prime mover who is God. The moral argument is that the experience of a moral law and conscience leads us to the idea of an eternal lawgiver and judge. And, finally, the argument of general human consensus states that the fact that belief in the Divine is widespread carries authority.

None of these arguments will persuade the non-believer. Logic rarely does. And a God of rational proof seems aloof to human needs, morals, and beliefs. As William James points out, there is always a "thisness" which philosophy cannot address.[28] But it must be remembered that theology is always a distillate of experience and reflection, not its substitute. Anselm's famous proof is part of a prayer, implying that, as a logical exercise, the proof doesn't "prove" anything, but merely gives form to an already present experienced reality. The rational proofs for the existence of God constitute a standard for lucid discussion of what we mean when we say "God," and amount to the assertion that God is unlimited, necessary, absolute, perfect, spiritual, immutable, simple (not composite), and eternal (has no prior cause). Any other formulation is both partial and incoherent. Thus, theology serves as a potential corrective to error and unreason. This too is tradition – the three-millennia-long intellectual and spiritual conversation of humankind.

From the perspective of tradition properly understood, there are clearly things wrong with traditionalism. Approaching faith with the preconception that the world is used up and barren, and with a desiccated personality afraid of total engagement, means "tradition" remains at best cosmetic, at worst a tiresome indulgence. Attending Tridentine Masses or the Divine Liturgy, desiring nothing more than to have the emotional stuffing wrung out of you, entails the loss of the human conversation to which tradition is a partner, and hence a loss of the opportunity to widen the present moment in any enduring manner. Enjoying periodically the "smells and bells," but without ever committing to an affiliation, for fear of contracting a bond which is felt to be wrong and colonizing, renders tradition a mere matter of present taste and style. Refusing to accept change in tradition embalms it, taking it out of the ordinary current of change, resistance, accommodation, and reformation, and rendering it brittle and ultimately inconsequential. The error is a confusion of change with spiritual compromise. The former – surely one must point out to the traditionalist – in no way entails the latter. Under traditionalism, tradition becomes an intellectual configuration, a political reformer's handbook, or – as when a work like *Black Elk Speaks* becomes scripture, or a baptism or bar mitzvah becomes unduly "special" – a trivial abstraction of a single aspect of a living tradition, falsely rendering it a placeholder for an entire cultural complex. Such distortions may even close down the contingent possibility that humankind might be granted another divine revelation superseding all others. Wherever these contractions deprive baby-boomer seekers of a real tradition, the search for a deeper engagement with reality is corrupted until it becomes simply the latest thrill in the jaded taste for novelty. Often, such assertiveness entails a decidedly undignified posture: wearing *Weltschmerz* on her sleeve, a baby boomer parades her desire for martyrdom, another denounces those who falter to exonerate himself, yet another abandons his family and seeks a surrogate in tribalism. Being homeless, many baby boomers have only their self-righteousness to keep them warm.

But, above all, traditionalism is guilty of taking us nowhere. Engaging faith because it is moving, touching, and fulfilling is unquestionably a seductive and addictive aesthetic pastime – even art inspires revolutions – but it is an empty gesture. It leaves in place our reductionist ideas of the body, mind, and world, while prettifying with gilding. It cannot supply order to human souls or communities because the spiritual options are clutched out of the air, with no ground beneath them, and thus are illusory phantoms of imagination. Meaning is not truth, feeling is not reality, even isolated collective certainty is prone to deception. Marx once wrote that every skepticism is a concealed dogmatism. He could also have said that every dogmatism is a concealed scepticism. Traditionalism is a dogmatism, and by letting sentiment stand in for intellectual demonstration, and psychological responses for spiritual phenomena, it only betrays its own insincerity: the faltering step which exposes the skeptical fear that the real and true can never be known. Traditionalism is an act of conjuring by sentimental association and is heavily mortgaged to homelessness and nostalgia. In the process, the more important task of engaging our present world more deeply, and of listening for the sources of revelation still lingering in our traditions, is being too hastily abandoned, even though its results are the more enduring ones. The question posed by the baby boomers' attraction to traditionalism is whether the enchantment with the "old and venerable," with a place that "looks like a church, smells like a church," takes a human being to the presence and opening of the world, or merely offers an escape from it.

·    ·    ·

For all its shortcomings, traditionalism does, however, also expose the now unacceptable trade-offs and short shrifts brought in by modernity. Marx, Freud, and Nietzsche may have cleared the ground of superstition and prejudice, but they did not rebuild a home fit to accommodate the complexity of human longing. Baby boomers have seen through the myth that human happiness would ensue once, as Marx wrote, man "will revolve about himself as his own true sun." The revolutionary processes of "demythologization" unleashed by these thinkers, while stimulating one dimension of liberty, equality, and fraternity, failed to leave intact the resources for a profound hallowing of life. In search of the subtle grace notes which confer weight and refinement on these goods, baby boomers find in traditionalism a way of restoration. Contrary to Marx, baby boomers appreciate that the tensions of life turn out to be interior as much as they are exterior, for there is a need for consolation and exaltation which no temporal organization of life can fulfill. And, though Marx thought otherwise, baby boomers' discovery of the human need for partnership with past generations, and of an inheritance which is bequeathed, to which one must add, and which one will pass on, is palpable and genuine. Having found spiritual directors and writers of great spiritual discernment, baby boomers have dismissed Marx's declarations of human sameness and solidarity as phony; their discoveries have revealed that there *are* gradations of perfection and discrimination within humankind that legitimately confer authority on the saints and holy persons of our times.

Dissenting from Nietzsche, baby boomers have found that humans cannot live in the perpetual zing of self-overcoming and creativity, but need roots and anchors to acquire depth. They might agree with Nietzsche that religion arises from suffering, but when baby boomers delve deeply into their brokenness, and desire union with transcendent beauty to be sanctified, they have not bared their self-hatred, but disclosed an avenue for emptying themselves – as a prelude to prayer. As the twentieth-century religious thinker Simone Weil wrote, "Even at the darkest moment of affliction, perhaps especially then, when we believe God has forsaken us, if we love, we are at that moment closest to God."[29] From the perspective of those rare moments where traditionalist baby boomers have obtained an intimation of the true eternal, Nietzsche's idea that we should be in the eternal joyful moment of a child at play, is exposed as childishness.

And against Freud, baby boomers have learned that burrowing away at the origins of desire and consciousness casts a person into an infinite vortex whose centre is empty, depriving individuals of the distinctions and subtle shades essential to discernment. The fallacy at the heart of Freud's deconstructions is precisely the insight which won him fame: that humanity's "higher" achievements were mere sublimations of primordial desires and apprehensions, and that the higher could only be understood in the light of the lower. In the homogeneous soup of our origins, he believed, were the clues to our being, albeit clues revealing that our nature was subhuman, and signifying that the repressions which assign us our human characteristics are inauthentic and colonizing, even as they are inescapable. Traditionalist baby boomers have experienced the lie of this dogma. They have learned of a sublimation vastly more profound – for it ascends rather than descends – where humanity, dignity, and shame are not effects of repression, but discriminating forms of freedom, and where the divine is not a substitute satisfaction, but the terminus of all desire and search for fulfillment.

Neither Marx, nor Nietzsche, nor Freud dug deeply into the experiential sources of faith, preferring for purposes of rhetorical flourish to remain at the surface of doctrine and theology. To their credit, they got their licks in against dogma and superstition, but they rarely engaged religion at its foundation, where anthropology, a reasoned account of the human, is involved. What traditionalist baby boomers have achieved is to signal to modern humans that there may be ways to restore a more profound way of being human. Marx, Freud, and Nietzsche were successful in shaping modern consciousness because their rhetoric capitalized on modern man's sense of terror in the wake of the breakdown of the ancient and medieval worlds and the resulting four centuries of turbulent dislocations and revolutions. It was a rhetorical ploy intended to suppress false pride and vainglory, in the expectation that fear was a more effectual passion than love to marshall human order. But a human soul cannot live on rhetoric alone, and what traditionalist baby boomers have discovered above all is that, contrary to modernity's persistent denial, there is a good higher than happiness, and its name is gratitude. At the heart of gratitude is love, and awe at the simple goodness of existence – not terror. To truly be human is to live the truth of gratitude.

The ghosts of Marx, Freud, and Nietzsche are being laid to rest in traditionalism. All three thinkers failed to see that religion, by positing something above humankind did not debase humans, but prevented them from degenerating to a state below the human condition. Unlike previous modern thinkers, baby boomers have lived through historical times and personal tribulations which illustrate the irrevocable persistence of sin and evil. Traditionalist baby boomers have recognized that there is no choice between God and humanity, because true humanity is summoned forth in the act of the "old and venerable" search for God. And while traditionalism is not tradition, it may just serve the didactic function of disposing baby boomers to real tradition, in much the same way as a night of the Boston Pops can awaken the need for Bach and Mozart.

# Tweaking Modernity

Widening the Present Moment

••••••••••••••••••••••••••••••••••••••••••••••••••••••••••••••••••••••••••••••••••••••••••••••••••••••••

R everend Bill Phipps is the former Moderator of the United Church. In 1997, during an interview with the *Ottawa Citizen*, Reverend Phipps said that Jesus Christ was not God.[1] At the same time, he was evasive on the truth of the Resurrection, on the reality of heaven and hell, and on the literal meaning of the gospels. Newspapers across Canada picked up the scandal, and invitations for spots on *Cross Country Checkup*, *Pamela Wallin Live*, and countless other media opportunities were instantly forthcoming. Retaliation by the faithful was also immediate and vituperative. The United Church's "theological watchdogs" – the Community of Concern and the Renewal Fellowship, still hypersensitive after the church's 1988 decision to ordain gays – denounced Phipps, leading to calls for his resignation. He may have had the ear of the liberal theologians in the progressive group Church Alive, but, for many rank and file members of the United Church, the split between the church and the people had gone too far. "I think people are looking for leadership," Phipps had said after his election as Moderator. After the *Citizen* interview, few members of the United Church thought they wanted that kind of leadership. If everyone is entitled to fifteen minutes of fame, as Andy Warhol once claimed, Reverend Phipps had his limelight in spades.

It is the tragedy of our sensationalist times that a man like Bill Phipps would obtain his fame in notoriety, when he has been working quietly behind the scenes for decades with the sick, the poor, and the imprisoned, exercising the virtues of a martyr and enduring the pain of personal tragedy. Born in 1942, he obtained his law degree and was admitted to the Law Society of Upper Canada in 1970. One year before this, he completed his bachelor's degree of divinity and was ordained. He worked as a poverty lawyer and as a chaplain in a children's hospital. He acquired inner-city street experience, and became deeply involved with aboriginal rights issues. He involved himself with United Church–Jewish relations, and developed an abiding commitment to the interface of spirituality and justice. As a minister, he sought to integrate pastoral and prophetic voices in congregational worship, and his early parishioners recall particularly his prophetic social ministry. The church, he believes, must align itself with the marginalized in society – the homeless, the poor, First Nations peoples, and environmentalists:

> If we are just doing Bible study and spiritual formation for our own individual enlightenment, then that's not what the Christian church is about. We do that to be in solidarity with the hurting people in the world, regardless of who they are and how they come to us.[2]

In his interview with the *Ottawa Citizen*, Phipps began by elaborating on these convictions: We've lost our moral centre, the church's role as a strong social conscience has been diminished, market-economy language has taken over, we need to revisit the language of compassion and solidarity, Jesus talks more about economics than anything else, apartheid had been justified on biblical grounds by high-minded Christians who claimed they loved Jesus.

The interviewer, however, would have nothing of this line of thought. Pointing to the button on Phipp's lapel – "Zero Poverty" – he asked whether as Moderator it shouldn't be a cross, and, before Phipps could answer, inquired whether United Church parishioners shouldn't have a true relationship with Jesus. Phipps answered that he recognized the importance of Bible studies, the Eucharist, and prayer service, but that Christians also need to be active.

"Unless you believe in Jesus you will not be saved. Do you believe that?" the interviewer questioned. Phipps asked for clarification of the question: "That Jesus is the only way to God?" When the interviewer nodded assent, Phipps admitted he did not believe that. Did he believe Jesus rose from the dead? He answered, "I believe Jesus lives in people's hearts and did from the moment of that Easter experience." "But did he die," asked the *Citizen*, "spend three days dead and rise from the dead and walk the Earth?" "No," Phipps answered, "I don't believe that in terms of the scientific fact. I don't know whether those things happened or not." Responding to the interviewer's push to have him acknowledge the literal facts of Christ's resurrection, Phipps added, "The gospels were written by people with a theological axe to grind and an agenda and, fine, that's what they are. But they weren't histori-cal records of anything."

At this point, the *Citizen* asked if he believed that "Jesus is divine, that he was the son of God," and when Phipps replied that they could have a whole discussion about that, the *Citizen* curtly retorted, "Well, I would think the head of a Christian church would have a clearly defined position on the issue. You have a clearly defined position on this world, but I'm asking about theology. What interests me about theology, an afterlife, is more important to me than a soup kitchen." Phipps's answer was equally terse: "It wasn't to Jesus and it wasn't to people of the Bible. Your soul is directly tied to whether you care about people who are starving in the streets."

In response to the interviewer's insistence that Phipps come clean on his views as to whether Jesus represents God, Phipps replied:

Christ reveals to us as much of the nature of God as we can see in a human being. Now that has some presuppositions to it, the major one of which is that life and death and God, the Divine and the Holy and all that, is a tremendous mystery of which anyone sees only a very small part. But as far as we are able to understand, Christ is that person who reveals to us the most about the nature of God, what God wants of us, who God is, of any human being.

The *Citizen* asked bluntly, "So was Christ God?" and Phipps answered, "No, I don't believe Christ was God." Seeking an explication, the *Citi-zen* asked, "He's not part of the Trinity? He's not the son of God?" Phipps answered, "I think that's ... I'm no theologian," to which the *Citizen* cattily replied, "You're head of a Christian church; you have to be." When pressed as to what he believed, Phipps answered that he believed in the unconditional love of God, poured into the person of Jesus, which establishes an ethical obligation to work for justice. Asked further, "Is there a heaven?" Phipps answered, "I have no idea. I believe there is." He then tried to return to the theme of unconditional love, but now the *Citizen* wanted to talk about hell. Phipps again refused the bait by saying:

> I don't think Jesus was that concerned about hell. I think we're concerned about life here …. I've got enough problems, and I think most of us have enough problems, trying to live an ethical life knowing all of the ways we compromise ourselves and all of the frailties that we've got. We've got enough problems trying to live ethically and well here to have any knowledge or understanding or worry about what happens after I die.

End of third degree, and beginning of controversy.

After the interview was made public, a public forum was held in London, Ontario. Phipps reminded participants of a study, *Reconciling and Making New: Who is Jesus for the World Today*, which the General Council had passed earlier that year. "Nothing I've said is particularly new." He was assailed repeatedly on the status of Jesus, to which he modestly responded:

> Jesus embodies all of God that can be embodied in a human being. That makes Jesus special, it makes Jesus unique …. [But,] Jesus is not all of God … the brilliance of the Trinity, for me, is that we understand God to be far more mysterious, holy, unknowable, and so on. In fact … I don't think it's necessary to believe in the Resurrection in that particular form [bodily resuscitation] in order to believe in the Resurrection and that Jesus lives and is alive …. The spirit of God in Christ energizes me, forgives me, empowers me to engage the dark corners of our life; to heal the broken, to stand in solidarity with the oppressed; and to embrace the weak.[3]

To the charge that, while he was entitled to have his own views, as Moderator he had to represent the whole church, he replied that the Moderator of the United Church is not a pope or a bishop.

A little over six months later, Phipps was interviewed by Pamela Wallin.[4] As with other interviews, some of his comments nearly have an ironic quality. He began by musing that the danger of going on the spiritual journey by oneself, in the absence of a community, is that one finds only one's own image, and warned that if one loses mystery, one loses religious power. How these opinions fit with the "social gospel" theme of his *Ottawa Citizen* interview was glossed over. Instead, and not surprisingly, Wallin wanted the straight goods on the controversial position he took during the *Citizen* interview. Phipps reiterated that, for him, Jesus was a pathway or window to God, and that he, Phipps, preferred to speak of God, who was so much greater, rather than Jesus. Then he explained that "legal language" cannot inspire the human spirit, which only poetry, music, and art can do. The Bible, he added, is the language of metaphor and poetry. God, he said, is there in the midst of suffering and pain, and in the midst of the political struggle. We are fragile, vulnerable, and broken, he added, and the gravest danger we all face is self-righteousness and arrogance.

The conversation with Wallin did much to repair Phipps's reputation. He emerged from the interview a figure of sincerity, guileless reverence, and compassion. Viewers acknowledged that his latitudinarianism was less impiety than Augustinian humility. Yet he was stumped when Wallin, in her usual astute fashion, located the Achilles heel: "Look [you're saying], 'Jesus is not God, [and] all human beings are God' [but] the only one who is not God is Jesus?"

A little later, Phipps was on *Cross Country Checkup*. Rex Murphy, always the consummate host, gave him an opportunity to expand on his understanding of religion:

> What's wrong is to think religion has answers. Sometimes the formulation of questions and possibilities is more important. It's not just truth claims, but adventures .... It is not enough to say that Christ is Gnostic, the question is why are people gravitating to it .... The best and oldest part of ourselves is not natural, it is part of God .... From Spinoza we should learn to love God without ever expecting God to love us in return. We're all in this together. Not a sparrow should fall. There are too many sparrows falling .... We need belief in miracles; they're a gratuitous gift .... It's about seeing the God in everyone, versus hate, greed, nationalism .... Religion gives perspective, hope, [amid] so much futility.[5]

Though his theology emerges in sound bites, a composite sketch surfaces from these assorted interviews. For Phipps, what needs to be protected above all is the utter transcendence of God. Any expectation we may harbour that God is obliged to reward us for good deeds, succour our needs, or reciprocate our longings, as if there were a cosmic order of commerce, arises out of our selfishness and arrogance. To project our humanity – whether our passions or our reasoning powers – onto God is to deny that God is God. But it is precisely our pride and overconfidence that, since we were made in the likeness of God, we can create, order, name, and judge as He did that has filled our human condition with misery and hurt. In our current state, a war of each against all, we fail to acknowledge our sinfulness and admit the pathetic pettiness of our individual and collective enterprises. In the process of accumulating riches and power, we think we are gaining security from death, and we even applaud ourselves for displaying a little charitable largesse by devising means for our overabundance to trickle down to the unfortunate. But we fail to realize that we are producing an environment where the casualties of our acts of self-assertion are falling between the cracks. And the next casualty may be ourselves. But God, whose goodness is incomprehensible, reveals Himself in acts of random benevolence, substantiating our hope that humankind may be redeemed. If God's relation with us is to mean anything at all, it is incumbent on us to imitate God's compassion and mercy by administering – in humility and forbearance – to the victims of evil and misfortune.

Every turn of this theology – so felicitously true to the writings of St. Augustine, Luther, and Calvin – speaks of the purity of simplicity, transparency, and gratitude. Perhaps his dedication to living at the rawest and most original moment of humankind's encounter with the divine explains Phipps's deep respect for Judaism and his ongoing work on United Church–Jewish relations. The Hebrew YHWH commands with direct and uncompromised authority. He asks nothing more than that humans fulfill their obligations toward Him and their fellow humans. Dictating neither individual salvation, nor the selfish calculation of rewards in heaven, He bids the faithful to obey and be thankful, communally, and for the sole sake of pure holiness alone. YHWH invites his created beings to enter into a *berith* (covenant) with Him and with one another, and not merely to socially contract a network of private needs and expectations. He is a God who commands social and economic justice, and, above all, historical responsibility. Not encumbered with creed and ecclesiology, the relation with YHWH is void of want and ambition. Judaism extends an invitation to encounter revelation at its source.

Reverend Phipps says as much during a talk I had with him in his office. "Judaism gives you an opportunity to listen to God, to serve God, as opposed to the baby boomers' search for 'It is good for me, satisfies me, fulfills me.'" Phipps's Christianity does not presume to correct, fulfill, and succeed Judaism. "Jesus embodies, represents, the Torah, the biblically based life," he explains. "Our task is still *Tikun*, to heal and repair the world." Indeed, Phipps elaborates, Social Gospel – the movement inspired by Walter Rauschenbusch's 1917 book *A Theology for the Social Gospel*, which emphasizes Christian social responsibility in the face of the evil propensities in social institutions, and which Phipps holds in high favour – has its roots in the Hebrew tradition. And a restoration of Social Gospel, Phipps adds, is decidedly overdue. Our present times are deeply impaired.

> Principalities of power infuse everything. We live in a sinful world. People think they can find the right solution, can insulate themselves, isolate themselves, from the primal – with money. But evil invades everyday life. Ours is a flawed doctrine of sin – we can't create a perfect world, we can't find the just way and just action. We must retrieve a more profound doctrine of sin. Nothing can be permanent.

Social Gospel offers a sound theology: Recognize the fallenness of human institutions. Acknowledge the perfectibility of humanity. Lessen the occasion for sin and evil. Walk humbly and modestly with God. But Social Gospel, Phipps admits, is also in need of a "fresh articulation." One way is through the Jesus Seminar. "The Jesus Seminar lets people appreciate the authority of Jesus," Phipps acknowledges.

Reflecting back on his speeches and interviews, it is easy to see how much Phipps respects the Jesus Seminar's work. The Seminar's Jesus is his Jesus: the Jesus who shuns legalism and metaphysics, the Jesus who is radically egalitarian and challenges the hierarchies of the world, the Jesus who is neither apocalyptic nor eschatological but ethical, the Jesus who is known in His transformational effect. If this reorientation means translating the religious tradition into morality, its compensating dividend is that – unlike the legions of today's moralists – it takes the religious context of ethics seriously.

That kind of seriousness is what enlightened observers see behind Phipps's controversial theological statements. Lying behind his denial of the divinity of Jesus is a position as old as Arianism – one of the options explored during the fourth-century debate about how to formulate the belief in Jesus as both human and divine.[6] Arius made two arguments. First, he observed, God could not become human without seriously compromising His divinity. Hence, it follows, Jesus was not divine. Arius's position was elaborated to protect the uniqueness and transcendence of God the Father, and diminish the idea of human self-deification. Second, he objected directly to the position taken by Athanasius, the Alexandrian Patriarch, who appeared to be de-emphasizing the historical Jesus, and unacceptably rewriting the church's teaching on salvation. Arius argued that the *imitatio Christi* (imitation of Christ) meant looking at the mystery of the human Jesus and imitating his exemplary human actions. Salvation came through moral perfection in conformity to the divine will as it was manifest in Jesus the man. From Athanasius' viewpoint, this de-emphasis of Jesus' divinity lowered the status of Christ. For Athanasius, the body was sinful and corrupt, but the Incarnation changed humanity and made possible conceiving a perfect divinity as the true meaning of the *imitatio Christi*. The humanity of Jesus was just an instrument used by the eternal Logos in the work of salvation. An initiate to the faith is invited to grow spiritually in the image of the divine Logos, and true faith requires shifting attention away from an engagement of the total personality in the world to inner spiritual activity. From Arius's perspective, this "spiritualization" not only overstated the divinity of Christ, while failing to do justice to the humanity of the divine and the sacred nature of profane life, but also entailed an undesirable increase in ecclesiastical control insofar as it reinforced the church's propensity to deem itself exclusively competent to monitor each believer's growth in spirituality. From the church's perspective, Arius was exaggerating the potential for redemption of this world, and encouraging a dangerous tendency to self-reliance. The Arian argument was denounced as a heresy in 325 CE, at the Council of Nicea. The Athanasian view prevailed, and the church to this day rules absolutely, as Cardinal Joseph Ratzinger, Prefect of the Vatican Congregation for the Doctrine of the Faith, confidently displayed in a recent admonishment to dissident Catholic groups:

On questions of faith and morals the only subject qualified to fulfill the office of teaching with binding authority for the faithful is the supreme Pontiff and the college of bishops in communion with him. Anyone who doubts or denies the doctrines as solemnly judged to be divinely revealed, written, and handed down by the Pontiff and the magisterium falls under the "censure of heresy" as defined by canon law.[7]

Phipps's standpoint is neither reckless nor unconsidered, but calculated and credible. His United Church detractors might want to consider shifting their devotion to the Church of England or Roman Catholicism.

Nevertheless, Phipps's Arian interpretation of Christology has major drawbacks. To preserve the uncompromised nature of God, God must withdraw from the world of human affairs. Such an argument is an old one, present even in the Platonic dialogue *Euthyphro*, in which Socrates explodes conventional definitions of piety by showing that to make the gods subject to our petitions and expectations is to limit and define them inappropriately. The remarkable conclusion of this discussion of why the gods should not be reduced to naturist revelations and the social functions of human society is that the gods may be too distant and too good to be worshipped, and that the greatest piety may actually be to disregard the gods. However, 2,000 years later, Friedrich Nietzsche had a blunt retort to the very historical process centred on the Protestant Reformation, which left God remote from the human world, uncompromised by the human desire for reassurance, consolation, and redemption. "God," he wrote, " – an idea no longer of any use, not even a duty any longer – an idea grown useless, superfluous, consequently a refuted idea: let us abolish it!"[8] And so God died, at least for Nietzsche, though also for many others. Maintaining too distant a god, the gods finally fade into oblivion, for – as Mircea Eliade points out – humans forget the gods as soon as they have no need of them.[9]

The other danger in Phipps's Arianism is the potential for a moralism turned irascible. Phipps's Jesus is the historical, social radical and iconoclast who calls the powers of the day into question, while working on behalf of the weak, poor, and unjustly treated. To say, as Arius does and Phipps echoes, that we are called to imitate Jesus' exemplary human actions, and that salvation comes through moral perfection, runs the risk of derailing into the hope that the Kingdom of God can be realized in the here and now. Indeed, when Social Gospel is justifiably criticized, it is for its overconfidence in human perfectibility. But virtue that forgets human fallibility transforms the healthy application of our moral duties to social engineering. The traditional position is that there are natural laws of justice that transcend time and place. But these laws are only guidelines and can never be totally realized without untold political mischief. There is always a gap between human actuality and reality, and the civic norms of tolerance and respect safeguard the legitimate heterogeneity of human pursuits.

What vouchsafes that transcendent goods are not treated as mere solutions to problems is mystery. In his interview with Pamela Wallin, Phipps started by saying that, if mystery is abandoned, religious power is lost. In his talk with me, he emphasized that justice issues and mystery must go together. When I asked Reverend Phipps how the United Church could retain those who sought mystery – the awesome experience of the infinite and the holy – he appeared at a loss, admitting that this was a problem for him. How does one hold the revived need for transcendence together with community, and give people opportunities to find public ways of expressing a life sanctified by grace, rather than leave them to explore mystery in private and in cults? He did not know. Indeed, this is what his detractors were saying, too, in their insistence that the United Church proclaim that Jesus is God. A mystery remote from life is just a mystery. A mystery incarnate in daily life – such as the mystery of the Incarnation, where Jesus is both human and divine – both enhances morality and acts as a brake to moralism. It may be that the suffering to which the United Church so visibly administers is only a signal of a deeper, darker affliction to which only the awesome mystery of transcendence is an answer. After all, even Augustine, one of the chief sources of Protestant theology, wrote that true charity is not merely succouring the miseries of the unfortunate: "I call 'charity' the motion of the soul toward the enjoyment of God for His own sake, and the enjoyment of one's self and one's neighbour for the sake of God."[10]

· · ·

The world was not created some six thousand years ago. The diversity of life species which now exist in their present form evolved over hundreds of thousands of years of adapting to their environments. Man was an afterthought. The physical remains of human cultures in Indonesia, China, and Egypt reveal that there were humans – as we now know ourselves – at least 250,000 years ago. There is no evidence of ancient Israelites ever fleeing slavery in Egypt and finding refuge in Judea. Herod was no longer king when Jesus was born, and the census of Quirinus took place a decade after Jesus' birth. The Christmas story has suspicious resemblances to the birth of Zoroaster, not to say of the Mesopotamian king Sargon of Akkad, Buddha, Krishna, and Dionysius. Little is known about who borrowed what from whom. The tale of God's descent into human form through a virgin birth, His life on earth filled with raising the dead and curing lepers, and His crucifixion and resurrection are so fantastic as to be beyond human comprehension.

While Peter may have been asked to be the "rock of the Church," and successive popes claimed their authority from apostolic succession, papal infallibility was only declared by the First Vatican Council in 1870. Until the eleventh century, Roman Catholic priests were not required to be celibate – Peter, the first pope, was married – and priests and popes continued to marry for hundreds of years after that. From 1378 to 1417, there were two popes and two papal lines, Urban VI and Clement VII, and their successors – one in Rome, one in Avignon – each claimed to be legitimate heirs to Peter. Today, Pope John Paul II's word is infallible, Catholic priests chafe at the bridle of their vows and cheat, Christendom is fragmented, and rival factions proclaim themselves rightful heirs to Christ. Who and what is one to believe?

Similar problems of succession and questions of divine transmission bedevil Muslims, with Sunnis tracing authority to the descendants of Muhammad, and Shia declaring spiritual descent from Ali, Muhammad's son-in-law. Sikhs who are unsure whether to follow the rulings of the *jathedar* (high priest) or the explicit teachings of Gobind Singh, the tenth and final guru, have recently faced similar dilemmas (as the altercation at Vancouver's Ross Street Temple over whether chairs and tables should be permitted in the *langar* – eating-area – of the temple tempestuously communicated). Worldwide followers of the Indian guru Rajneesh bicker over whether Osho was his rightful heir, Theravada and Mahayana Buddhists dispute whether Gotama Buddha's religious practices or his experience of enlightenment should be emulated, and Jews are divided between the Orthodox, who subscribe to a strict adherence to the *mitzvoth* as the literal word of Y H W H, and Reform and Reconstructionist Jews, who see the Pentateuch as redacted, and hence not God's definitive word, and live by the conventions of an evolving Judaism. The manifold disputes between Protestant denominations, which arise from the dogged insistence that one scriptural passage rather than another reveals God's true meaning, shatter any hope of Western Christendom's unity.

Facts which are said to be indisputable, and claims to be the one, true religion – the unique, unsurpassable revelation of God to man – are almost never so. The human encounter with divine revelation inevitably leaves a yawning gap for quarrelsome interpretation of its meaning, not to say the machinations of palace politics. As with many complex phenomena, delving too deeply below the surface breeds doubt and skepticism. Nietzsche once warned that a historical fact examined too closely reveals "[its] madness, its injustice, its blind passion, and especially the earthly and darkened horizon that was the source of its power."[11] What can a reasonable person believe?

Rather than adopt the fideist response – acknowledge the fallibility of reason, extinguish the human presumption to judge, accept God's word on faith – three artful solutions are put forward to cope with these predicaments. The first is to reinterpret scripture existentially. The second is to look at sacred text mytho-poetically. The third is to rescript faith, acknowledging defeat on the expectation of definitive verification of the facts and transforming religion into moral teaching.

Rudolf Bultmann is the theologian associated with the first solution. Using the philosophy of Martin Heidegger as a stencil, he gave the Bible an existentialist twist, seeing its histories and parables not as records of actual events millennia ago, or as intellectual and spiritual teachings of essential truth, but as paradigms of human existence in the contemporary world.[12] Following Heidegger, Bultmann is concerned with the problem of how contemporary human beings can live an authentic existence. "Authenticity" entails freedom from the past and a radical openness to the future. It means acknowledging that traditional compass points verifying the closed and fixed world of the past are now useless. Our lives, he writes, are irrevocably characterized by impermanence. We live only toward our death, and we must acknowledge that our struggle with *Sorge* – anxiety and burden – cannot be overcome. All our efforts to find an exit are doomed to failure. So far, Bultmann sounds like other followers of Heidegger – Jean-Paul Sartre, Albert Camus, Simone de Beauvoir. But unlike other existentialists, Bultmann does not believe that mere human recognition of our real situation is enough. Humankind needs the actions of a transcendent God, and in our free capacity to choose to live with faith in the *kerygma* – the proclamation of the redemptive power of Christ – lies authenticity. The *kerygma*, Bultmann insists, cannot be confirmed by historical investigation. The message is in the myth, and for that reason Bultmann focuses primarily on the Gospel of John and Paul's letters, rather than the more factually based gospels of Mark, Luke, and Matthew. Bultmann's take on faith, which transforms a mythological world view into a set of existential propositions, clearly affirms that religion is not about the supernatural, or about facts verified by irreproducible miracles, but wholly fits within a contemporary frame of reference – in the present reality of existential states of the contemporary individual. Are the events and persons true and real? Bultmann "brackets" those unanswerable questions, and – to satisfy the demands of today's paradigm of truth – faith becomes "empirically non-falsifiable."

Northrop Frye, Victoria College's illustrious literary theorist, offers the quintessential mytho-poetic reading of faith, premised on the judgment that, other than through art and myth, no avenues of transcendence remain open to us. In his famed major work, *Anatomy of Criticism: Four Essays*, Frye suggested that all literature appeals to universal archetypes, symbols, and rhetoric. The literary universe, he proposed, is divided into desirable and abhorrent visions – the one captured in comedy and romance, the other in tragedy and irony. The Bible, Frye claims, must be taken as a work of literature, indeed the supreme example of comedy. As he suggests in *The Great Code: The Bible and Literature*, the facts of the Bible are not empirical and historical, but elements of a *Heilgeschichte*, a spiritual and mythical narrative whose truth is experienced in its transforming power. Indeed, it is not given to humans to have certainty, for truths can be demonstrated only through personal example. Thus, he adds, myth and metaphor are the only way of educating a free person in spiritual concerns.[13]

The third approach to displacing the centrality of messy religious facts and theological interpretations is to look at faith primarily through the prism of ethics. Here is a view of faith that attends less to the mystical and cosmological understanding of God, but bears witness to a radical truth with direct bearing on the social, political, and economic powers of the day. Observing human suffering and affliction, brokenness and injustice, the religious believer sees faith as conscience, as the voice of dissent and protest, and as a catalyst for transforming the compromised forces of immanence. "By their fruits you shall know them," says Christian scripture, enjoining the believer to live faith in moral action and adopt the Hebraic idea of history as the dynamic conduit of YHWH's covenant with humans. Herein lies the image of a God of righteousness and justice, who defines historical responsibility as defeating the sin and evil in temporal institutions, as progress in the perfectibility of humans, and in the social relevance of faith. Such an approach is evident in Peter Berger's *The Homeless Mind*, where he argues that there is a universal need for a "sacred canopy" which sanctions how we act morally. The "school" most famously associated with this approach is the Jesus Seminar.

In 1993, a new multicoloured version of the New Testament surfaced in bookstores. *The Five Gospels: The Search for the Authentic Words of Jesus* had a distinctive characteristic: The sayings of Jesus appeared in four colours and, as the editors explained, reflected the judgment of the Jesus Seminar's Fellows as to the authenticity of the sayings. The conclusions they reached followed extensive examination and discussion of the 2,000 quotes attributed to Jesus in the gospels of Mark, Matthew, Luke, John, and Thomas. When talk ceased, 125 scholars cast votes using coloured beads placed in a box. Red signified that Jesus undoubtedly said this or something very like it; pink meant that Jesus probably said something like this; grey denoted that Jesus did not say this, but the ideas contained in it are close to his own; and black expressed the judgement that Jesus did not say this and that the saying in question represented the perspective of a later or different tradition. For believers, the New Testament gospels are inspired by God. For the Jesus Seminar, things are not as clear-cut. By their reckoning, only 18 per cent of the sayings could be justifiably attributed to Jesus. Of the Lord's Prayer, only the words "Our Father" emerged unscathed and were deemed authentic. Predictably, hostile public outcry by faithful believers, particularly Christian evangelicals, fundamentalists, and traditionalists, was immediate.

The Jesus Seminar was founded in 1985 and was led by Robert Funk. Other major figures associated with the Seminar who have become media personalities include John Dominic Crossan, Burton Mack, and Marcus Borg.[14] The Seminar's work was intended to apply literary interpretive analysis (Higher Criticism) to the Bible, as well as the most recent archeological, historical, sociological, and anthropological findings to knowledge about Jesus and his followers. As significantly, the Seminar's avowed task was to separate the sayings of the "historical Jesus" from the religious interpretation which followed his death. They accepted the current scholarly consensus that the Gospel of Mark was written around 70 CE, the Gospel of Matthew in the 80s, the Gospel of John during the 90s, and the Gospel of Luke, together with the Acts of the Apostles, in the early second century. They took as decisive to debunking his authority that Paul, whose epistles form the foundation of theological and institutional Christianity, does not mention Jesus' miracles or parables; indeed, Paul's writings contain nothing of Jesus' earthly life. Evidently, the Jesus Seminar concludes, Paul did not know the human Jesus. Cardinal "Pauline" texts like 2 Corinthians, Hebrews, Philemon, and Philippians are equally suspect, judged now to have not even been written by Paul. Can it be confidently maintained that any of the Gospel writers knew Jesus directly? Are the names Mark, Matthew, John, Luke, and Paul not mere placeholders for later redactors? The Jesus Seminar adopted the evidence that the extant versions of the gospels can be dated to 175 years after Jesus' death. In the strong likelihood that they are not the "first edition," interpolation by successive editors is likely. Lacking firm evidence as to what Jesus *really* said and did, and dismissive of the "legend" surrounding Jesus, the Jesus Seminar felt it necessary to look at supplementary evidence.

The search for the "historical Jesus" is nothing new. In 1835, David Friedrich Strauss published *The Life of Jesus Critically Examined*, advancing the position that the real words and actions of Jesus had to be distinguished from the history of doctrinalization informing the formation of the historical church. In 1906, Albert Schweitzer wrote his acclaimed book, *The Quest of the Historical Jesus*, in which he excoriated liberal Protestant theologians for reading their own prejudices and commitments into their historical depictions of Jesus as an ethical teacher. But, in his own account of Jesus as a misguided apocalyptic prophet, Schweitzer also dwells on the historical Jesus and excludes any discussion of the Resurrection and its larger theological meaning, thus reinforcing the turn from orthodoxy. For both Strauss and Schweitzer, theology and metaphysics fall by the wayside and "faith" is reconfigured to placate modern skepticism. Bultmann's own work offered a way to accomodate theology to modern tastes. In his thought, the historical Jesus supplies the immanent reference for faith and theology, and humankind's historical – in opposition to its essential – condition is pushed into the foreground. Cosmic events – supernatural reality, eschatological prophecies – are bracketed out, while existential predicaments, in the here and now, are showcased as the exclusive site for the human-divine encounter.

All of these studies have in common the desire to distinguish Pauline Christianity from Jesus, and the "Jesus movements" from the Christian Church. Not surprisingly, nearly all the writers are Protestants. Observing that "The gospels provided a historical point of origin that supported the institutional claims of Christianity as the church,"[15] each exploration of the life of Jesus was at the same time a search for a Christianity prior to the Catholic Church. And all of them cast doubt on what cannot be verified by empirical evidence or offends the natural order of things, an effort as old as John Locke's famous seventeenth-century effort to question whatever in scripture could not withstand modern scientific testing, and particularly miracles, whose non-repeatability leaves them with a failing grade. Sticking to "just the facts" – the political, economic and archeological data – prevents flights of fancy and patenting truth in a shot at consolidating power. As John Meier, a scholar of religion at Catholic University of America, wrote, "You are not putting your faith in a fairy tale or some historical symbol, but in a real person who was crucified in the first century."[16]

The quest for a pure, unadulterated Christianity was not exclusively an expression of hostility to Catholicism. It equally served to differentiate Christianity from Jewish apocalyptic thought and Hellenistic mystery cults, whose similarity at key points – dying and rising gods, the rite of baptism, sacred meals – undermined Christianity's claim to be a unique revelation of God.

Added to this push for a more critical reading of the New Testament was new historical evidence, supplied by the extraordinary archeological find in 1945 of the Nag Hammadi codex collection and the Qumran scrolls. Among the manuscripts discovered was a fifth gospel – the

Gospel of Thomas – comprising a "sayings collection" of 114 sayings of Jesus, a Book of Peter, Coptic-Gnostic writings, and an apocryphal Acts of the Apostles. These texts stimulated reassessments of the significance of additional manuscripts – such as *The Didache, or Teaching of the Twelve Apostles*, found in 1875 in Constantinople – previously judged marginal to an interpretation of the four gospels. While most of the sayings in these texts confirm passages in the "synoptic" gospels, there are also sayings not found there.

Equally revolutionary were the conclusions drawn from years of careful text-proofing of the four gospels by laying similar and identical scriptural passages together and speculating on the meaning of these comparisons. It is now widely accepted that Mark's is the oldest, and the evident source of Matthew's and Luke's texts. But Mark was not a disciple and, like Matthew and Luke, was not a witness to the events he describes. Moreover, there are materials in Matthew's and Luke's gospels absent from Mark's, which suggests the plausible theory that there must have existed an earlier document – the Q, or *Quelle* (Source) Gospel – which Mark himself used as his source. Since the narratives in the four New Testament gospels add up to only thirty-one days of a thirty-three-year life, it seems no great stretch of imagination to conclude that other texts, including this century's discoveries, may contain evidence beyond that conveyed in the present configuration of approved scriptural texts. And, to hammer the final nails in the coffin of orthodoxy, much modern sociological and anthropological study of ancient Palestine exposes extensive inaccuracy in the gospels.

The Jesus Seminar, then, was hardly breaking radical new ground. In many cases, its scholars merely made public what had been brewing for fifty or more years in academic circles. Even the assumptions governing their analysis were reasonable and moderate from a modern perspective: Accept only those passages which are attested to by two or more sources, reject those monologues of Jesus where no witnesses were present, focus on sayings more feasibly arising in an oral rather than a literate culture, discount statements linking back to ancient prophecies or projecting forward beyond Jesus' death, ignore the boundaries of contemporary academic disciplines. Other assumptions – to emphasize the more radical statements of Jesus, to ignore "Christian" formulations, to refuse all perspectives on the gospels arising after Constantine's 313 CE edict of toleration, and especially to disallow the dogmatic agreements of the Council of Nicea in 325 CE – may have been more problematic, but were certainly not outside the pale of plausible, defensible interpretation. Above all, the Seminar's touchstone, "When in sufficient doubt, leave it out," abided by the modern canons of cautious and tentative inference.

Notwithstanding the dissident nature of their enterprise, the ambition to seize the higher ground by decrying other "ideological and idolatrous" versions of Jesus, and their claims to detached objectivity, there is among the members of the Jesus Seminar a surprisingly homogeneous consensus about who the real Jesus was and what his life amounts to. And bootlegged within the innovative image of Jesus and Christianity they all subscribe to lies a commitment to a specific theology and metaphysic, all protestations to the contrary notwithstanding.

The most significant feature which Jesus Seminar Fellows share is the substitution of an "eschatological" for an "apocalyptic" theology. An apocalyptic theology states that Christ expected the world to end, and that Christ's death and resurrection fulfilled the promise of a new age. The messianic kingdom was established in the hearts of the community of believers in the resurrected Christ, and reinforced by the Church's official teachings. An eschatological theology, by contrast, states that the flesh-and-blood Jesus, who lived in the city of Nazareth, and subverted all existing religious beliefs and political authority, was a wisdom figure whose radical life comprises a "realized eschatology," which is to say that the Truths he brought were by no means "truths" based on symbolic interpretations of the Resurrection and Pentecost, to be officially promulgated by a Church, but a call to a radical witnessing of his own life and teaching. Jesus taught a revolutionary mode of life intended for the immediate present. In his book *Myth of Innocence: Mark and Christian Origins*, Burton L. Mack depicts Jesus as a Cynic sage, more Hellenistic than Jewish, who limited himself to pithy aphoristic statements uttered to challenge conventional wisdom and subvert the dominant social structures of the time. Marcus J. Borg bases his conclusions on the hypothesis that Q was a book of wisdom sayings, like those produced by other first-century philosophical schools, such as the Cynics. He claims that the apocalyptic teaching was later added by Mark in the wake of the Jewish rebellion against Rome, and the destruction of the Jerusalem temple, to respond to rising eschatological expectations. Borg sustains this depiction of Jesus as a subversive sage and teacher of an alternative life by pointing out, in his 1984 book *Conflict, Holiness and Politics in the Teachings of Jesus*, that Jesus was born, lived, and died a Jew.

Despite his unorthodox views on the *Halakah* – Jewish law – his enjoyment of table fellowship with his followers, independent of social class, and his ambition of replacing the dominant Jewish ethos of holiness ("Be holy as God is holy"[17]) with an alternative paradigm of compassion (Be compassionate as God is compassionate), Jesus can be understood wholly within the framework of a Palestinian Jewish world, possibly within the *Hasid* tradition. The "real Jesus," it follows, was not the anti-Judaic Jesus of Christian theology. John Dominic Crossan, whose study *The Historical Jesus: The Life of a Mediterranean Jewish Peasant* situates Jesus in the context of a pre-industrial peasant world – an honour-shame culture, a patron-client society – sees him emerging from colonial protest movements struggling on behalf of a radical egalitarianism. Crossan proposes that no single "Jesus," least of all the theological Christ, sufficiently acknowledges the dynamic, living experience of Jesus: "The 'real Jesus' is, for me, the perpetually renewed interaction of the historical and theological Jesus within communities of Christian faith."[18] The theological Jesus, who requires the entertainment of fantastic beliefs like the resurrection, is not needed; it is sufficient to uncover a historical Jesus whose words and actions can be religiously transforming. Harvard professor Elisabeth Schussler Fiorenza's book *In Memory of Her* is an application of this idea: God is Sophia and Christ is her spokesman. Jesus was a wisdom prophet who, by questioning patriarchy, and giving higher status to women within a "discipleship of equals," revealed his capacity to see from a woman's gestalt. Perhaps we are all free to find the Jesus we need.

The important point for the Jesus Seminar Fellows is that Jesus did not clearly see himself as the Messiah and expressed no intention of founding a church. The apocalypticism one finds in the gospels, they contend, is a secondary development in the early Jesus movement. Once Christ was said to be the anointed one, then began the long process of institutionalization and doctrinalization which gave orthodoxy its power base and its claim to exercise that power until the end of time, *ad majorem gloriam Dei* (for the greater glory of God) – sanctioning, too, centuries of inquisitions, pogroms, witch hunts, and forced conversions.

The second essential characteristic of the Jesus Seminar is the whole-sale subscription to empiricism. "The Christ of creed and dogma, who had been firmly in place in the Middle Ages, can no longer command the assent of those who have seen the heavens through Galileo's tele-scope," reads the introduction to *The Five Gospels.* Did Jesus raise Lazarus from the dead? No. Did Jesus feed thousands from a handful of fish and bread? It cannot be. Did Jesus heal lepers and perform exor-cisms? Probably not. Was there a virgin birth? Impossible. Dead people do not come alive, food does not multiply, and prophecy cannot happen. Quite simply, the natural order of things – mechanical cause and effect, wholes exhibiting no more than the sum of their parts – cannot be suspended. And when narrative cannot satisfy the tests for historical objectivity and historical proof, it must just be myth.

Since the Resurrection is the prime event of Christianity, and every-thing else rests upon it, it is instructive to observe how the Jesus Semi-nar handles the mystery. First, writers note the discrepancies in the Resurrection story: Matthew says the resurrected Jesus first appeared before Mary Magdalene and other women; Luke says he appeared before Peter; and Mark has no post-Resurrection appearance at all. Luke says Jesus appeared to the apostles in Jerusalem, Matthew says they were in Galilee. Amid such confusion, how can anyone be certain of what happened? Second, members of the Jesus Seminar simply deny the event, either through silence or explicit dismissal: It was highly unlikely that Jesus was buried, the story of Joseph of Arimathea was invented, and Jesus was probably devoured by dogs or buried in a mass grave. Christian beliefs such as vicarious human sacrifice and atoning death are mere myth and superstition.

The problem with these two sallies is that the Passion narrative is the central mystery of Christianity. Thus, the challenge the Jesus Seminar faces is how to deal with the evidence that, after his death, the disciples, not to mention nearly two millennia of Christians, continued to expe-rience Christ as a living reality. The third solution put forward is neat, even while – in light of our earlier discussion of the tendency in modern times to surmount hard fact with sentimental myth – it is predictable. It runs as follows: Why people continue to feel the pres-ence of Christ does not depend on a physical resuscitation. The Jesus Seminar shows that, with a little creative reinterpretation, the Resur-rection can be understood functionally and subjectively: Does the vision of the Risen Christ give an individual a moving spiritual experience, and achieve the transformative effect of binding together a community of believers? If so, that is all that belief in the Resurrection requires. Today's believer can avoid a questionable belief in the Resurrection as an event while embracing it as an experience of the living presence of Jesus.

On many fronts, the Jesus Seminar wants to have its cake and eat it. Its Fellows, for example, are favourably disposed to Jesus' moral code – at least, the component more inclined to social reform – but would happily jettison the foundation which substantiates it. With just cause, one might judge this to be an act of bad faith, for in the absence of a more assured grasp of the ultimate reality in which time is cradled, the historical moment upon which they seize – Jesus' life and his utterances of acceptable sayings – is arbitrary. Indeed, the idea that a given juncture in time has a paradigmatic meaning at all is actually derivative of the Christian theology that the Jesus Seminar rebels against. As Augustine explained, the very idea of history as composed of unique events with universal validity, and situated within a progressive sequence of time, is derived from the mystery of the Incarnation and the teaching of salvation promised in the Resurrection. Secularizing the theology may give the moralist a clear conscience, but, in the final analysis, it renders the selection of one interval of history over another a purely private act, inconsequential to anyone who is not a Christian.

Equally, relegating Jesus to the status of a holy man, sage, or healer, while denying him metaphysical status as the guarantor of reality, renders him indistinguishable from Mother Teresa, the Sai Baba, or Oral Roberts. If Jesus is God, then he is no mere role model of what a human being should aspire to. Nor is he a psychopomp, or a saintly being. He is instead the essence of what is true and real. Another "holy" being cannot substitute for him, since he is not a prototype who can be imitated and copied, but the source prior to all instantiations of existence. This is why the Gospel writer John depicts Christ as the Logos – the primal speech and reason grounding all creation and giving each existing being its form.

It is all very well for the Jesus Seminar to proclaim that they have provided people with a bridge back into a wholehearted participation in the Christian life, especially those "for whom the older image of Jesus is no longer functional," or to have heard over and again from readers that "You've made it possible for me to be a Christian again." However, just because something works does not mean it is true or real. Marcus Borg likes to write that the Jesus Seminar Fellows ask themselves whether a vote on the admissibility of a scriptural passage "can be cashed out" for the average sitter in the pew. But recruiting for Jesus is really not what is at stake in the Jesus Seminar's debate with orthodoxy. Accommodation to modern consciousness and culture, on the other hand, is. Suggesting that it is immaterial whether Jesus is God or a commendable teacher and activist as long as the image "works" fails to distinguish Jesus from all the other "Christ-cults" which arose throughout Greece, Syria, and Asia Minor and, hence, runs roughshod over the distinctions between truth and meaning, reality and perspective, essence and experience. The first term of the distinctions denotes what is objective, while the second term conveys what is expressive and subjective. Functionalists generally are distressingly insouciant about inherited and widely attested distinctions – and the result is the loss of the distinctive uniqueness of a phenomenon, as well as hierarchies of objective value and rank. A shoe, as the political philosopher Hannah Arendt liked to say, is not a hammer, however well it drives a nail into a wall – and failing to distinguish between purpose and function, as the Jesus Seminar tends to do, reduces all phenomena to their pragmatic utility, rather than their power to reveal reality. But Christianity stands or falls by its claim to explain reality in all its gradations and distinctions. It must persuade seekers that its judgments of higher and lower – such as the higher status of charity over justice, or love over reason – represent the true order of being.

Even accepting that the work of the Jesus Seminar stimulates an individual "to be a Christian again," one has to ask, "What kind of Christian?" Central beliefs of Christianity – that we are individuals with free choice, that our bodies and the earth are good and redeemed, that history bestows a progressive disclosure of truth, that love will conquer anger, that patience must endure weakness, that forgiveness ends the otherwise limitless consequences of sin and evil, that peace should prevail over war – are guaranteed only because of the central mysteries of the Incarnation and Resurrection. The call to saintliness, the teaching of justice, the message of salvation, and the judgment against perfidy all come as a complete ontological package. All these aspects of Christianity are "meaningful" and "empowering" only because Jesus is God, because the historical and theological Jesus validate one another. It is mystifying to read that, in the minds of the Jesus Seminar Fellows, even if the Resurrection did not occur, Easter can still be celebrated for its symbolism of hope and new life. What confers ground and direction for such hope? When Robert Funk writes that the aim of the Jesus Seminar is "to set Jesus free from the Scriptural and credal prisons in which we have entombed him," he insufficiently appreciates that the normative content which remains of Jesus once the Seminar has completed its deconstruction, and upon which Fellows still wish to capitalize, is heavily mortgaged to the theological Jesus. They are the legacy of theological Christianity, albeit in a secularized form.

But the most severe problem with the Jesus Seminar's work, in my judgment, is the "reversal" of apocalypticism and eschatology. It is a "reversal" because there is an ancient history to the two options. After Jesus' death, and in the wake of uncertainty as to what his followers ought to do as a fledgling church, his brother James proposed that they define themselves as an eschatological community – they would wait for the pending catastrophic events prefigured in Daniel, and expect that this world would be replaced by the kingdom of saints. They could be iconoclasts and rebels, rejecting institutional authority, whether political or ecclesiastical. Others argued they were an apocalyptic community which, through the death of Jesus and the descent of the Holy Spirit at Pentecost, had already entered the new age simply by living as a community bound by faith in the resurrected messiah. The apocalyptic option prevailed. The "community of the faithful" naturally evolved into the church – the institution that had to work out the new faith's complex worldly relation with the Roman Empire and equip itself with formal doctrines to define and safeguard the faith vis-à-vis other sects and cults. James' more radical eschatological option went underground, though wherever there is an antinomian spirit of protest against doctrine and the institutionalized church, and the claim that a new age is imminent, the spirit of James' alternative persists.

The apocalyptic reading had the drawback of committing revelation to the exclusive keeping of the church, but, because it acknowledged a future event, the "Second Coming," which would fundamentally alter reality, it had the advantage of subduing the presumption of individuals or sectarians within or outside the church inspired to believe that they independently possessed direct wisdom from God that promised their salvation.

The church was particularly adamant in denouncing the heresy of Gnosticism, the belief that humans can obtain *gnosis* (definitive knowledge) that will here and now save them and unite them with God. The Catholic Church, for all its failings, has never presumed that it is the Kingdom of God. Like John the Baptist, it has always said that its forms of worship and theological doctrine only point to that kingdom. In principle, the Catholic Church is "agnostic," though in practice it has often assumed itself to be in possession of God's wisdom.

When the Jesus Seminar dredges up the abandoned option, it usefully reins in any Roman Catholic tendency to presumption – especially in the papal power to speak *ex cathedra* (the Council of Florence's stipulation *extra ecclesiam nulla salus*, "There is no salvation outside of the church," legitimately outrages non-Catholics) – and adopts the sober policy of cautious, tentative reasoning in matters related to the divine. But paradoxically, through its commitment to "realized eschatology," it closes down the radical transcendence of revelation because it stipulates that reality was totally comprehended, and revelation about the end fully fulfilled, in the wisdom teachings of Jesus, leaving to posterity merely the task of applying these teachings to changing historical circumstances. Or fixing up some details in the new age initiated by Jesus. Since, in the past, these teachings were faultily applied – how else could social hierarchy and injustice (such as the exclusion of women from clerical office) have endured? – today our greater clarity in really understanding Jesus' teachings, and truly reaching the climactic moment of world history in which God's kingdom is announced, means that we are presently in a situation where the truth can, for the first time, become actual.

But if this is a credible interpretation of what the Jesus Seminar means by "recovering" the historical Jesus – with the evident proviso that no member of the Jesus Seminar expresses himself or herself so baldly – it is not untoward to conclude that the Jesus Seminar can be accused of a strong tendency to "presentism," elevating, even divinizing, the present state unjustifiably (some would say "undeservedly") to an absolute mode of truth and reality. The philosophical position of the Jesus Seminar is *historicism*, the viewpoint that truth changes as it unfolds in history. Today, historicists contend, we are in a better posi-

tion to unlock the secrets of revelation than ever before. The philosophical position of the church, on the other hand, is *metaphysical,* the
judgment that truth is eternal, if transcendent. We are no further along
today, the church says, than we were when Christianity was first theologically expounded.

It is an open question whether historicism or metaphysics is the
more aggressive instrument of intervention in the world. Modern taste
inclines to favouring historicism on this point, for it relativizes all projects, thus restraining the impulse of believing anyone is in possession
of Truth but an equally plausible case can be made that traditional
metaphysics is more moderate and tolerant, because it always leaves a
gap between present reality and transcendent truth.

. . .

One might wish that the skirmishes over the wording of our Constitution were more informed by an understanding of what is really at stake
in declarations of fundamental principles. The circumstances of the
most recent debate are as follows: In 1999, Member of Parliament
Svend Robinson tabled a Commons petition on behalf of his
constituents of Burnaby–Douglas – or, more precisely, representatives
of the Humanist Association of Canada – moving that reference to
God be removed from the Canadian Constitution.[19] "Whereas Canada
is founded upon principles that recognize the supremacy of God and
the rule of law," begins the Canadian Charter of Rights and Freedoms.
Robinson and his associates believe otherwise. "It is inappropriate to
include a reference to God in the Constitution when Canada is a secular society, and includes people with no religious belief. Our Constitution should be as inclusive as possible."[20] Sheila Ayala, in a special plea
for Canada's humanists, underscored the point: "Leaving the word
'God' in the Constitution interferes with our freedom to be humanists.
The Charter belongs to all Canadians. How can we be part of something that is contrary to our beliefs?"[21] For his efforts, Robinson was
shunted to the backbenches (as the *Ottawa Citizen* quipped: "God is
dead – MP Svend Robinson. Svend's career is toast – God").[22] Though
it is doubtful that Robinson's brief banishment had anything to do
with the New Democratic Party's espousing religion, and everything to
do with avoiding bad publicity and revenge at the ballot box, it

revealed how problematic many Canadians' understanding of the relationship between religion and politics is.

In the wake of the controversy, four spiritual leaders – Rabbi Reuven Bulka, Archdeacon Shane Parker, Reverend Brian Kopke, and Associate Pastor Clint Curle – were subsequently asked by the *Ottawa Citizen*, "Why should we keep the reference to God in the Constitution?"[23] Rabbi Bulka suggested that the principle of the supremacy of God simply "refer[s] to a historical feature of the birth of our country." He proposed that this does not demand that belief in God be mandatory to be a Canadian. "A society in which God is supreme," he added, however, "is more likely to be a caring, sensitive, virtuous society." Archdeacon Parker suggested that the debate had little to do with "the efficacy of our Constitution" and added:

> Since the debate over keeping the reference to God in the Constitution is not about the corruption of justice, it has become a tiresome and at times vindictive harangue that embarrasses sensible people. I do not believe that keeping a reference to God in the Constitution makes Canada a "faithful" nation; nor do I believe that removing the reference makes it an atheistic nation. Words on a page are of little consequence unless they reflect or inspire human lives.

Reverend Kopke suggested that removing the reference is unacceptable historical revisionism and reverses the historical fact that Canada was founded and shaped by men of religion. The reference "simply recognizes our historical roots. To me it's a no-brainer, God stays." Pastor Curle suggested that the preamble helps give Canada its identity, "along with hockey, doughnut shops, and free health care," specifically "protecting the rights and freedoms of the individual from incursion by the state."

It was Rabbi Bulka alone who identified the fatal flaw in the humanists' position. He pointed out that atheists who continue to subscribe to the inviolable dignity of the person, our obligations to the less fortunate, and the duty to respect teachers, parents, and elders are living off the heritage of religious values. His astute observation recalls the statement of Alexis de Tocqueville:

There is hardly any human action, however private it may be, which does not result from some very general conception men have of God, of His relations with the human race, of the nature of their soul, and of their duties to their fellows. Nothing can prevent such ideas from being the common spring from which all else originates. It is therefore of immense importance to men to have fixed ideas about God, their souls, and their duties toward their Creator and their fellows, for doubt about these first principles would leave all their actions to chance and condemn them, more or less, to anarchy and impotence.[24]

With the exception of Rabbi Bulka, none of the spiritual leaders even saw the problem Tocqueville identifies, a sign of how seriously secularized the world (including, perhaps, the seminaries), and how restricted the definition of religion, has become. Tocqueville's point is simply that our ideas of what an individual and our humanity are, and what our moral obligations and our ties of community amount to, depend on the idea that we live in an ordered, rational cosmos where events and actions are not random occurrences left to chance. "God" is our guarantor, and whether He or She is Allah, YHWH, Sophia, Brahma, the Divine Logos, or Christ, the essential point is that, somewhere amidst the perpetual alterations of existence, and the fickle changeability of human conduct, there needs to be a foundation of an incorruptible nature. If rules were simply wallpaper over chaos, we would be unable to grasp their inner reason, or discern their power to sanctify us, and would subscribe to them only half-heartedly at difficult moments of temptation and vice. Without a "God" before whose legislative might we stand in fear and trembling, or within whose loving compassion all living things have a place to express their gratitude for the simple goodness of creation, our world would be torn apart by ruthless self-assertion and arrogance. If we could not trace our moral duties and reasoned norms back to an extra-human arrangement, then they would have no higher status than mere habit or social convention. Or our rules would simply be legislated by those with political power, who "dignify" the raw force they are exercising by calling their mandates "laws."

A community can remain blissfully oblivious to the fact that its laws are substantiated by nothing more than will – and often individuals' tacit consent is accepted as a sufficient vote of confidence in the prevailing norms – but, sooner or later, usually during times of crisis, the incoherence at the core of a civilization must come out. That is when the perception that random chance has prevailed brings on the "anarchy and impotence" to which Tocqueville alludes. The crisis may appear dramatically, as the widespread breakdown of civil order, accompanied by flagrant violations of human life and dignity. It may express itself as pervasive freeloading – by those who have reckoned that the only bad consequences to cheating occur if one is caught. Or, equally enervating to the human order, it may manifest itself as utter indifference to the legal and political processes by which we govern ourselves.

Now, it is true that in liberal democracies, since the eighteenth century, the official and public rationale for our laws and duties has not come from an appeal to the rational orderliness of creation or a tablet of holy commands, but from a doctrine of "the general will." We restrain our inclinations and acknowledge our moral duties to others because, unlike animals, we have the choice of rising above our natural desires and willing a universal law of reason. The "general will" is not merely the aggregate of our interests, nor enlightened self-interest, but a moral rule stipulating that no principle of action is legitimate unless it can be adopted by everyone without contradiction of its own premises. I may assert myself in regard to others as much as I will permit others to assert themselves against me. I am not entitled to anything unless everyone is entitled to it in similar circumstances. In emphasizing our freedom to choose self-limitation, the "general will" endows us with self-respect and acknowledges the dignity of others. One might say that the "general will" is a modern adaptation of the golden rule: "Do unto others as you would have them do unto you."[25]

The unfortunate case of the matter is that at present one looks for a "general will" in vain. Indeed, one looks equally in vain for anyone who would even endorse the idea of the "general will" as a goal to strive for. In the last few decades, universality has all but vanished under the unrelenting pressure of local and regional interests. The decline of the very concept of universality is in no way peculiar to Canada since it is happening all over the world, as liberal democracy enters a period of transition and, once again, reconfigures itself to fit a new environment – in this case, a world where culture, ethnicity, race, gender, and lifestyle preferences are being reintroduced to the political arena. Moreover, the turn from universality is especially understandable where "universality" has come to mean the global availability of a homogeneous collection of consumer goods and services and the ethos of the marketplace, rather than an enlightened search and understanding of standards of truth, goodness, and beauty.

If the moral project of the "general will" has broken down, and if a condition of "anarchy and impotence" has to be forestalled, then the renewed spiritual searches of baby boomers comes exactly at the right time. Those many baby boomers drawn to the work of the Jesus Seminar, and who endorse the direction Reverend Phipps is nudging the United Church in, or who more generally find in their spiritual searches a reinforcement of their hopes for justice and equity, are discovering that what this world needs above all is heroes – or, more precisely, martyrs and witnesses of Truth. "Jesus" may no longer be the cosmic Jesus of St. John's Gospel or Paul's Epistles, but His moral teaching – of peace, love, and justice – is a window to the divine presence of God. Having relearned that "I am dust and ashes and full of sin" (Luther), they can no longer triumph in modernity's shameless rush for money, sex, and power, while the victims of greed and ambition fall between the cracks. Surrounded by chic cynicism and world-weariness, these baby boomers admit that the encounter with the divine has restored their sense that something must be done. Though they may despair of a fallen world, and acknowledge that they had underestimated the power of sin and evil to mar the dream of a perfect society, many baby boomers sense that somehow the social contract must still be rewritten. The profound experience of the divine has exposed how shallow this-worldly moralities are, and how incomplete the duty to be stewards of creation remains. They return to social action both chastened and reanimated with the need to heal a broken world. Often a simple trigger provokes the renaissance, such as Vaclav Havel's prophetic call for an "existential revolution" of spiritual awakening to conclude the "velvet revolution" of economic and political reform, or Archbishop Tutu's saintly handling of the South African Truth and Reconciliation Commission. These two remarkable statesmen of our times inspire renewed spiritual purpose, reminding many baby boomers not only of the harrowing presence of evil, but also of the miraculous power of forgiveness.

And for these baby boomers, Reverend Phipps's suggestion that the civic world and mystery must go together is right on the button. The reciprocity entails a mutual enhancement, yet also a mutual correction. It recognizes that there is a cosmic, not merely human, context to the historical work of advancing justice, and thus reinforces the hope that, despite the transience of all human enterprises, some eternal good is achieved in social action. Acknowledging the mystery of the divine being not only elevates the moral and political projects we undertake, but also moderates the zeal with which such enterprises are sometimes undertaken. To recognize the divinity in human beings is not to be blind to Golgotha, the inextinguishable human propensity to sin. Only by acknowledging the infinite distance of humanity from God can the phenomenon of evil in the world really be taken seriously, and extravagant dreams of a perfect human world moderated.

That Reverend Phipps would speak of "mystery" rather than specific theological and doctrinal formulations protects the unadulterated sanctity of Jesus' teachings. Indeed, though it was a baneful sight for many United Church members to see their Moderator deny the divinity of Christ, it was also a refreshing moment of de-doctrinalization, permitting an "unpatenting" of God and religion, while retaining the metaphysical mystery of divine transcendence. At the same time, Reverend Phipps's statement situates mystery in the world, thus transforming personal experience into a humanly meaningful form. Glossolalia and mystical encounters are fine if they can be transformed into symbols. Without a link to the world where symbols are formulated and interpreted, and where other human beings can see the good that mystery works, mystical experience remains an anomalous, private affair. Reverend Phipps's formulation of the United Church's responsibilities offers the valuable critical widening of the present moment because it unearths the deeper, philosophical, and theological roots of modernity. Unlike other Protestant religious leaders, he does not undertake the secularizing move of emphasizing the moral teachings of religion alone, but accompanies this action by remembering the religious roots – the experiential encounters with divine mystery – of ethics. Of all denominations, the United Church is the litmus test for the future of progressive modernity.

Rabbi Bulka understood how much was at stake in Svend Robinson's actions, recognizing that the issue was one of metaphysics – divine mystery – and not just history. When Reverend Kopke and Pastor Curle, on the other hand, proposed that the reference to God in the Canadian Constitution could be justified on the grounds of heritage, they failed to appreciate that historical defences of principle are notoriously problematic. Why should one historical moment be privileged over others? Why should we permit heritage *per se* to trump healthy moral and political progress, rather than examine reasoned arguments on behalf of conflicting beliefs? Nor, with due respect to Archdeacon Parker, is the issue one of increasing or diminishing faith, a tack which can only aggravate sectarian controversy, since one person's faith is another person's apostasy. If our national anthem contains the words "God keep our land glorious and free," and our motto, *a mari usque ad mare*, is taken from Proverbs' reference to the universality of God's dominion, it is not the historical, but the metaphysical significance of these nods to the divine that is being remembered.

Without a centre and foundation, human rights, moral obligations, laws, and civic manners are a precarious house of cards, ready to tumble at the slightest disturbance. We need to know, as Alexis de Tocqueville recognized, that, at some level, all is well in the cosmos and we are at home in it. Svend Robinson and the Humanist Association may have exposed flaws in the language of the Constitution – especially if it appears that the reference to God is to a parochial god, which would be unpalatably divisive – but dispensing with metaphysics, in a final push at secularization, is not the answer. The problem with Robinson's actions is that the convictions which members of the Humanist Association endorse – moral decency and compassion, alleviation of suffering and exploitation, rational criteria for behaviour, free inquiry and truth at any cost, freedom from fear – are mortgaged to the Christian inheritance, residing within it, as under a "sacred canopy," to use Peter Berger's fitting metaphor.[26] Both ignorance of the more subtle and refined elements of that inheritance, and overly dogmatic assumptions about its legacy, hamper these critics from understanding what is really at stake when the foundations of our moral and political practice are destroyed.[27]

·  ·  ·

Regrettably, the pressure to remove God from the Constitution is not an isolated incident. Intense embarrassment concerning the Christian heritage permeates Canadian society. In 1985, the Supreme Court of Canada declared the Lord's Day Act unconstitutional – out of fear that those who do not reserve Sunday as a day of rest would be offended. When federal ministers of the Crown are sworn in, they are not obliged to swear an oath of service and secrecy to God, but instead declare they will act "faithfully, honestly, and truly." A similar development is occurring in the push to eliminate God from the courtroom. Brosi Nutting, Chief Judge of the Saskatchewan provincial court, wants the oath on the Bible eliminated in favour of a simple promise to tell the truth: "The reason for this is the dramatic change in the fabric of Canadian society, which reflects the multicultural character of Canada."[28] His campaign stems from a 1995 federal-provincial working group on multicultural and race relations in the justice system which concluded:

> The idea of swearing on a Bible is rooted in a time when religious belief was central to society's institutions and few questioned the existence of God. In general, religious beliefs are neither as widespread in modern society as they once were nor as strongly held, and they certainly cannot be assumed to play the same unifying role as they may have played in the past.[29]

Justice Peter Nasmith of the Ontario bench now just asks for a promise to tell the truth: "My oath ceremony is designed to suit everyone."

While some individuals who refuse to take an oath do not see themselves as perjurers, but as opponents of ceremony, one suspects that for many would-be liars, Justice Nasmith's proposal is inestimably convenient. It goes even further than the "heritage" argument, now reducing the foundation of legal practice to mere taste. If it does not "suit" a person to take an oath to God, but to base his or her promise on personal values which might include hopes of reward, public esteem, or even whim, what is to prevent that witness from altering their evidence as they see fit from one day to the next? It is well known that personal values change as circumstances change, for they are grounded on willpower alone. Justice Nasmith's practice is noteworthy for its confidence (many would say "extravagant" confidence and innocence) that personal values can stand in for the uncompromisable stability offered by divine wrath. For an alternative, and more persuasive account of what binds individuals to their political and moral obligations, observers attracted at first glance to Justice Nasmith's initiative might read chapter 8 of Machiavelli's *The Prince*. Even Machiavelli recognized the value of a God who inspired fear and trembling.

But then, fear and trembling no longer fit in most baby boomers' comfort zone. Reverend Phipps had to call our talk short because that morning he was giving a press conference at which the United Church was formally apologizing to aboriginal peoples who had endured abuse in residential schools. Apologies are, of course, *de rigueur* these days: In 1993, the Primate Archbishop Michael Peers apologized on behalf of the Anglican Church to aboriginal peoples for the church's attempt to assimilate natives to European culture; in 1998, Archbishop Michael Peers and 100 Canadian Anglican bishops signed an apology to homosexuals for "any sense of rejection that has occurred";[30] delegations of Christians on a crusade-cum-apology campaign, are travelling through the Middle East, wearing T-shirts with "I apologize" in Arabic script; and there is now even an International Forgiveness Institute, funded by a $5-million grant from the Templeton Foundation, which sponsors forgiveness research projects within the emerging field of "forgiveness studies." Undeniably, many of these appeals for forgiveness are just and long overdue. Avarice, dominion, fear, and abuse of power have often marred historical judgments, causing unconscionable pain to many. Enlightened thought is, fortunately, remedying past error.

One wishes that the acceptance of these apologies was as charitable as the offer, but often the whiff of financial compensation overcomes civil manners. "Talk is cheap," was the official retort of the president of the Congress of Aboriginal Peoples to Reverend Phipps's apology. While aboriginal peoples' suffering is shameful, where are we as a society when the sincere act of asking forgiveness – the sole act which can stop the infinite processes unleashed by historical actions – is scorned?

At the same time, it is impossible to rectify every historical error. For every decision, there are usually two sides to the coin. Every chronicled incident is equivocal. Without in any way condoning the Crusades, it must be remembered that the Crusades were first launched in 1095 by Pope Urban ii after Muslims restricted the access of Christians to Jerusalem. Reversing mistakes of the past is especially dubious when the "error" was committed in good faith by a decision that was appropriate to the state of knowledge and public consensus at the time. It is wrong to apply the responsibilities we have adopted today to an individual or nation not subject to them in the past. Retroactive applications of penalties are not permitted in law; why should they be tolerated in politics? Were we to proceed farther down this path, we would soon realize that even our own principles might turn out to be culturally relative, and as likely to be superseded in the future as past doctrines and behaviours that are now being repudiated. Our will and determination to fight injustice would be stymied and wither at the root.

Moreover, in acquitting putative past injustices, we are placing ourselves in risk of perpetrating new ones. Today there are class-action suits of up to $1.5 billion against the Anglican Church by former Ontario residential school students. How many food banks, hospices, or school-lunch and street-kid assistance programs will vanish if these suits are successful? There are currently more demands for entitlements than any viable economy can support; how can we expand these entitlements with any prudence to "victims" of the past? When apologies are merely a salve to a fabricated bad conscience – as some, regrettably, are – do they become ways of neglecting our present moral obligations?

What is certain is that the apology industry has a way of running roughshod over distinctions – confusing psychology and sociology with metaphysics, blacklisting all branches of Christianity as if they were identical, distilling religion to just another ethics, mistaking institution with theology, detecting hypocrisy in Christianity alone, misconstruing authority as authoritarianism and tradition as traditionalism, and failing to separate the political act of apologizing from the social question of financial compensation. When distinctions disappear, however, the human perception of reality is flattened, and all subtlety or opportunity for healthy, discriminating judgment is lost.

Particularly evident in the spate of apologies of the last decade is the ever-widening hostility against historical, institutional, and theological Christianity. Often it seems that only Christianity is accused of not living up to its own teachings of loving one's enemies and turning the other cheek.[31] These days, nearly any cudgel is good enough to beat down Christianity. The censoriousness takes many forms: the brandishing of charges of colonialism and imperialism, the persistent call for apologies and compensation from the Christian churches, a condescending and derisive attitude taken by the press and intellectuals to evangelical and conservative Christianity, the unrelenting cry that the churches accommodate the liberal and progressive movements of modernity, the depiction of opposition to homosexuality as hatred and bigotry, the insistence on declaring the Lord's Day Act unconstitutional (and removing the Lord's Prayer from schools and reference to God from the Constitution), the indifference of the public media to religious issues (unless it is coverage of the bizarre and spectacular – such as the 1998 incident of hundreds of people herding around the Tim Hortons doughnut shop in Bras d'Or, Nova Scotia, to see an image of Christ's face), and the conscious and deliberate provocation of Christians by such practices as witchcraft and Satanism, to name two. Even the restoration of healing practices, spiritual labyrinths, unofficial shrines, mystic saints, and interest in the historical Jesus – while resplendent in their vitality – are not signs of a renewal of Christian faith, but further evidence of protest against institutional religion.

While any schoolchild can easily pick out Christianity's faults – its triumphal militarist campaigns of colonization, its lingering patriarchy and top-down authority, its uncompromising stand on the sanctity of life, family, marriage, and sexuality, its glacial reassessments of dogma conflicting with scientific fact (evolution, heliocentricity[32]), excessive intellectualization at the cost of personal experience – one looks in vain for public figures who go beyond affirming their faith (as courageous as the Parliamentary Bible Fellowship's or Reform member of Parliament Jason Kenney's public witnessing of their Christian faith may be) to extrapolating its intellectual principles as ways to provide shades of discernment and discrimination often lacking in our public debates. Dogmatic restatements of professions of faith have their place in public discourse – if only to stake out a place amid the plethora of contenders in our public world – but what is needed above all are public intellectuals to work at T.S. Eliot's challenge to us: to sift through the legacy and heritage we have inherited from the past and identify those cardinal principles to which rational assent can be given and which define what it means to live in a "Christian society." Pursuing T.S. Eliot's challenge need not mean a literal subscription to Christian beliefs. It requires exercising an intellectual discipline and theological *esprit de finesse*, which would distinguish what is foundational from what is a dispensable accretion, while fostering respect for the tentativeness and multiplicity of all human efforts to understand the divine-human encounter – a task elegantly initiated by the Anglican bishop Michael Ingham, whose book *Mansions of the Spirit* is a model of thoughtfulness and charity.[33]

Disparaging Christianity is, among other things, one variation on a widespread tendency to self-hatred in contemporary Western society. We should be looking at the rich sources and complex histories of our institutions in the hopes of finding restorative possibilities which might serve to reanimate the intellectual and moral bearings of our civilization; instead, we seem caught in an ever-widening gyre of the hermeneutics of suspicion. While skepticism is a healthy antidote to ideological partisanship, the fashionable cynicism which parades as enlightened thinking in our day risks disinterring and consuming the sustaining roots of everything which has made us a great civilization. Western civilization is neither flawless nor uniform. It is made up of melodic counterpoints which intersect, reinforce, clash, correct, and moderate one another, permitting continuous self-critique and periodic revitalization. But our prevailing inclination to forget or to dispense with it all, in the hopes of a future unconditioned by past choices and commitments, risks destabilizing the uneasy balances in our civilization, unleashing far more problematic tides of immoderate zeal. Hegel once wrote, "To supersede is at once to negate and to preserve." We have become very adept at negation, nearly inept at preservation. Ignorance of tradition, and immoderation in impugning it, are particularly conspicuous in the case against Christianity.

As T.S. Eliot pointed out years ago, we live in a Christian society. This does not mean, of course, that we necessarily hold Christian beliefs, but that our culture is intellectually rooted in Christianity. When we subscribe to the idea of the singularity of the person, put a premium on the merit of individual choice, adopt the view that history is a process of incremental steps from anticipation to fulfillment, believe that charity ought to be extended to the disadvantaged, and contend that we should be caring stewards with respect to the natural environment, we are expressing a profound debt to Christian theology and philosophy. Even when we dispute these convictions, we cannot help but deploy a subsidiary vocabulary and arguments which are in the same family of theoretical concepts that distinguish Christian thought. Indeed, the most important modern critic of Christianity, Friedrich Nietzsche, infamous for his statement "God is dead," aimed his devastating blows not merely at the overtly religious dimension of Christianity, but at its world view, whose legacy includes modern science, empirical and rationalist philosophy, liberalism and socialism, art and culture, and even our distinctive grammar and syntax. What Nietzsche succeeded in doing was to remind us how, in even the minutiae of everyday life, we cannot help but be thrown back onto the central mystery of Western life, the mysterious origin of our being: God became man, so that man may become God.

In the absence of an intellectual assessment of the legacy of Christianity, antipathy and aversion to Christianity will persist only in their most infantile form. And our public representatives, perplexed as to how to govern a multicultural society, end up resorting to equivocal practices in an appeal to "sensitivity," as the debacle over the special memorial service for the victims of the 1999 Swissair jet crash demonstrated. Christian religious leaders were asked to read from the Hebrew scripture, but they were told that they could make no references to Jesus and use no New Testament readings.[34] Avoiding offending non-Christians ended in offending Christians. Just as with Canada's failed policy of multiculturalism, which gave us a potpourri of washed-out cultures void of all critical perspective vis-à-vis one another, so now – in the interests of "inclusiveness" – religion risks being reduced to nothing more than a generic "spirituality" for all believers. As with multiculturalism, the operational meaning of "inclusiveness" has become "dismantle and discard," rather than "embrace and co-celebrate." The problem is that there cannot be an undefined faith. Faith is faith in something. Without an anchor in beliefs, religion's true purposes – namely, the worship of the divine, and the sanctification of the human soul – are reduced to mere effects, signifying nothing, entailing nothing. With Mies van der Rohe, one can say that God is in the details.

And the churches, equally thrown on the defensive, are taking recourse by banding together in frightened solidarity – in interfaith dialogue and ecumenicism. While neither initiative is an illustration of secularization *per se,* both enterprises have become the means through which different faiths find common ground, with the consequence of furthering two trends – more conformity to the limits of the world and escalated disestablishment. They also contribute to a phenomenon of increased "unitarianism" or "Bahá'ísm" by taking the churches in the direction of a unified world faith – a "reasonable" religion beyond all creeds – in which the only precepts subscribed to are a "god" and universality of conscience, while all other differences are bleached out.

On the surface, these initiatives are growing in number and intensity, especially as baby boomers on spiritual searches begin asking why, if God and reality are one, human-made religion is manifold, and why, if nearly all the faiths of the world embrace virtually identical moral precepts, doctrinally they are miles apart.

One of the more interesting undertakings involves a group of seventeen churches, temples, and synagogues in Toronto's "Bayview corridor" that calls itself Mosaic. Meeting in one another's places of worship, with a speaker who presents the cardinal principles and theology of the faith, and with the occasional presentation of a devotional rite, the participants in Mosaic plan events around a shared meal, where inclusiveness and commonality are particularly heightened. The desperate need in our times of a moral reawakening appears as a common theme among the members of Mosaic, providing a bottom line of agreement. My host at one of these events explained:

> Take precepts from three different faiths – "What is hateful to you, do not do to your neighbour. That is the entire Law; all the rest is commentary," (Hillel, Talmud – Shabbath 31a), "I am a stranger to no one; and no one is a stranger to me. Indeed, I am friend to all," (Guru Granth Sahib), "This is the sum of duty: do not do to others what would cause pain if done to you," (Mahabharata 5:1517) – and you have a complete meeting of the mind.

However, polite interest and periodic animated curiosity in the more "show and tell" aspects of the evening, rather than reconciliation, seemed to be in ascendancy. As one baby boomer whispered to me, "It's all a bit of a freak show."

Yet interfaith dialogue is by no means just spectacle. Consider the

Roman Catholic Church's extensive repertoire of overtures to other Christian denominations: the Lutheran–Roman Catholic Commission for Unity, the Joint International Commission for the Theological Dialogue between the Catholic Church and the Orthodox Church, and Catholic-Evangelical dialogues, to name just a few. Since 1970, the Anglican–Roman Catholic International Commission has been seeking a basis for reuniting the two churches. One particular campaign among Christian churches – "intercommunion," or reciprocal sacramental opportunities in any Christian church – sustains the ambition of restoring the one universal church.

The likelihood of reunion, however, remains impossibly slim. And this is where the fervent wish for reconciliation, union, and universal creeds falls to the ground. To illustrate, Anglicans cannot and will not accept papal authority, nor are they comfortable with Roman Catholicism's lingering "magic," such as Pope John Paul's commitment to "indulgences" (promising, for example, that pilgrims coming to Rome for the millennium year would obtain a remission of sins). A similar reservation dooms ongoing dialogues with Protestant denominations: Regardless of how many imaginative spins are put on interpretation, most Protestants will not accept the Catholic's idea of sanctification through sacraments (as opposed to justification by faith alone), nor the subordination of scripture to tradition. Only by rescinding history, overturning theology, and distilling religion to vague generalities, can the "unitarian" or "Bahá'í" option be realized. In the meantime, internecine conflict, schism, and further splintering are far more evident than concord – conspicuous in the tensions between the Anglican Renewal Ministries and the Anglican Prayerbook Society, the United Church's Fellowship of Covenanting Congregations and Church Alive, the General Conference of Mennonites and the Old Mennonite Church, the Regular Baptist Churches of Canada and the Fellowship of Evangelical Baptist Churches, the World Council of Churches and the International Council of Christian Churches, and the list could go on *ad infinitum* without even including the breakaway para-church groups like the Promise Keepers, WomanChurch, and the "home-church" movements. Too much money, power, and history has been poured into the differences. Overcoming the division of sect, denomination, and religion is a hope – but it is a hope that has, in reality, all the reserve of a "save us, though not quite yet."

Or, more emphatically, it is a "yes, but …" At the 1998 meeting of the North American Interfaith Network, in Edmonton, one session in particular showcased the kind of impasse reached in any serious interfaith dialogue. After years of work, the United Church had just released its discussion paper *Faithful Witness: United Church–Jewish Relations Today*.[35] The presenter began by setting out the grounds of interfaith engagement: There should be no judgements of superiority and inferiority, commonalities were to be emphasized, and theology was to be ignored. He then summarized the discussion paper as follows: The relationship between Christianity and Judaism has to be understood exclusively in its historical context. There was a need to take the Jewishness of Jesus much more seriously. It is not that Christians have to accommodate Jews – they have to reform their theology in light of the continuity from Jewish origin. The old theology of seeing the New Testament as a correction and fulfillment of the Old Testament must be superseded. The "fulfillment" alluded to by Luke and Matthew meant that the life of the Jewish people was to be recapitulated as experienced today, but not that God's covenant with Jewish people had been revoked through the appearance of Jesus. Indeed, the church's rejection of Jews was an act of disobedience to God. The United Church, in its support of multiculturalism, pluralism, and a more inclusive ecumenicism, acknowledged responsibility for anti-Judaism, white supremacy, the pogroms, anti-Semitism, the desecration of synagogues and Jewish cemeteries, and misunderstanding and insensitivity with respect to the importance of the *Shoah* (Holocaust) and land for Jews. As a sign of the United Church's new sensitivity, it would change its language – such as using the terms Older Testament, First Testament, Hebrew scriptures, or Tanakh, rather than Old Testament – and acknowledge that it is not obvious that God's promises to the Jews needed fulfillment beyond what was given in the Jewish texts. Indeed, it would adopt the new interpretive rule, "In the New Testament, what does not fit the Old Testament should be challenged." And it would reverse its doctrine that conversion from Judaism to Christianity is necessary for salvation.

Derision is perhaps too strong a word for the reply of Rabbi Eliezer Segal (one of the invited commentators), but restrained incredulity, together with firm though civil opposition, were evident in his response to the United Church's extended palm leaf. As if saying he did not know whether to laugh or to cry, he admitted that though the Christian–Jewish relation was more difficult than with other faith relations, the discussion paper represented an unnecessary move from the stringent to the more simple. "It should not be an objective that we will all agree and get to a point of being the same." He protested that the United Church document went too far to be accommodating, especially on the question of promise and fulfillment. For Jews, he reminded the audience – looking pointedly at Reverend Phipps (one of the authors of the report) – there could be no possibility of accepting the divinity of Jesus, whereas for Christians the factuality of Christ's life has the salvific status of Law. The better tack, he proposed, was to just respect otherness, and not demonize it. "That's all we want," he concluded. "People who are going to agree on everything are not going to dialogue." After that brief theological lesson, in which Christians were advised, at the very least, to be true to themselves and to be alert to the danger of zeal without knowledge, silence descended on the room, though one voice piped up to say, in an enigmatic non sequitur, that the Orthodox Jewish response to Roman Catholic accommodation has not been reciprocal, since it sees Catholicism only as medieval Catholicism.

It is not difficult to understand Jewish sensitivities. For centuries, Jews have suffered religious persecution and hatred at the hands of Christians, who have seen them as killers of Christ. The crusades, inquisitions, pogroms, and "final solution" marking Western European history have all been directed at Jews. The slimmest compensation for these horrendous phases of persecution is that these have also been the times during which a refined, subtle Judaism flourished in the form of mysticism and Hasidism. Yet, even today, Jews are targeted for conversion by evangelical Christians, as a sign the messiah is coming. Even among some dissident Jews like Jews for Jesus (who believe Jesus is the messiah), a belief prevails that if enough Jews are converted, it will mark the beginning of the Last Judgment – despite the efforts of Jews for Judaism, a Toronto group which seeks to bring messianic Jews back to Judaism. A thousand and one signals betray insensitivity to Jews: the planting of Christian crosses at Auschwitz/Birkenau, one of the Nazis' most horrific concentration camps; the canonization of Edith Stein, a Jewish philosopher who converted to Catholicism but was killed at Auschwitz as a Jew; the invitation extended to Jörg Haider, leader of

Austria's right-wing (reputedly neo-Nazi) Freedom Party to visit Canada. In the context of such varied shades of enmity and thoughtless slights, and the desperate need for rapprochement between the two faiths, Rabbi Segal's curt rebuttal of the United Church's initiative seems poorly conceived, and nearly churlish.

At a deeper level, of course, Rabbi Segal is absolutely right. When religion is drained of its theological form, it loses its coherence and integrity. For better or worse, Christianity demands the belief that Jesus was unique and that His word was the decisive and final revelation. The mysteries of the Incarnation and Resurrection cannot be rescinded without putting everything else in jeopardy – the idea of a dynamic history of progress, a morality of love, compassion and forgiveness, the recognition of the singular person (apart from race, gender, or tribe), the concept of individual responsibility, the sanctity of the body and the earth, and the hope that, at the end of time, the just will be rewarded, while the unjust will suffer punishment. To diminish the foundation in any way insinuates the corrosive viewpoint that Christianity is merely one perspective among many.

Rabbi Segal's judgment was not merely the free gift of an edifying lesson to Christians. More profoundly, he was saying that recognition of the depths of one's own religion leads one to acknowledge what is worthy of being respected in another religion. By seeing truths with significant consequences in the distinguishing characteristics of a religion, rather than restricting one's assessment to the features a faith shares with all others, one dignifies the unique revelation that is its inner core and that endows it with its living character. The United Church's sensitivity and inclusiveness notwithstanding, Rabbi Segal was perhaps the one showing the true charity, if charity is understood not merely as attending – in the interests of unity – to those who are marginalized and excluded, but also as recognizing the diversity of gifts and manifestations of truth and goodness admitted in the human-divine encounter.

Ecumenicism and interfaith dialogues are vulnerable, as the session on Christian-Jewish relations shows, to becoming instruments rather than critical appraisals of modernity. Instead of leavening modernity with a richer account of human personality and justice, they can become exercises in disestablishing religion – withdrawing its public profile and its status as a radical witness to a truth uncompromised by this-worldly forces. A major reason for this is that they are often laced with a poisonous hermeneutics of suspicion – of seeing their own heritage as a legacy of colonizing bonds to be discarded at the earliest moment.

Many baby boomers are drawn to the Jesus Seminar's iconoclasm, and Reverend Phipps's mission of social justice, for they serve as ways of tweaking modernity. Already armed with the judgment that the world is out of kilter, that boundaries reinforced by aggression have destroyed the natural synchronicity of the globe, that the inherited wisdom of the past is defective and about to be subverted by truths not yet revealed, and that in adopting the challenge of becoming stewards rather than owners of the earth they are playing out their own historical destiny, the message of an immanent faith strikes a deep chord.

And baby boomers aroused to action by this new faith are demanding a reassessment of many of modernity's cardinal beliefs – the myth of the isolated individual, the contractual origin of human society, the irreversibility of historical progress, the abbreviation of morality to utility or rules, the rationalistic dismissal of alternative ways of knowing and understanding, and the reduction of mystery to problems responsive to technical solution. Spurred to social action, these baby boomers are also focusing on the political dereliction of modernity: the failure of national democracies to achieve a global fellowship beyond compromise and sectarian interests, the inauthenticity of political representation in present models of governance, and the injustice of lingering gaps of social distinction between which the unfortunate fall. One observes baby-boomer frustration with "business as usual" in the popularity of a recent trend – the grassroots, quasi-religious "voluntary simplicity" movement. In this protest against modernity, the opposition to overwork and consumerism links up with the grievances buried within the environmental, self-help, natural food, alternative health, and alternative school movements to produce the latest rainbow coalition, distinguished by its additional subscription to post-denominational, "celebration" spirituality.[36]

But many of these baby boomers have gone too far in taking their analysis of the defects of modernity and applying them to the entire history in which their religious faith is rooted. In deconstructing root and branch, they not only leave themselves with only the most generalized and innocuous religious sentiment, they also lose the substantive claim to validity to which each religion legitimately lays stake. This politicization of reality leads them to see the theoretical options exclusively in the black-and-white ideological dichotomy of liberals versus conservatives. As a consequence, tradition – the inherited conversation of humankind, the source of reasoned arguments for truth and significance, and the likeliest candidate of a third option of understanding reality – is summarily foreclosed. By cutting themselves off from a foundation that is not only felt or experienced in its affections, but "known" – such as through Bonaventure's "third eye" of contemplation, or, as Simone Weil phrased it, by "an intelligence enlightened by love" – religion is reduced to sentiment and subjectivity. It has become an aesthetic, not perhaps the aesthetic of the traditionalist, who desires sensual beauty, but the aesthetic pose of the *provocateur* of permanent revolution, for whom the sempiternal frisson of anger and revolt stands in for true eternity.

Such a pose is evident in a recent statement by the Catholics of Vision, a group which, dissatisfied with the Roman Catholic's resort to tradition in matters of doctrine, presented the Council of Catholic Bishops with an extensive catalogue of grievances: "We see a serious crisis developing in the Church in Canada …. [We have] accurately read the signs of the times … [and have] high expectations of engaging in continuing *aggiornamento* [updating] of the Church."[37] Here, in this manifesto, as with the other illustrations I have presented of faith accommodating to the limits of the modern world, traditional piety is assumed to be unavailable as a consequence of secularization, leaving only "remythologization" to correct the demythologizing effect of modernity. But, in the process, a far more problematic "faith" is asserted, one which is based exclusively on its transforming power – even though all manner of beliefs, even untrue and pernicious ones, can produce results – and whose iconoclasm is far more destructive of the diversity of faiths than "tradition" ever was. Indeed, one might say that ecumenicism and interfaith, as the primary tools being used to turn the corner on tradition, are today's Tower of Babel – humankind's hubristic attempt to produce one inclusive voice and communicate directly with God, for which it was punished by God by being returned to the condition of human plurality. Given the depths to which the opponents of tradition aspire to push the processes of liberalization, it is a wonder they stick with Christianity – a religion poorly suited to being deprived of its metaphysical basis – at all.

· · ·

Indeed, it is surprising that many more baby boomers seeking an immanent faith to tweak modernity have not found the answers they are seeking in Bahá'í, where, on my reading, the phenomena that I have been describing logically end up. Starting with the premise that truth is consciousness of the oneness of humankind, and observing the present reality of unrelenting competitiveness and a glorification of struggle in all walks of life, the Bahá'ís conclude that "the turmoil now convulsing human affairs is unprecedented." That turmoil has economic, political, and religious manifestations. Limitless acquisition and consumption, and a work ethic that divides people, have set tribes, cultures, classes, and nations against one another, diminishing global prosperity and the prospects for world peace, and producing an environmental crisis. The classical economic model of an impersonal market in which human beings act as autonomous makers of self-regarding choices is incompatible with a world motivated by unity and justice, the Bahá'ís say. The political models of the nation-state, nationalism, partisan democracy, and the advocacy principle of civil law have prevented the emergence of an "organic whole, a collective trusteeship." Moreover, the Bahá'ís add, "Society does not need and is not well served by the political theatre of nominations, candidature, electioneering, and solicitation," which only "arrest the momentum of the integration of humanity."[38] But the greatest censure is reserved for religion:

> Exponents of the world's various theological systems bear a heavy responsibility not only for the disrepute into which faith itself has fallen among many progressive thinkers, but for the inhibitions and distortions produced in humanity's continuing discourse on spiritual meaning.[39]

Spiritual and moral issues have in the past, the Bahá'ís contend, been bound up with contending theological doctrines not susceptible to objective proof. The "spiritual impulses" of Krishna, Moses, Buddha, Zoroaster, Jesus, and Muhammad, the Bahá'ís allege, have been "obscured by dogmatic accretions" and "diverted by sectarian conflict."

All these distortions – economic, political, and religious – must pass: "The human race is being urged by the requirements of its own maturation to free itself from its inherited understanding and use of power .... Humanity stands at the threshold of maturity."[40]

Fortunately, the one good man amid so many "inhibitions and distortions" – Baha'ullah, the nineteenth-century founder and Messenger of God – cut through the veil of illusion and saw the future: "O ye that inhabit the heavens and the earth! There hath appeared what hath never previously appeared." An intellectual breakthrough, the "potentialities latent in the consciousness of the world's peoples," and a "gathering momentum of an emerging unity of thought in world undertakings" have made it possible to live by "new spiritual concepts and principles" to serve the real interests of the generality of humankind.[41] The new unity will create a magnitude of force never before seen – though what this new force will be required to do is somewhat thin on details.

Two constituencies are singled out for particular attention – women and aboriginal peoples – for their inherent predisposition to unity, integration, inclusion, and holism. The pivotal importance of women arises from the contribution they, in particular, make to peace, productivity, social integration – in short, to the healing of families and community. Wendy, a baby boomer who converted to Bahá'í after a Pentecostal minister diagnosed a "God-size hole" in her, went in search of a loving, inclusive God. She explains to me: "Men suffer as long as women are not equal. Full humanity is like a bird with two wings – the bird is weak if it is not aloft with two wings."

The Bahá'ís have a special relation to the aboriginals, and indeed, of Canada's 20,000 Bahá'ís, 7,000 are aboriginals. As the Bahá'ís avow, both espouse the essential equality and spirituality of human beings, and both understand spirituality to be manifest primarily in standards of moral conduct. Canada's aboriginals are the carriers of a new valuation which emphasizes collective rights and the organic nature of human society. And aboriginals' aspirations to enter into relationships with the global village directly, rather than through the intermediary of a dominant culture or government, is a harbinger of dramatic impending challenges to the established international and worldwide institutions of governance. Indeed, Canada's aboriginal peoples' self-determination is a first strike against parochial politics. As the Canadian Bahá'í community divulged in its submission to the Royal Commission on Aboriginal Peoples, "Canada's political institutions, including the Canadian parliamentary system, were conceived for the needs of an earlier and very different age."[42] Local self-determination and world citizenship must replace the distorting intermediary institutions to which we still atavistically cling.

If the Bahá'ís generally have less to say about the specifics of spirituality, and more about the hurdles and blockages impeding it, what is not left to imagination is the reason why the world has turned out the way it has and, in particular, deprived itself of the truths abounding in the spirituality of aboriginals: Judaism and Christianity. Here again, just as in the other religious movements I have referred to in this chapter, Western civilization is blamed for kick-starting and reinforcing the economic, political, and cultural forces that clashed and foreclosed a more enlightened understanding, not to say world unification. And, as is implied in the prediction of impending chaos, and the search for a faithful remnant which is still in touch with a truth absent from this world, Bahá'ism embraces a subversive apocalypticism. "This is a terrible time. There is going to be lots more upheaval and destabilization," Wendy comments, "but there will be a world order within the next century. There are tremendous capacities engraved in us, and only if you realize you are noble, a gift from God, will you take control and take on responsibility. You can show people what is possible." Spoken like a true baby boomer.

Is there only cause for despair in the future of an immanent faith? Since so much good is done in the world by people of faith – in charities, hospices, food banks, and philanthropic agencies – it may be premature to lament the passing of a faith which commits itself to working within the limits of the world. And despite fears that the "politics of difference," with its corrosive suspicion toward tradition, will abet the depletion of goodwill and undermine attempts at marshalling the opportunities among faiths for a concerted stand, at least one singular event of 2000 suggests otherwise. The Great Jubilee Project – initiated and pushed by as unlikely and varied a quartet as the Pope, the rock group R E M's Michael Stipe, Muhammad Ali, and Archbishop Desmond Tutu – harks back to Leviticus: 25. Every fifty years, scripture directs, society must be renewed by freeing slaves, returning seized land, and forgiving debts. With the collaboration of the World Council of Churches, the Project has been seeking Third World debt forgiveness – indeed, the cancellation of global debt entirely – thus relieving the burden of less fortunate nations in their struggles for economic and social development. Given these nations' current plight – where payment of interest on current debt alone is crippling the capacity to invest in the infrastructure for health, education, and social services – it is hard to think of a worthier initiative, and one more consonant with the spirit of gratitude, magnanimity, and forgiveness which unreservedly emanate from the core of spirituality.

But … enterprises like the Great Jubilee Project are sustained by more than goodwill and resolution. They are also anchored in a metaphysic which underwrites the idea and experience of moral obligation. Justice, gratitude, compassion, respect for individuals, forgiveness, and all the other moral attributes we esteem are only conduits for the self-disclosure of the divine. Reverend Phipps recognizes that "social gospel" hinges on the truth of God's revelation, and not only on an affective experience. But his God is so transcendent that, while He humbles our tendency to own God and constrain Him by our needs and wants, He is at risk of becoming a *deus absconditus*. For those modern "believers" like the members of the Jesus Seminar, or the Humanist Association of Canada, who would eradicate the idea of a supernatural being, but maintain the commitment to reason, compassion, democracy, free inquiry, and the scientific method, God *is* absconded and the idols which remain – our practices of promise-keeping, truth-telling, and gift-giving, to name a few – have only a shadowy existence. To recall Nietzsche's reasoning, once God becomes so remote that we have no need of Him, we are led to forget Him, even to "murder" Him. Once "God is dead," reality is no longer permanent or universal enough to let us confidently say we are in possession of truth. But then "duty" and "promise" may also be abolished in clear conscience – if only timidity or intellectual laziness do not hold us back from this final fateful act.[43] In the final analysis, an "immanent faith," depleted of its metaphysical core, is insubstantial. As Nietzsche says, it has become like the shadows at the back of a cave that linger after God is dead.[44] One tenet after another deteriorates and fades away, and individuals feel liberated to mix and blend forms of worship and ideas from conflicting traditions according to taste. And then, *voilà*, one reaches our time's most renegade option, where even a god of one's own making is permitted – namely, fusion faith.

# Fusion Faith

## Renegotiating Modernity

.................................................................................................................................

> A theology that chooses to meet our time, a theology that accepts the destiny of history, must first assess the theological significance of the death of God. We must realize that the death of God is an historical event, that God has died in our cosmos, in our history, in our *Existenz*.[1]

Room 106B at the Blackfoot Inn in Calgary is a typically sterile hotel meeting-room, blandly appointed for the business transactions, market strategizing, and go-for-it rallies of Shriners, Amway distributors, and car dealers. Today, however, it is shrouded in cave-like darkness – with the exception of pencil-thin light beams dancing off a glitter ball, illuminating a dais at the front of the room garlanded with gold cloth, sprinkled with glittering sequins, and surrounded by harps, mandolins, and horns. Above the makeshift altar are white Christmas lights blinking like stars. Around the periphery of the room are Day-Glo-spackled mandalas, overstuffed Turkish cushions and stalls offering crystals, smudge pots, and dream catchers. The room is congested – with baby boomers.

Billed as SpiritFest '99, the Council of Shambhala has issued a calling of the clan – and Calgary's New Age movement is out in full force. Looking around the room, one cannot help but be overwhelmed and perplexed by the soup of symbols: here, to one side, some Ju-Bus (Jewish Buddhists) examining a Tibetan prayer wheel; there, near the front, feminist shamans examining a smudge pot; at the rear, a healing quilt being sewn. "There are ways to kill spirituality," explains the person seated next to me. "Build a church. Today, we need an unabashed transcendence away from prescribed, habitual patterns. It's true if you live it. If you don't live it, what's it worth?" Here, at Spirit-Fest '99, we can enjoy the lived experience of the sacred, he adds.

Enlightenment comes at a cost. Full attendance for the three days comes in at just under $1,000, providing one has not been tempted to buy handfuls of crystals, costing $27 each, or a divining rod, or amulets, or even a meditation blanket. I start to question my interlocutor about this, but he advises, "Language is a mask. Sitting in silence makes it safe to be together – the screen of fear and suspicion begins to dissolve. Just *be* the communion of silence." I fall silent.

A gong sounds, and the moderator stands up, abruptly asking, "How many of you believe your blood family is your real family?" Not a single hand is raised. "How many of you do not?" All one hundred baby boomers put up their hands. "And how many of you believe that you have a secret truth you are trying to get in touch with?" Again, nearly everyone present raises a hand. "We are all victims of social consciousness," the moderator notes.

> We forget who we are and then we give our power away. But the cosmos will fall in line with what you want, the magic and energy of what you are. We have challenges and blockages. When you are challenged by people who don't understand what you're doing, it's fear. Here we're permitting you to move to your higher self. It's frightening, terror, like jumping off a cliff without a parachute. I urge you to jump. I urge you to the terror.

At this point, a woman gets up, throws her arms around the moderator, and cries, "I need your support." Another woman lies prostrate on the floor. The moderator continues:

> Judge, critic, saboteur – they all came in when I started my jump. They started *decreeing*. And the mind is always making up stories – it's all nonsense. How does the unconscious conspiracy reinforce your story? It's mental masturbation and you never get an orgasm. This thing up here [he points to his head] drives us crazy. In your heart, you want to move. You need you to support you. You must say, "I want to love myself, I want to tidy up my inside closet." The

rest is a big smokescreen. Tell me what you came to the planet for,
tell me who you are, how you feel. I don't want to know your story.
You're right on the edge of what you want to do.

With each further step in the call to enlightenment, people in the
crowd raise their arms and wriggle their fingers.[2] The woman in front
of me dips into her satchel and pulls out some anti-stress lotion,
dabbing it on her temples. Moments later, she pulls out a crystal on a
chain and proceeds to douse. "It's the magic. It's the ju-ju," she explains
when I stare uncontrollably at her.

The centrepiece of Spiritfest '99 is the channeller Craig Russell, who
discloses that he channels for two angels, and that he is on a metaphysical, not spiritual, path. What this means, he explains, is that he dreams
of being someone else and of his previous lives. During one of his
dreams, he was told – by no less an authority than the Archangel
Michael – that he was a friend of the ascended masters. Soon after, he
had his "core perception" and made contact with Akasha, the divine
mother angel, and Asan, the divine father angel. He learned that angels
can acquire humanity and descend, just as they can provide the means
of ascension. Our task, Russell relates, is to let the angels move into our
"heart-space," thus preparing for the possibility of "heaven on earth."

> We must become the messenger to each other until we become
> gods. Something wonderful is about to happen. You are participat-
> ing in the opening of the seventh seal. Look to the power of your
> higher self, not your outer self. Watch your mind – you are often not
> the conscious creator of your thoughts. The ego files the data, starts
> making decisions. You have to tell the ego you're in charge. Yamma-
> yamma will appear less.

While Craig channels, syrupy, tingly New Age music wafts around the
room. The lights have been dimmed, leaving only the glitter ball to
refract its beams through the thickening incense smoke-ribbons. Many
of the participants wander off into their own mode of bliss – one man
spreads himself out on the floor, makes like a snow angel and then rolls
into the fetal position. Another begins deep-breathing. A third repeatedly makes the sign of the cross. Two women, wrapped in a quilt
(Linus's "security blanket"?), dance affectedly around the room. As we

move into the second hour, Craig starts to utter stream of consciousness – nearly glossolalia – with a husky ethereality:

> Overcoming all consciousness of duality, left the plains of bliss, and
> entering the deep sleep of the third dimension. In the presence of
> Mother Mary – she is the mother who allows your soul-flames to
> walk through her flames. It's a purification, to experience the
> consciousness of the One. A wish to awaken, lacking in human
> consciousness, to gain a new momentum in the becoming. You are
> architects of truth. The mother goddess of feeling and heart has not
> been in the human mind. We have to come to full balance source.
> The will of the Mother had to come into the space of the Father.
> The yappy voice – thoughts – the altered ego: an old warrior of
> attack, defend, offend, and afraid of the unknown. The solar plexus
> is the gateway.

At this point, the angels Akasha and Asan have quite evidently
enflamed Craig with unprecedented visions of grandeur:

> I am the open door, what Jesus intended. I am the Resurrection of
> the life, your higher self. I am your beloved, I am presence. I am
> allowing the electronic energy to pour into you of the Holy Spirit,
> the flame of your physical atoms, your Christed self. You must clear
> the cellular history of your life, undo the duality of consciousness,
> live beyond the human good. Good and evil are only products of
> the mind. You must come out of the ancient contracts into grace. I
> own the part of me that wants to fly and I hop along with a broken
> wing. We must put the Christ back on the throne of your flame.

And, in a final paroxysm of overwrought emotion, he ends:

> The angels give you cosmic hugs. A violet-flame angel dissolves and
> consumes all the negative energy, like molten liquid lava, consum-
> ing like a forest fire. It's necessary to ascend these bodies. A rose
> pink flamed angel, the divine protector of the Christ child. To fly
> again – that is your destiny. Someone has to push your button to get
> the human stuff out. This is coming from the eleventh dimension. It
> will help the cellular structure of your body to return to grace.

Looking around, in the aftermath of this meteor shower of babble, I am dumbfounded to see looks of enchantment and rapture on baby-boomer faces. I realize now that the whole room has been decorated and musically enhanced to evoke a mystical womb – and my SpiritFest compatriots are swaying, rubbing their eyes, and looking about with the kind of primeval wonder Adam and Eve must have manifested, as if they had just undergone a meltdown, from the pedestrian everyday world of familial and professional responsibilities, to primal ooze, as a prelude to rebirth as a new, spiritual self.

Arguably, nowhere does the search for sacred reality exhibit itself in as pure a form as in mysticism, a mode of religious experience equally at home in the *kataphatic* as the *apophatic* traditions. As the acclaimed scholar of Jewish mysticism Gerschom G. Scholem comments, "It is religion in its most acute, intense, and living stage."[3] And nowhere is the incompatibility between faith and modern consciousness as stark. The great mystics – Rabia in early Islamic times; Isaac Luria in medieval Judaism; Meister Eckhart, Jacob Boehme, Juliana of Norwich, St. Teresa of Avila, Hildegard of Bingen, and Catherine of Siena in Christian Europe – have left us with precious testimony of their enjoyment of direct and intimate consciousness of divine presence. But this evidence – of "seeing through" and "seeing within," of ineffable, paradoxical experiences and images where opposites coincide and antagonistic principles co-exist, and of calculated attempts to confound the mind through non-thought and non-speech – is anathema to the common sense of the empirical and inductive, or the rational and deductive methods of modern reason and science.[4] As importantly, New Age enthusiasm for mystical experience departs from the sublime mystical tradition in its utter lack of spiritual discipline. At SpiritFest '99, freestyle self-enchantment replaces the long, arduous paths taken by Luria, Eckhart, Boehme and other mystics. Not only the modern mind, but equally the traditional mystic's mind, must see the antics of SpiritFest '99 as indistinguishable from the irrational and delusive arts of clairvoyance, spiritualism, occultism, and magic.

If the stylized gestures, arcane incantations, insipid music, free-association babble, and precious affectation of SpiritFest '99 have the putrid scent of sensual decadence, it is all nonetheless conducted with a grim earnestness, unleavened by the slightest hint of irony. And though, from any balanced point of view, the antics can only be judged as over the top, they nonetheless contain important signals about the baby boomers' spiritual quests, resonating powerfully with ideas and themes to which I have already referred. Here at SpiritFest '99, one encounters a resplendence of baby-boom culture and consciousness: We are destiny; we will tolerate no "men in hats"; we seek the challenge beyond all challenges; our spiritual guides must walk the talk; we want ritual, not doctrine; we need to release the child within us; we will be as *bricoleurs* picking and choosing what works for us; if religion at all, it has to fit our comfort zone; spirituality must be nurturing and embracing; we need to get back to a pure beginning. SpiritFest '99 epitomizes the anti-rationalism, anti-institutionalism, romantic idealism, and fascination with the primordial so integral to baby boomers' way of being. Above all, SpiritFest '99 is wrought with world despair, its participants evidently open to the prophetic call for the destroyer-god. The illusion that so many hold that they were not generated by their natural parents and not part of their family's natural, continuous bloodline is telling. It reminds one of Freud's discussion of "the changeling fantasy," in which individuals dream that they are fairy children kidnapped by adoptive parents who parade as natural parents. The fantasy lies in believing that there is a mystical other self which is the true self. There can be no spirituality for baby boomers without a sense of drama.

In 1993, James Redfield published *The Celestine Prophecy: An Adventure*. It was the number one international best-seller of 1996 and, together with the sequel *The Tenth Insight: Holding The Vision*, spent seventy-four weeks on the *New York Times* best-seller list. It could have been the script for SpiritFest '99, for both expressions of the new spirituality are unrelentingly Gnostic – not simply expressions of faith or intellectual intuition, but of a secret knowledge of ultimate truth, which will permit a radical change in human nature, the conditions of existence, and the structure of being. Redfield prefaces his work with the prognosis that "Human society will take a quantum leap into a wholly new way of life." The choice of words is apposite – like the unpredictable and indeterminate quanta in the thermoelectric field, humankind is invited to take an impulsive, capricious spiritual leap into a realm of pure energy, where nothing is solid and everything permutates.

*The Celestine Prophecy* is about an ancient manuscript found in the rainforests of Peru, containing nine key insights whose adoption would move us toward a completely spiritual culture on Earth. The reader is invited to awaken from the Modern Age, be part of a critical mass of dissenters, and launch into a new (old?) phase of consciousness.

So, what is the great prophetic insight? The philosophies and ideas of East and West will integrate into a higher truth. We will learn to project energy on to others and avoid addictions to other people. We will attain a social organization where needs will be met without waste and without currency. And we will have "meaningful encounters" by having learned to "vibrate at a new level."[5] As we learn the lost truths, we will evolve, having let go of the ego, the mechanism which drives us to control, and we will be in a state where we can "reconnect [our] energy – stay full, stay in a state of love."[6] A certain amount of social engineering will be required – each parent is to have only one child, we must be the kind of being who receives our opposite-sex energy, we must minimize actual human contact in case this evolution is thwarted, we must overcome the fantasy projection about the other gender, and we must break all codependent relationships, especially romantic ones.

In the process of progressively disclosing the celestine prophecies, Redfield spins an adventure story replete with lost treasures, magical plants, stalking gunslingers, and government agents – a kind of Crocodile Dundee meets Shirley MacLaine. The key dilemma for the protagonist is that the "government" is "concerned about this Manuscript" – not surprising, since Redfield's gospel is antinomian and communistic, requiring that the new cognoscenti initiate a program of eugenic breeding and a total remake of creation, specifically human nature. And, like all Gnostic myths, the prophecies hold out the hope that, once they are fulfilled, we will finally be like Christ – or, at least, the divine Christ – for the ninth prophecy makes it possible for us to transcend death by overcoming the density and timeliness of the human body. We will be able to expand the physical world into the spiritual and be so light we can walk on water. By then, we will have been taken beyond a world competing for energy and power, and thus to a time where human conflict is ended. At that time, we, like Redfield's protagonist, who has evaded his opponents, will stand on a ridge, and experience a great epiphany, "being suspended, floating, amid a space that existed in all directions," an inner buoyancy, not bounded by earth's gravity.[7]

*The Celestine Prophecy* plays on all the phobias and intoxicated dreams of baby boomers, wrapping them in surreal mythology – which, though akin to Tolkien's fantastic adventures in *The Lord of the Rings*, lacks all of that author's nuance and spiritual discipline. Here are secret elixirs, esoteric wisdom, guardian monsters, dangerous adventures, and the ultimate promise of absolute reality, sacred power, and immortality. The world is sclerotic, its author says, and its salvation lies in taking human nature to a state of being where we are no longer differentiated, dependent, and determined, and thus limited by attributes. In a flash, baby boomers are offered everything they could ever have wished for and are rid of a world in whose redemption they have lost faith.

On the positive side, the book points to renewal of the human spirit, offering the prospect of breaking the apparently inexorable necessities of modern society. Its protagonists exemplify the human power to act and initiate new beginnings. Against the cynicism of contemporary philosophy, *The Celestine Prophecy* speaks of hope.

While promising much wisdom, *The Celestine Prophecy* offers little. Instead, its "prophecies" are little more than a shopping list of all the grudges and garden-variety disappointments which make up large parts of human life. What is particularly striking about the book is its utter lack of charity with respect to the human condition, leaving neither an opening for the deepening of possibilities in reality, nor their imaginative transformation through human virtue.

Tone, rather than substance, is all one gets from *The Celestine Prophecy*: breathless, panicky reportage from the brink of the apocalypse, and syrupy mysticism as reward – *The Fugitive* meets Deepak Chopra. The book works like a crucible, dissolving the corrupted and compromised state of the world and transmuting the molten core to a new golden state. Trading on the unwarranted hope for an as yet undiscovered salvational truth, and extravagantly promising a return to a paradise where there are no conflicts, no limits, no lack, no forfeited choices, no hurtful discrimination, no "I-It" relationships, and no ambiguous speech, *The Celestine Prophecy* is a dream of returning to a pre-adult world. In its offer to take readers to a place, unencumbered by the past, where all needs are met and all desires indulged, *The Celestine Prophecy* is finally a mad bid to repeat the act of creation, to remake what the first Creator so misshapenly produced. Its romantic idealism –

overcoming our worldly condition, restoring the child's dream of staying at a condition of oceanic oneness forever – is finally inhuman, for to
live without lack is to live without time, in other words, to live in animal
contentment. The human world of work and obligation, war and
honour, are conveniently occluded.

And little of this tale is particularly original. From Aldous Huxley
and George Orwell to Anthony Burgess and Kurt Vonnegut (not to
mention films like *Blade Runner, Brazil,* and *The Matrix*), there is a
literature where New Age mysticism touches up against twentieth-
century totalitarianism. But where Aldous Huxley's *Brave New World,*
for example, was intended to be a warning, showing the limits imposed
by human nature, and not a utopian blueprint, now, for Redfield, the
nexus of spiritualism and absolute technology becomes a path of
human development to be seriously considered. The surprising thing
about *The Celestine Prophecy* is not the dreamy message – as old as the
ancient Gnosticisms of the first-century common era – but that the
book is so poorly written, so juvenile in its aspirations, and yet so
wildly popular among baby boomers, evidently striking a responding
chord. The frightening prospect – in the context of cloning and genetic
engineering – is that Redfield's misty-eyed "prophecies" could be actu-
alized. The God of the Torah, the Old Testament, and the Koran is
transcendent and judgmental, defining our humanity by His distance.
*The Celestine Prophecy*'s invitation to self-divinization places us in that
dangerous unlimited state warned of by Ivan in *The Brothers Karamazov:* "If God does not exist, everything is possible."

Somewhat less known, though as immensely popular, is a do-it-
yourself spirituality package called "A Course in Miracles." If baby
boomers need to see themselves and the world from a place of love
and forgiveness, and if their every whim and indulgence is taken to be
a sign of grace, the Course is the baby boomers' ultimate religion. The
Course's message has, of course, a credible pedigree. In his book *The
Varieties of Religious Experience,* William James distinguishes the "religion of the healthy-minded" from the "religion of the sick-souled."
The "healthy-minded," James writes, embark on the *via positiva* and
enjoy the experience of the gradual ascent to the divine, from sensual
pleasure at creation, to the intellectual recognition that there is intelligible design and purpose in the created world, to an ultimate holistic
union with God. The spiritual search is one of affirmation through

the hierarchy of existence culminating in the pure being of God. All existence takes the place fitting for it, each created being is good, and collectively existence is very good. A believer experiences only beneficence and kindness at the hands of God, and the believer's growth and development is the theatre for God. The "religion of the healthy-minded" is a religion of nature and joy, where the miraculous is found in everyday life. Where the finite world is shot through with manifestations of the infinite, happiness and holiness coincide harmoniously. Existence is a great chain of beings, a continuous graduated reality, which is orderly and good. Humans share so deeply in God's divine mind, they need only read their own minds to read God's. Evil, as well as sin and dread, are treated as perceptions which can be banished by acts of will and positive thinking. There is even a specific image of the deity that corresponds to the healthy-minded religion, God as fullness of being: "The gods we stand by are the gods we need and use, the gods whose demands on us are reinforcements of our demands on ourselves and on one another."[8] A more technical term for the healthy-minded religion is *kataphatic* – the believer is drawn through creation toward God.

Like James's healthy-minded religion, the Course in Miracles focuses exclusively on positive thinking as the medium of spiritual exaltation. "In the real world," reads Jerry Spears's primer on the Course, "there is no sickness, for there is no separation and no division. Only loving thoughts are recognized …. The power of your valuing will make it so."[9]

The author (or redactor) of the Course, Helen Schucman, was a Columbia University psychologist who channelled lessons allegedly dictated by Christ. In 1965, she began to set them to text. Proximity to the true source meant that institutionalized and organized religion could be supplanted, and Schucman was clear that the teachings were never to be patented, nor a new church instituted. Indeed, in evident opposition to the inevitable worldly compromises of all establishment churches – and, in particular, evident in the trend to megachurches – the Course builds on the radical potential of the model of the twelve apostles and the primitive church, directing its teaching to "refugees from various worldly based motivational systems."[10] Nevertheless, profane ambition is not lacking in this movement. Like so much of the spirituality industry, the message of love and forgiveness has the

quicksilver property of translating into big business, and the Foundation for Inner Peace – the Course's current proprietor – peddles a vast
array of program options, retreats, publications, and counsellors. And,
though hardly unique to the Course, there is vituperative debate on
who is actual heir to Jesus' and Schucman's work.

The objective of the Course is "taking individuals from a life of pain
and disappointment to a life of joy and open, evolving relationships."[11]
The key to this transmutation is the rediscovery of miracles as gratu-
itous gifts, as invitations to have a relationship with some kind of god,
and to enjoy life-affirming opportunities. "Miracles occur naturally as
expressions of love. The miracle abolishes the need for lower-order
concerns."[12] But "lower-order concerns" like fear, pain, and disappointment are for most of us a daily diet. Before miracles can start to
happen and be lived, a new orientation toward God and society must
take place. "God is not vengeful; it is all right to make mistakes and you
are not going to be punished for it," explains my ex-Catholic host,
Raymond, offering an introductory sampling of the Course in Miracles. "Institutionalized religion holds nothing for me. I needed something more freeing, not so restrictive. Catholicism had little to do with
love, and the Course connected for me that God was loving. It's simple
and straightforward – a God who's not keeping score, but who is
loving. When you're tired of suffering, you turn to love. You become
naturally Christed."

However obdurate concrete reality may appear to be – friends and
lovers who abandon you, bosses who humiliate you, the necessity of
labour, sickness, and death – it is solely our perception that matters.
"We're in a rut and have to break the cycle. I have invented the world I
see," Raymond explains, and the Course teaches that "my salvation
comes from me."[13] But rediscovering miracles requires recognizing
that the source of our misery is the activity of the ego. "Ego is the
conditioning being. We have to let go of judgment. Judgment is a
setting of price and, as you set it, you will pay for it. The world is an
illusion that we look at through the ego." As the manual for the Course
reads: "What is the ego? Nothingness, but in a form that seems like
something …. The ego's opposite in every way – in origin, effect, and
consequence – we call a miracle."[14]

The world of darkness, forever compromised by fear and ego activity, must be countered by "finding the light inside of you." "Clarity

comes from meditation," Raymond expands. "It frees you from structure – there are no penalties, no contradictions to life. You make them
and you'll grow out of them. The point is to be freed from fear, from
limitation and conditioning." The Course teaches that "reality belongs
only to the spirit and the miracle acknowledges only truth."[15] "The
Holy Spirit is the motivation for miracle-mindedness – the decision to
heal the separation by letting it go." And by "letting it go," the Course
offers the prospect of "return to the eternal formlessness of God."[16]
Neither the uniquely historical person of Christ, nor the God-initiated
gift of grace are any longer prerogatives of God's power alone, says
Raymond: "Your Saviour is everyone you look at, to doctrinalize is an
ego activity. Everyone can do miracles."

In the absence of miracles, and their modus operandi of love and
forgiveness, we are confined in our egos: "We're driving towards a
brick wall. We're going to reach a point of environmental crisis, of
depletion; we're going to be forced to change dramatically. We have to
go global and universal – to restore the inner-connectedness of all
things, the need for respect and reverence; we've become so separated."
As the Course promises, "Through forgiveness the thinking of the
world is reversed."[17] Indeed, the Course, in a sense, leapfrogs over the
world, since it offers in effect a "religious" version of the middle-class
nostrum "Think globally, act locally" in the advice "Be spiritual, experience the god indwelling."

Raymond concludes, "It's the fifty monkeys thing, the whole balance
will shift. As each of us changes, society will change. We have to change
ourselves and the structures will change." The Course in Miracles is
not a new testament, nor a new set of doctrines – "It's simply a vehicle
to get you back on track." But "back on track" cannot mean traditional
religion. It is too late for historical Christianity, Judaism, or Islam, for
their inanition is the destiny of history.

The Course in Miracles would seem to be an obvious candidate for
Nietzsche's derision of a religion designed for spiritual waifs, if it were
not so derivative of Nietzsche's philosophy of life – "joyful science."
Though the language of the Course is "grace" and "love," in the absence
of any idea of atonement, what is really meant are "recovery" and
"growth." Nietzsche had said, after all, that a god on the cross is an
abomination. In the Course, there is neither evil nor demons, nothing
ontological about the fall, nor inescapable fault in our souls. Human

perfectibility substitutes for original sin, and self-divinization replaces sanctification by God. The Course demands neither commitment to theological doctrine nor ecclesiastical authority. In their stead are personal meaning and morality. Separation, distance, and alienation are not permanent or integral aspects of cosmic reality, but psychological tensions within oneself. By healing oneself – by extending "grace" to oneself – one can, in the absence of divine initiative, overcome the separation from God, a far cry from both Judaism's injunction *Tikun Olan* (repair the world) and Christianity's appeal to *caritas* (charity). Casually neglected in the Course is the Jewish, Christian, and Muslim recognition of humankind's ineradicable distance from God as a consequence of human sin and apostasy.

In the service of recovery and health, the Course tolerates a farrago of techniques, allowing a flexibility of private worship and devotional practice appropriate to their utility – "By their fruits you shall know them." It is a pragmatism congenial to the baby boomers' eclecticism, confirming the idea of a personal religion whose core – experience and feeling – is more authentic and real than theology and ecclesiastical organization. Baby boomers' desire to pick and choose has, of course, a long pedigree. Like the toys they played with as children (Tinkertoys, Lego, Meccano), their "child-centred" education was often an exercise in modular self-design, reinforcing the idea that the world and its things were supremely malleable stuff. The language students were taught elevated youth and novelty, as if the conditions of existence were negotiable and could be subjected to their indulgences. What was reality? What was illusion? A popular poster hanging in many Canadian classrooms at the time displayed variegated patches of bland colours which, looked at one way and then another, permitted a gestalt switch of rabbit to duck, duck to rabbit. It made a huge impression upon many baby boomers, since it conveyed to them the idea that they lived in a sepia world with few clear demarcations. Decades later, their made-to-measure spirituality is concerned less with the truth of doctrinal proposition, or how it reveals reality, than with its functional value: "Will it work to illuminate my daily life and the range of my experiences?" Such functionalism, while hardly unique to Nietzsche, permits the Course to share one other important feature of his thought: What is real and true is so to the extent that Life Itself is sanctified.

Of course, Nietzsche's "joyful science" was not intended for "every-man" – quite the contrary – but the migration of his philosophy to North America and its assimilation to an ethos of practicality and democratic equality has meant, ironically, that all of us could "give birth to a dancing star," even religious believers.

That Nietzsche has had such a colossal impact on North American religious culture is, in great part, courtesy of Matthew Fox – the theologian, former Dominican priest, and author of the acclaimed *The Coming of the Cosmic Christ* and *Creation Spirituality*. In these works, Fox calls for a new cosmic story, "to cut through the addictive enslavement of overdeveloped cultures." Fox's most beguiling contribution to contemporary society is the idea that there is a wounded child within us, a wounded earth around us, and a wounded Cosmic Christ. He invites the child in us to worship, bidding us perform a deeply healing act for the wounded child in all of us. The artist *manqué* in each one of us must combat "adultism" and become young again. We must, Fox writes, "teach adults to play again in church," to re-sacralize and re-enchant their lives and "return to the Original Blessing of creation" before the messy advent of original sin. "Creation [spirituality] is the spiralling, dancing, crouching, spring-ing, leaping, surprising act of relatedness, of communing, of respond-ing, of letting go, of being."[18] We must seek a "New Creation where ... all paradoxes are reconciled in a living, whirling, laugh-filled dance to the erotic Godhead who painted us all, sang us all, gifted us all, imag-ined us all, and still laughs at us all."[19] Here, in the primal fluidity, a "morphic field ... a kind of cumulative memory from the past," lies the power to "relaunch the species."

Fox's primordialism, apocalypticism, and messianism lie at the heart of A Course in Miracles. Arguably, they inform nearly all of the spiri-tual searches baby boomers are undertaking.

. . .

Another "spiritual path of self-purification and transformation," the Pathwork, takes the "protestant" emphasis on private conscience, indi-vidual choice, and personal responsibility, and the Nietzschean cele-bration of joyful Life, as the means of assuming responsibility for oneself and all humankind one step further – into the sphere of secret conspiracy and occult wisdom. The 258 lectures – channelled teachings from "the Guide" written down by Eva Pierrakos – are particularly popular among women's spirituality groups. Here, too, traditional spiritual disciplines are only tools for self-confrontation. More radically than the Course in Miracles, the Pathwork speaks to a deep, subjective interiority, whose esoteric, nearly clandestine quality has no ambition to renew the world.

Pathwork Lecture N° 204 captures well the overall flavour of these lectures, dwelling on our profound alienation from ourselves, while invoking a deeply hidden recess of the self that will supply the necessary salvific power. The ego-self, the Guide says, is steeped in negativity and destructiveness. Fortunately, deeper within us lies a "dormant potentiality" – "a feeling or sensing that another, more fulfilling state of consciousness and a larger capacity to experience life must exist." But we are at war with ourselves and there is something within us which prevents us from experiencing true spiritual bliss. We must go into the dark areas of the self – the pain – and "ferret out the underlying beliefs behind any strong resistance or revulsion," and experience our naked vulnerability. There we will find "real aliveness" and "inner truthfulness." Reminiscent of the baby boomers' adage "No pain, no gain," the Guide relates: "The deepest pain is a revivifying experience. It releases contracted energy and paralyzed creativity. It enables the person to feel pleasure to the degree he is willing to feel pain." And, in so doing, we will be "fulfilling the task you came to fulfill through your birth." The Pathwork – the Guide adds – must, of necessity, be a "secret society." It "cannot be a popular movement for there are very few capable or willing to follow such a path."

Sniffling, hugging, and "blissing" her way through this session is my host, Deborah, a convert to the Pathwork from the United Church. Later, we have herbal tea at her remote wilderness log cabin, and I learn how thoroughly she has lived by the Pathwork injunction, "You must go through and into your darkness." In the next two hours, we enjoy a tour of her spirit – a labyrinthine soul tormented by chaos, energy flares, past-life recall, vibrations, realigning planes, fairy visitations, archangels, and "a part of me that freaks the shit out of me" – an utterly mad recitation made all the more remarkable by the fact that, in dozens of prior conversations, I had been struck by how balanced and moderate this New Democratic Party activist's political and social views were.

Sitting in a living room refracting the light from over twenty burning candles, we are positioned in front of a self-designed altar on which are positioned crystals, a knife, gems, an Amazon goddess, various pouches, a pendulum, a feather, a shell, and ivory skulls. Each item has been deliberately placed to evoke the cardinal directions of the cosmos. Chimes at the doorway keep out spirits, and the furniture is arranged in accordance with the principles of feng shui. Altars are the centre of the world, where cosmic levels intersect, and the site for hierophanies (the revelation of the sacred and divine), Deborah explains. She ignites some sweetgrass, and its pungent aroma wafts through the air. Given the derivation of the hodgepodge of artifacts – running the gamut from animism to native and Celtic spirituality, Santeria to witchcraft – I am not surprised when Deborah admits her spiritual path has been a busy one. She has experimented with Esalen, the human potential movement, alcohol and drugs, psychiatric counselling, Alcoholics Anonymous, personal development seminars, yoga, macrobiotics, breath and silence therapy, emotional regression, Celtic spirituality, Gaia spirituality, archetypes, and Shiatsu – all in search of transcendence and wholeness.

Born with a silver spoon in her mouth, Deborah shunned the world of her socialite parents, opposing its hypocrisy and *amour-propre*. Pretending to be perfect, but unable to deal with situations and preoccupied with looking good for the community, her family provided scant opportunity for developing a sense of inner direction. And the charm and passion of her first love affair, comprising a whole life-world of experience and standards, ended up a poor substitute. Her first boyfriend precipitously left her and moved in with another lover, and Deborah, utterly devastated, went into a tailspin and attempted suicide. It left her unable to move and act, yet with a huge sense of purpose. For years, she explored this in psychotherapy, with therapists who became surrogate fathers, mothers, and lovers. One day she felt within her a burning flame, and a colleague explained that her heart *chokra* had opened, an inner spirit released. Pursuing personal development seminars on Gabriola Island, Deborah became convinced of a "god indwelling" and began to devote herself to "moving physical energy," be it material, emotional, or mental, from macrobiotics to inner child therapy to yoga. "As humans, we're constantly moving. When we get stuck in a group, we stop moving. We are born with a journey, I just finally got it."

Working with Gaia and Celtic spirituality and archetypes, Deborah adopted the premise that everything in existence is spirit, and decided to become more earth-conscious and attuned to its cycles. Each of the cardinal directions, she found, emanated energy, and it was important to honour these energies and their different forms of manifestation: the east as air, an egg, birth; the south as fire, the playful child spirit with energy to burn; the west as water and the harvest; the north as spirit, the dark and quiet; the centre is the earth. Primary plants and roots – garlic, ginseng, ginger – rejuvenate and enspirit. Now, so perfectly is her nervous system in alignment with the environment that her energies reproduce its cycles: "I can't communicate after December twentieth, from February second I'm locomotive, by April a lunatic – just flowing with energy and strength. After June, everything slows down and I work with my garden and animals." Even the organization and appointment of her house honours the different parts of herself and of the earth. A dream catcher hangs in her window, a smudge pot nestles next to her hearth.

When all of being is recognized as synchronized, many older ways of seeing and knowing must be jettisoned. Time is no longer made up of discrete successive moments. Instead, past, present, and future are simultaneously present, making it possible for her to experience past-life recall – "a spirit has been in training with me" – seeing events in the past and visions of the future. Space is alive and animated. Out in isolated Ontario farmland, she knows and works with unknown spirits, and has overcome her fear of them. She can call on the spirits, invoking them by name. There is a magnet under her nose, providing her with a sense of discernment previously denied. "When you're aware it's there, you believe in it." The silence makes it possible to hear, and, as Josef Pieper once wrote, prepare the soul's power to answer to the reality of the world.

Vegetarianism, benevolence, stewardship of the earth, loving kindness to all sentient beings – all constitute ways of living in synchronicity. Duality is an illusion, and unwanted "vibration increases when there is more duality." Even pain can be gone into, released, and rendered a positive experience. "I learned to take ownership of my co-creation of my family. Now I don't blame them. I must now get away from sorrow, pain, and suffering, must grow from what they bring. There's a part of me that is wounded and dysfunctional. I try to go into the experience as fully as possible, to release it, and it becomes a positive experience." Of course, synchronicity also has its drawbacks. When the 1998 eastern Ontario ice storm occurred, Deborah's nervous system was totally depleted: "I learned that I need to do my energy work, be in this energy place. I can't allow myself to be depleted, de-energized again."

What of evil? "What goes around, comes around," she repeats many times over – acknowledging that everything she does, feels, and experiences resonates with all of existence, and is governed by reciprocity and compensation.

> Evil resides within us and is projected out as reality. What is outwards leads me to work on my self. Everything negative has to be brought within. To acknowledge the synchronicity of all things means asking, "What is in your energy that wanted this experience?" I am always getting cues and working with them; everything negative has to be brought within. They are all beautiful problems and opportunities to awaken to the journey. You have to ensure you are not blocking the energy current. I've just turned my will over to the beings of the light.

Institutionalized, patented, doctrinalized, and timetabled religion is redundant: "I walk the ritual now, so I don't need ceremony." Since all history and place is coterminous, and her being is the influx of all the energy of the cosmos, Deborah claims to have lived Christ's passion and reincarnation experientially. She also noticed she had become the carrier of other's detoxification, and realized she was an empath. "Some people just know I'm a healer. I don't have a power; I align to a power." And also:

> More and more people are approaching diseases with a desire to have spiritual awareness. Pain, fear, death being experienced in a wholly new heightened way. There is a new Christ-consciousness building steam. All kinds of planes are coming into new alignment, an acceleration of time is going on, beings are all being moved into higher levels of consciousness.

"To go back home in union with God is what all spirit longs for." For years, Deborah was involved in the peace movement and environmental causes, but she finally concluded that these initiatives on behalf of social justice were fear-based and chaos-inducing, and risked stagnating her energies. She also fled from the city, immuring herself in isolated wilderness, to escape the distractions of urban life. Where Deborah experienced ambiguity in the world as conflict and stress, her new life is one where a "nucleus of consciousness" encounters cosmic energy directly (Pathwork Lecture Nº 204). Bypassing the world of politics and social interaction, she "grounds her energy in the earth, opens her crown *chokra* to the universe." "I cannot serve the distorted paths of others."

Notwithstanding her aloofness from the world, as we share a bowl of lentils and greens, I appreciate that Deborah has achieved that state of voluntary simplicity where not only a modest lunch, but all of life is a *feast*, exhibiting, to use Karl Kerényi's definition, "the union of tranquillity, contemplation, and intensity of life." Her elaborate daily ceremonies endow the passages of her life with transcendent significance, cutting through the hypocrisy and shallowness of modern life. "What this is all about," Deborah concludes, her hand circling the room, is "to be in the rawness of what one is as a human being."

I have dwelled on Deborah's New Age spirituality, not to ridicule, but to illustrate both its sanity and its madness. It is very easy to caricature or debunk the New Age movement. It is much harder to see at its core something authentic and serious. Before judging New Age out of hand as naive and juvenile, one needs to ask whether one has mistaken an attractive simple grace for mere simplicity. Often, New Age is a complex statement on what it is to be a human being particularly in the late modern age, recalling that modernity's grand project of collapsing the transcendent into the secular realm – as if just fixing up the profane would confer the wholeness humans hope for – is exposed as a myth. What is attractive about New Age is that, unlike the partial societies of autonomous and discrete beings characterizing modernity, the world its practioners inhabit is animated by a living drama, wherein all the aspects of existence can be occasions for divine revelation and transcendence. Theirs is a spiritual world where chthonic deities, sorcerers, fetishes, and idols, and also nutrition and sexuality, are interconnected. Deborah's world stimulates a capacity for devotion. While from the hindsight of the scientific outlook, this may be mere "enchantment," it can also be seen as living organic life as sacrament. In Deborah's often inchoate longings, one senses an ardent desire for a holistic sympathy of all aspects of being, not to say a powerful human desire to be in touch with the sources of richness out of which our religions emerged. It is a desire barely different from that which attracts mystical Jews to the *hekhalot* tradition's invitation to celestial journeys, or Christians to Hildegard von Bingen's erotic, lyrical music, the *Symphony of the Harmony of Celestial Revelations.*[20]

Even the enchanted gestures and stylized rituals – so precious and self-indulgent on the surface – may speak of a higher mytho-poetic understanding. Consider Krishna's comments in the Gita: "The world is imprisoned in its own activity, except when actions are performed as worship of God. Therefore you must perform every action sacramentally and be free from all attachment to results." To suborn God to our needs and wants – which we do every time we apply a standard of utility and reason to our attendance to God – is not to perform sacramentally, but to presume that our actions are all-important, meaningful, and significant in the cosmos. Observing Jews understand this spiritual obedience perfectly: To comply to the *halakhah* (divine commands) – no walking between private and public, no work, no carrying, no lighting a fire on the Sabbath, observing kosher laws – is not right because it is rational, efficient, or hygienic, but because, in conquering one's own self-interest and passions, acquiescence confers purity and holiness.

That Deborah preoccupies herself with fetishes and communing with semi-divine beings may leave her open to the charge of committing the error of "misplaced concreteness" – or indeed the indictment of practising magic, fetishism, and superstition. But even so enlightened a thinker as Saint Bonaventure acknowledged that, while a profane object should not be literally engaged, but rather seen as a window to the divine, there is nonetheless an intimate connection between nature, human artifacts, and God. The whole, he writes, is a cosmos hierarchically ordered as a ladder of ascent to God. In *The Mind's Road to God*, he writes of a person who first encounters physical nature, then identifies traces of God's presence in it, and then reaches upward beyond the physical world into his own intellect, where he encounters God's signature. From his own intellectual world, his mind rises to the archetypes of the eternal essence, and sees through these to the very mind of God. Finally, the individual encounters God himself. The whole iconic, sacramental cosmos is a ladder of ascent. Bonaventure does not draw the conclusion, as do iconoclasts, that the lower rungs are abandoned during the ascent. Bonaventure's depiction of the spiritual encounter with God also means that the greatest themes of human life are not the exclusive possession of the philosopher or theologian, but are already present in the all-too-human proportions of everyday life.

The ascent need not be expressly intellectual – in the Sufi *qawwali*, where devotional song has the power to generate ecstasy, or the practice of *zikhr*, where repetition of the names of God to the accompaniment of tabla and harmonium excites union with the divine, a similar mystical ascent through creation toward the divine is experienced. The Jewish kabbala spells out the means whereby the mystic encounters Y H W H by practising endurance, loving-kindness, wisdom, and humility, thereby ascending the very Tree of Life from which Y H W H descended. At the festival of Sukkot, Jews wave four species of plant (palm, willow, myrtle, and etrog) in every direction, reunifying Jewry and re-sanctifying the chosen people's relation to God, so that they may be "a light unto the nations." Christian Orthodox plainchant employs modulations to evoke the grandeur and glory of creation, and the nothingness of atonement, to integrate all aspects of reality. The Nazarene and Holiness churches use spontaneous ecstasy to draw out God's power and meet Him halfway, thus sanctifying the point of contact between Creator and creation. And Vaishnavas – Hindu devotees of Vishnu, the preserver god – perform *pujas* ensuring that each aspect of reality is present to the other, thus experiencing not merely the oneness, but the relationship, of union with the divine.

In Deborah's actions lies the argument of the iconodulist, the defender of icons: Gods too remote from human life, too radically transcending of experienced and known reality must eventually be forgotten, as we can have no need of them. Her need to make all of life a sacred drama has a noble parentage. For Orthodox Christians, who have made icons one of the primary means of *deosis* (human participation in the divine), the Gospel of John's profession that "The Word became flesh and dwelt among us" signifies that it is possible to represent God iconically, for Christ's incarnation redeems and sanctifies all material life. Indeed, failing to include the earth, body, and matter in

God's redeemed creation is judged by the Orthodox to be the "heresy of docetism" – the erroneous opinion that the historical Jesus' body was merely "docetic," or semblance (*dokein*, to seem), not divine, and thus must be pushed into the background. According to Irenaeus, the second-century Greek theologian who expounded on the intellectual errors in diverse heresies, the icon – like earth itself, and historical time – "recapitulates" the mystery of Christ, manifesting the ongoing transformative power of Christ. Sanatanist Hindus, whose oblations to vivid representations of the gods and goddesses are particularly festive, subscribe to a similar understanding of the living involvement of the divine, with all of existence a source of sanctification. Deborah's actions exhibit a similar logic.

One feature of Deborah's liturgical life is the vast amount of time devoted to theurgical activity – ritual that draws out the saving divine power. Such activity is not utterly surprising, since it is the very absence of the gods in contemporary life that may produce, particularly among the highly sensitive, the preoccupation with calling them forth. As the famed scholar of classical religions E.R. Dodds once pointed out, "In an age of faith no one thinks of proving that gods exist or inventing techniques to induce belief in them."[21] Deborah may be but a vivid example of the fate of those with high degrees of discernment, in an age without faith. Beyond this explanation – which unfortunately runs the risk of sanctioning the acts of saints and neurotics indiscriminately – one might also recall that spirituality does not demand passive piety. Central to Judaism, for example, is the requirement to be a partner to God in the ongoing act of creation. This means not only repairing and preserving the created world, but even playing a part in perfecting it. The rite of male circumcision, for example, is predicated on the notion that God did not create a perfect world, but left something for humans to do. And the renowned Rabbi Judah Low, employing supernatural means to vanquish enemies, used the secret seventy-two-letter name of God to transform clay into a golem, a living being, to assist him in overcoming the abuse of Christian neighbours. By extension, Deborah's alchemical actions do not need to be censured as acts of hubris, but could be affirmed as acts of human ingenuity and participation in completing creation. While there are dangers in believing oneself to have the power of divination – it may destroy the virtue of hope and take away the power of accommodation – theurgical action is a bid to cause the numinous to stir in us, and an expression of the human need to be an active participant in the divine-human encounter.

While theurgy always risks being censured as presumption and arrogance, as if the priestess exalts herself as the magus who does not worship the divine but seeks to master it, what mutes this danger in Deborah is the background presence of an unwavering sense of the infinite, an awe of the sacred, and a sentiment of absolute dependence – call it, as William James does, a "faith-state." The sense of power and autonomy that may accompany devotional technique is not, in her case, permitted to run ahead of piety. Her experience of the sacred, for example, is one that both replenishes and terrifies, affirming both the potential for union with, and the utter transcendence of, the divine. Even her syncretic crafting of devotional practices and spiritual experiences is less an attempt to impose her own taste and style than a desire to suffer the vital unity of all existence and to bind together the fragments of life and existence.

Nonetheless, Deborah's magical conjuring of gods and goddesses – an intention and action replicated across the country in New Age sweat lodges, sweetgrass ceremonies, vision quests, Tantric sex workshops, yoga sessions, and Sufi ecstatic dancing – corresponds expressly to the syndrome so characteristic of baby-boom culture and consciousness: the strange conjunction of, and wavering between, assertive autonomy and enchantment. On the one hand, Deborah's life says, "I can go it alone," and she abjures community, church, and tradition. As another baby boomer commented, subscribing to a sense of devotion and opposition to authority similar to Deborah's, "It is easier for me to be ritualistic than doctrinal." Picking and choosing from among incompatible rituals and beliefs, Deborah elevates a "self" before whose bar of values all existence is to be summoned. The gods, her actions imply, are commanded to manifest themselves and trigger the moods, "meaningful" experience, or "special belonging" she desires. In this mode, the spiritual journey appears confined to self-realization, not self-transcendence – the traditional hallmark of religion. For Deborah, there is no clash between wanting to be spiritual and choosing one's own way, between worship and proud independence. And thus, perhaps, nothing truly lays its claim on her.

On the other hand, Deborah's life is a process of unending enchantment, as physiological functions, emotional states, animal behaviour, biological cycles of growth and decay, random events, fortuitous coincidences, and cosmic processes all indiscriminately become sources of delight and rapture, and she gives herself over to them entirely. That she sees herself solely as "a container for the influx of energy," has turned her will over to "the beings of the light," perceives all duality as illusion, and intones repeatedly, "Who knows what will happen," are indications that, at least in her interpretation, the most exalted state is one where she is nothing but a cipher, resonating instinctually with the modulations of beings around her. Unlike the sense of mystery where, in the face of wonder, one's intellectual curiosity is piqued and one remains detached and capable of acknowledging the claim placed upon one, enchantment renders one impassive and acquiescent.

The danger with enchantment is the loss of distinctions – between the fantastic and the significant, the irrational and the sublime, and, ultimately, between the human and the subhuman – for the power of judgment is significantly undermined. What is gained in immediacy is lost in depth and complexity. Her awe is not reverence, which would demand so much more of her than naturalistic magical effects. Deborah's spiritual experience, while vivid, displays little tendency toward maturation, either through an appreciation of the historical context of her beliefs or through a scale of value which would permit her to distinguish the more from the less developed. Despite the fact that one can see in her stylized rituals the long shadow of John Wesley's "holiness movement," most often it seems that many of her preoccupations, particularly those dwelling on physiological and emotional reactions, seem wholly out of proportion with their actual significance. There is a pattern of immoderation to her spirituality, an excessive materialism giving rise to an excessive supernaturalism.

There are tens of thousands of baby boomers like Deborah, who are content to forsake the world of facts and common sense and take a "leap of faith." This should not surprise us. In comparison to all previous generations, baby boomers may have been given the purest dose of modernity's confidence in technological progress and social revolution, but the boosterism was laced with an equally strong dose of absurdity. Literature and drama classes were heavily preoccupied with a philosophy of madness found in Samuel Beckett, Harold Pinter, and

Arthur Miller, among others. Baby boomers read out loud, performed, and editorialized on *Death of a Salesman, The Sandbox, The Birthday Party, Waiting for Godot.* From Joseph Heller's *Catch-22* and Ken Kesey's *One Flew Over the Cuckoo's Nest,* to Thomas Pynchon's *Gravity's Rainbow* and Kurt Vonnegut's *Slaughterhouse Five,* they were led into a widening gyre of lunacy. Ego-loss and madness, the literature said, are the only way to overcome the schizophrenia and absurdity of the world. Baby boomers festooned their bedroom walls with prints by Salvadore Dali, and those of the rediscovered Hieronymus Bosch, right next to the Apollo xi posters of the dark side of the moon.

In an age of widespread, paralyzing cynicism, the enthusiasts at SpiritFest '99, the persuaded readers of *The Celestine Prophecies,* the followers of the Course in Miracles and Pathworks, and Deborah all enjoy the enviable condition of having something to believe in. They have conviction in their hearts, even if scientific proof remains out of reach, akin to what St. Paul means by faith – "the assurance of what we hope for, the proving of what we cannot see."[22] Yet, at the same time, belief does not make truth. There is among many New Agers a tendency to conclude that "Since I believe it, it must be true." This fideism – the will to believe something, anything, even the most irrational, in preference to believing in nothing at all – risks rendering New Age devotees vulnerable to those whose shrewdness has honed in on the baby boomers' credulity. One of the striking paradoxes of baby boomers' spiritual searches is that most of them will not accept institutional or creedal authority, but are willing to hand over their minds and hearts to a spiritual director.

And much baby-boomer belief is conditioned by what it negates. Many baby boomers' early experience of the church – or at least the false memory of that experience – was that of the removed, judgmental, and punishing God. Now they wish for a loving, rather than a fearful, God – a nurturing, caring and affectionate divinity. They recollect their religious experiences as passive – empty ritual, authoritarian naysaying, hand-me-down faith – and now are nearly hyperactive in summoning forth the gods. Having lived without commitment to anything, even actively avoiding commitment, they now desire to commit totally. Responding to a God too exclusive and judgmental, they embrace a god so willowy as to be inconsequential. Rejecting religion that is one-sided – intellectual, authoritative, opposed to the body

– they adopt a spirituality equally unidimensional in accentuating only the beautiful, fulfilling, and moving. While affirming the opposite seems like a refutation of the first option, in reality the second option is only the reversed mirror image of the first, and thus is as incomplete as what it rejects. Only a synthesis at a higher level of affirmation could achieve what the baby boomers desire. Counterposing romance to reality does not change reality.

New Agers' romanticism and sentimentality, predicated on the desire to return to that oceanic bliss preceding entanglement with a malevolent world, are particularly evident in their view of nature and society. Returning to the body, physical nature, and primal elements (crystals, herbs, the original sounds of creation) invokes an image of nature for which one looks in vain in the complex reality of creation. The view overemphasizes beauty and harmony, while neglecting nature's tyranny, cruelty, and destructiveness. And it tends to reduce nature to the primitive, while ignoring nature's impulse toward complex organization and purpose. The chimerical view of nature is matched by a whimsical view of human society. Many New Agers long for covenantal communities – special settings of harmony and peace – consonant with their spiritual experiences of wholeness. Unfortunately, their dreams, like those of many academics who are "communitarians," are usually of human society without corruption, injustice, and domination. Like modern philosophers who dreamt that historical progress would culminate with heaven on earth, and whose fantasies have been invalidated by reality, the New Agers recall Buber's "I-Thou" relation – whose existential "mutuality" was intended to be a corrective to the detachment and manipulation of the "I-It" relationship – but unconvincingly fail to take evil seriously, an intellectual error Augustine diagnoses with unsurpassed clarity as human *amor sui*, self-infatuation. Omitting the facts of reality – in this case, the inescapable certainty of human mischief – renders the dream of perfection mere "idealism," and harbours the presumption that humans can recreate reality. After all, fairies, wizards, special powers, messages from the dead, and angels, apart from their whimsy, are also expressions of extravagant hope that the order of the world can be miraculously suspended. Often isolated in solitude, dwelling on the most interiorizing sensation – pain – it is little wonder that New Agers like Deborah come up with such unworldly, fantastic imaginings.

Their musings have an antediluvian quality, evoking the image of Adam, with all his magical and divine powers, before the Fall.

Self-divinization can take many forms, and even the most credible of those – individuals who turn to the East, and are specifically attracted to the teaching of finding the indwelling god – exhibit distinct New Age characteristics and reinforce cardinal features of baby-boom culture and consciousness. Take Harold, a university professor, an infinitely gentle, charming, peaceful person who was raised Anglican but is now, after many years of study with a Zen master and then some of Tibet's most enlightened lamas, a respected Tibetan Buddhist monk. He explains why he left Christianity: "The Church wasn't going along with the paradigm shift." First, there was the censoriousness of ministers. "Censoriousness is the hole that never lets the cup overfill with joy – the mind naturally goes where it is happy." There is a human need, Harold suggests, for a deep sense of joy – "Spirituality as joy is at odds with doctrine. Spirituality is beyond words." Second, Western thought persists as "mere monophasic consciousness, permitting only those experiences that are culturally mandated. It has no place for transformative experience. It insufficiently recognizes that consciousness confines and traps us."

As if executing the formula "abandoned by lover, turned to God," it was a shattered, disastrous romantic relationship that triggered Harold's recognition that consciousness was merely produced by acculturation, and that meditation allowed one to step back, become the watcher, and finally "taste of bliss." An early semi-psychedelic experience of a dove flying toward deep restfulness, a peaceful ocean, suggested to Harold that one's approach to being human entailed cutting off hindrances: "What engaged me, trapped me." Only Tibetan Buddhism gave Harold the experience of being "sweetly empty, knowing all things." "Buddhism doesn't foreclose. Its teachings are lies, but they produce realization. The thing is to penetrate through the illusion of objects and permanence. It's illusory to think you can specify experience with words."

"Maps are not terrains; Western thinking mistakes the pointing finger for the moon." For Harold, the error is particularly evident in Western religions. "Rituals are symbolic control systems. My generation was raised in legalistic Christianity. For most Jews, the ritual is never transcendent for them. All these realities are relative realities. We have to be conscious of the vehicle as vehicle." Harold came to the conclusion that "Western religions are religions which restrict consciousness and people in them are not joyful. Ministers and priests may have heard a bell, but they didn't know where it was coming from. The Jesus that matters is within you, he's just a map, a raft which you wouldn't want to keep when you get to the other side. Buddhism is not institutionalized. It's highly experimental, like the period of the early Gnostics. We're into another process of awakening."

That is also the view of the wandering kabbalah and Hassidic master Rabbi Laibl Wolf, who offers breathing and visualization tapes to bring the mind into the "quiet zone." His lectures provide techniques that "allow a meditative guided internalization of the powers of the four archangels, so that like the Creator we can create angels, access the 'letters of thought' of dreams." Hebrew letters as symbols of higher reality, altered states of consciousness, near-death phenomena. Mitzvoth and interconnectedness. How to identify the sefirotic flows comprising the spiritual energy of love. Breathing in the healing light of Ohr Hashem.

Notwithstanding the power of kabbalah, during the evening Rabbi Wolf spent with a crowd of baby-boomer professionals in the Nepean council chambers, he made the prudent announcement that "Kabbalah is not a compendium of magical potions, rules of tarot, zodiac-based predictions or techniques to gain clairvoyance." Faces visibly fell; the woman beside me rolled her eyes. "It is an ancient wisdom explaining the laws of spiritual energy in the cosmos." Attention riveted again on Wolf, and my neighbour smiled contentedly. Rabbi Wolf explained that the kabbalah contained a "psycho-social model" providing "ten tools for spiritual self-management leading to optimal mind and emotion expression." Tapping into his audience's evident years of experience in human development psychology, yoga, and cynical corporate projects to stimulate greater productivity, Rabbi Wolf continued:

You might have tried technologies of change, but none provided deep fulfillment. Now, the principles of Hasidic psychology, drawn from the Chabad Lubavitch Hasidic school, offers four keys: *emunah* – you must believe that you can change; *ratzon* – you must draw upon the strength of the personal will; *avodah* – you must know a technology of insight; and *oneg* – you must practice a technology of insight. In a world that lacks self-confidence and spiritual purpose, a proven system of transformation leading to fulfillment is essential. If we are to survive, society has to undergo a revolution in the perception of life's meaning. We must study the success stories of people who have survived challenge and societal change. Jewish history, the Diaspora – no other people has suffered such prolonged adversity and enjoyed such disproportionate success in host societies.

The kabbalah, he said, offers a "maintenance schedule for the temple of the soul. The world doesn't change independently of you. Only through your own personal transformation does it change shape." The single biggest stumbling block, Rabbi Wolf diagnosed, is the lack of unity and balance between mind and emotion. The energies of the sefirot (the ten aspect's of God's – or our own – inner being) must be arranged in a pattern of relationships, comprising *shekhinah*, God's presence in the world.[23]

> The individual is like an umbilical cord which is connected from the Unknowable Infinite, *ein sof*, to the spiritual realm humans inhabit, *assiya*. *Assiya* is the lowest of the four spiritual realms below *ein sof* – pointing upward to *yetzira, beriya, atzilut*. The mystical teachings of the kabbalah relate to the secrets of the fourth level, *atzilut*. The mind has the capacity to trick the body. We need re-balancing. The cornerstone of creation is "differentness," absolute individuality. A lot of people seek sameness, "differentness" frightens them. To be ensouled is to be different. But we experience many dualities – internal/external for example. Our purpose is to resolve all dualities into unities, bridging the chasm of "differentness."

Hebrew, Wolf continued, is a holy tongue. The twenty-two letters of the Hebrew alphabet correspond to vibrational forces in the sounds formed by the five parts of the mouth.

> When you call someone by name and get them to turn, you are touching their essence. Words are a blessing, a means to draw down a channel. We need to be wordsmiths, saying the right thing at the right time, bringing wisdom into the moment of decision.

Rabbi Wolf ended on a high note:

> The spiritual quest and search beckons so many in the world today
> as we approach the new millennium. There was a development of
> spiritual power during the sixties and seventies in the West that was
> "outward transforming." The eighties and nineties brought inward,
> egocentric transformations. I hope my humble contribution will
> help pave the way for all of us to sing the new song of personal and
> relational redemption.

Not surprisingly – in the context of Jewish mysticism sidling up to
New Age, and baby boomers needing to meet their inner selves, over-
come anger, abnegate the ego, bond in relationships, and awaken to a
New Dawn, all by a dash of word magic, secret truths, and supernatu-
ral powers – Rabbi Wolf's parting shot was to link kabbalah to *The
Celestine Prophecy*!

For Harold, like the self-expressed New Agers and would-be kabbal-
ists, prayer and meditation lead not to the presence and opening of the
world, but escape from it. We are back to ground zero, they all appear
to be saying, so let us go forth and recreate. Yet, one cannot help but
speculate that here is the wounded healer speaking, persuading others
that they need healing. And as *bricoleurs* – exhuming the shards of the
past, while roaming the world for stimulation – their actions resemble
those of Gnostic magi, reconstituting reality.

· · ·

If New Agers like Deborah and, arguably, Harold, were more self-
conscious about their experiences and devotional practices, they could
make a useful contribution to the re-spiritualization of ritual and
doctrine in mainstream religions. After all, on one reading, they enjoy
the exhilaration of contact with a depth of reality equivalent to that of
the prophets and seers of the germinal period in which most of our
major religions developed. But these baby boomers will never be self-
conscious because they are so deeply handicapped by ignorance of
their heritage. Sensitive to what is unacceptable about Christian institutions and traditions, they are usually utterly blind to what is best in
them, since, for many baby boomers, there is no historical context to

their beliefs. Leaving aside the irony that in all their escape from Christianity or Judaism – or, at least, a child's version of them – many baby boomers remain obsessively attracted to their rituals (think of Madonna). It is also the case that the spiritual searches of many baby boomers are exact re-enactments of old theological debates and ancient sectarian finger-pointing. In the first two centuries of the common era, there was lively debate between Encratites, Carpocratians, Cappadocians, Docetists, Gnostics, Arians, Nestorians, Colossians, Corinthians, Donatists, Alexandrian Jews, Pharisees, and Saduccees – not to mention the whole gamut of magicians, prophesiers, messianics, millennialists, and alchemists – with points of view encompassing nearly all of today's options. When many of these sects were denounced as heresies, thoughtful and persuasive theological and philosophical argument was marshalled to defend the position finally adopted. The great value in reacquainting oneself with the range of sectarian disagreement, and the arguments made on behalf of orthodoxy, is not only to understand what were often very sensible justifications for a line of theological argument approved by the church, but also, when those justifications are not sensible at all, to unearth restorative possibilities hiding in wait in this material with which present errors can be corrected. One author who has made a consummate contribution to such work is Elaine Pagels, whose study *The Gnostic Gospels* made plausible and attractive the docetic, gnostic, and spiritual Christianity rejected by the early fathers of the church when they favoured a Christianity that was catholic, universal, and incarnational. Another more informal assessment of the century of ferment in which Christianity took its present form is Paul William Roberts's elegant book *The Journey of the Magi*, which suggests that there were complex interactions between Persian Zoroastrians and Christian and Jewish sects, reassessment of which might serve as an antidote to today's resurgence of excessive doctrinalization among fundamentalists.

Instruction in the historical and philosophical origins of religious belief should be paramount in religious education, pastoral work, catechism classes, marriage encounters, and seminary training. But many faiths departed decades ago from this "dry" approach, focusing more on the experiential and personal dimensions of faith. In the absence of efforts to pass on a heritage of reasoned principles and systematic theology – especially to a generation with unprecedented levels of post-secondary education, and thus impatient with pat formulas and assurances – many faiths are leaving their followers with the mistaken impression that beliefs, doctrines, and practices are simply up for grabs (just a "bag of tricks, let's see if it works" as one baby boomer suggested to me). The reality is that there is hardly a denomination or sect whose theology is not built on an intelligible premise, with first-order principles and secondary practical precepts logically derived, or symbolically entailed, from that starting point.

In their spiritual searches, baby boomers generally work so hard at "cutting off hindrances to consciousness," to use Harold's felicitous phrase, that they are blind to the supports Christianity and Judaism, in particular, can provide. Especially those faiths now seeking to recruit lapsed believers and converts would, one expects, make every effort to make their religions rationally attractive, for without this basis, faith – however vivid and enthralling – is just another flavour of the month. A deeper knowledge of this heritage would go far in grounding and refining baby boomers' spiritual searches. It is questionable, however, whether the mainstream religions are in a position to offer such maturation.

Apparently legions away from the New Age spirituality exhibited in SpiritFest '99, *The Celestine Prophecy*, the Course in Miracles, and Pathwork is the Anglican Church's Alpha Program, one of the most successful and popular "seeker-sensitive" programs devised to lure baby boomers back to church and to address head-on the decline in participation in Christianity. The Alpha Program is the brainchild of Reverend Nicholas Gumbel – ex-lawyer and now pastor at Holy Trinity in Brampton, England – who designed it after assessing the answers to a questionnaire surveying what baby boomers wanted in religion. It comprises a ten-week course, plenty of personal testimonials, a "Holy Spirit" weekend away, and accompanying videos. At the Alpha Program, Gumbel avers, "It doesn't matter what denomination you belong to. What matters is your personal relation with Jesus." Christianity with a velvet touch? Proselytizing with gentleness and fun? Perhaps. Yet, as we will see, at many cardinal points, the Alpha Program and New Age keep close company.

The first video begins with "Nicki," casually dressed in chinos and a polo shirt, conducting an Alpha class. He offers his own case as testimony. As a lawyer, he had pondered why Christianity was boring and whether it was true or irrelevant. The church services he attended had not been "the most exciting, riveting, and inspiring occasion that I've been to." In his estimation at the time, God had left the Church and no one cared. Citing Robert Louis Stevenson's crack, "I've been to church today and wasn't depressed," Nicki admits he had other objections to Christianity, primarily that God was totally irrelevant to his life. But he also added that during this time he rarely enjoyed the present for the present's state, was always looking for the next goal, and felt that something was missing. The sense of aching loss and isolation, despite all his wealth and success as a lawyer, was only answered by Jesus. Answering the hunger for meaning and providing an answer to life's great riddle – this is what experiencing a relationship with Jesus offers. And such a relationship is finally what prevents the saddest thing in life – to go through it and miss the point. Looking back at his own rational objections to Christianity, Nicki advises that it is not intellectual assent, but a matter of the heart that is required. "I've spoken to him, I've experienced a relationship with him," and this above all provides the answer to the question "what meaning has my life that death does not question?"

Nicki's claim is supported by the testimony of two participants, James and Julia Thomas. As the camera scans the audience of young, laughing, beautiful people, James discloses that God was no part of his life until the Alpha Program and that he only attended, as a skeptic, to be a devil's advocate. Yet, after a number of weeks, James decided to pray for a physical sign. He wanted to "experience the Holy Spirit" and did not want "just an intellectual experience." Wonder of wonders, James was "hit by a 5,000-volt charge, thrashing through his body." Julia attests that she too prayed for the Holy Spirit and suddenly burst into tears, experiencing a great wave of relief, and knew it was God. They then discovered that church was "full of lively and normal people, a tremendous atmosphere." When Nicki asks, "Is there any proof that Jesus exists?" they cite the Holy Spirit and healing. Like Nicki, they now enjoy freedom from guilt and addiction, and get their freedom "through God and Christianity." The first talk ends with a prayer, "I am sorry for the things I have done wrong in my life .... I now turn from everything which I know is wrong," and an invitation to the Holy Spirit to descend.

The second lesson addresses "Who Is Jesus?" Nicki begins by citing a psychologist who says all of us are hungry for love, security, and significance. And "People are looking for someone upon whom they can model their life." Jesus satisfies this search in a way that no other personality can, because He was not merely a great human teacher but divine. How do we know? Nicki reminds his listeners of the miracles Jesus performed at parties, weddings, picnics, and funerals. And He appeared to 550 people on eleven different occasions. Under the circumstances, "Following Sherlock Holmes, when you've eliminated the impossible, what remains, however improbable, must be the truth." Jesus is God. "We thank you, Lord, for leaving us evidence, [that lets us know that it's] not just a blind leap."

Lesson three is, "Why and How Should I Read the Bible?" Again playing to baby boomers, Nicki enumerates the way God speaks to humans: peace, angels, audible voices, dreams, wills, and actions. Once this intervention in a seeker's life has transpired, Nicki comments, he or she must proceed to "go and tell, go and make disciples," and succour the discomforts of the casualties of society. As Christians, he advises, you are called "to be a light in the dark world, to be in but not of the world." Nicki ends by praising Billy Graham's conversion to Christianity, and proposes that, like him, "You can settle all your questions and problems by accepting Christ. You will be totally transformed." The illustration he offers is of a wife who was fed up with her husband for not being a Christian. Nicki calls the man up, who testifies that he has now converted from being an atheist, to which his wife adds, "He's gone from one extreme to another … it's the best present I could have received."

There is a lot of seductive pathos in Nicki's class, and a large part of it is a product of style and delivery. His charm and self-deprecating humour create an environment of jolly camaraderie and bonhomie. He is clearly on the side of the angels, gladly offers the helping hand of the Good Samaritan, and he walks the talk. He is neither censorious nor authoritarian, just "one of the chaps." The beautiful-people converts around him exude (conveniently for the uncommitted seeker) loneliness, confusion, and the frisson of discovered salvation. What baby boomer, craving belonging and desiring a high-volt blast of purification and transfiguration, could demur?

But the real draw of the Alpha Program is the message, for in so many ways it touches on baby boomers' deepest wishes. This in itself is, of course, no surprise, since the Alpha Program was designed to "meet the seeker where he or she is at." On the surface, the Alpha Program converts with a message that has a long pedigree: We are sinners, we can be reborn, Jesus Christ is the saviour, salvation is at hand, repent and convert. But lurking in the Alpha Program's delivery of this mission are the mordant additives of baby-boom culture and consciousness, threatening many traditional elements of mainstream Christianity. Who is this Jesus, for example, whom the Alpha Program says you can have a personal relationship with? He is not the Jesus of the Anglican Church (though there are many), for He is not a Jesus who represents the whole of Christendom with its ecclesiastical hierarchies, sacerdotal authority, and established books of prayer and hymn. Indeed, the Alpha Program is virtually silent about the church – as if God goes directly from heaven to the soul of the baby-boomer seeker, and as if the charismatic gifts that are necessary for the perfect life will reach men without administration of sacraments. He is not the Jesus who mediates God and the world, and ties Christians to their worldly vocations, since the world is "dark," and converts are to be in, but not of it. This is also not a Christian teaching which adopts the traditional view that grace perfects nature. Instead – much like Protestant fundamentalism – the Alpha Program conceives a cataclysmic and miraculous intervention, with deliverance from the darkness of nature.

Despite Nicki's comments to the contrary, Alpha does ask for a leap of faith – not a blind one, but neither is the process of conversion a systematic review of the reasoned principles of one's life and the rational adoption of new ones. It is essentially picking a new paradigm – and what a paradigm shift! Like James, the star of Alpha's first video lesson, the convert can anticipate a "thrashing" change of being – no baby boomer will have her or his "ecstasy deficit" ignored. But Alpha also successfully fits a baby boomer's "comfort zone." As Janet, Alpha's coordinator for Canada, comments, "It's very non-confrontational. Churches are growing, ministers are excited. It's so cheering sharing faith with people you don't know." Indeed, by her account, many "computer programmers, robotic engineers, many very scientific people are finding a personal faith in the Alpha Program," evidently finding no contradiction between their technological jobs, which sustain man's dream of the total conquest of existence, and their Christian stewardship. Janet, a baby boomer who, at the start of her spiritual journey "did the New Age, yoga, mysticism route," also disclosed three other reasons for baby boomers' attraction to Alpha: "Not following doctrine and rules, Jesus is empowering you …. Christ pays the penalty for us. It's as if we haven't sinned at all …. I've felt closer to this group than any other in my life." And, reminiscent of all baby boomers impatient with the non-finality of the Human Question (what is the meaning of life?), and in constant, nearly obsessive, search of closure in the Big Answer, she concludes, "I've arrived now; there's nothing else out there – this is it."

Well, not quite arrived. There appears to be one niggling issue upon which she broods. "In Greek, Holy Spirit is neuter. Jesus makes a deliberate grammatical error in calling the Holy Spirit 'he.' The Holy Spirit is not an it, the Holy Spirit is a person." It is not surprising that Janet should focus on the Holy Spirit to voice both her enthusiasm for, and expectations of, the radical potential of the Alpha Program. The Alpha Program's highlight is the "Holy Spirit" weekend. Whatever else can be said of this glowing, God-intoxicated, weeping, speaking-in-tongues, bonding vacation to *illus tempore* (primordial time) – still raved about years later when many Alpha participants graduate to the "Cursillo" – the focus on the "Holy Spirit" itself is a suggestive concept. No Thomas à Kempis's *De Imitatione Christi* for baby boomers here, when the "Holy Spirit" offers an infinitely more obliging image of God: who hovers over the primal chaos when God created the world; who spoke through the prophets; who descends like a rush of wind and flame, incinerating old personalities; who, as an agent of regeneration, renews creation and fulfils all the biblical promises by creating a new heaven and earth; and, who evokes the sense of movement and the prospect of recreating the world continually. Thich Nhat Hanh, a Vietnamese Buddhist monk of much renown among baby boomers, writes, "It is safer to approach God through the Holy Spirit than through theology …. Discussing God is not the best use of our energy. If we touch the Holy Spirit, we touch God not as a concept, but as a living reality."[24] And, most importantly, as Reverend Barbara (not her real name) of St. Paul's Episcopal Church in Vancouver explains, unlike God or Jesus – the one as Father, the other who carries the baggage of saying "you're not okay, you're not part of the church" – "the Holy Spirit is generic and non-gendered."

Reverend Barbara's own pet project speaks directly to the first term, indirectly to the second. Earthy, gutsy, and outspoken, the Reverend is deeply committed to a re-spiritualization of the Anglican Church and to social justice. Fortunately, so is her bishop – Bishop Michael Ingham, famous (to some, infamous) for his private approval of same-sex marriages, multi-faith and multicultural ecumenicism, and a general liberalization of Christianity. He was also one of the disappointed delegates to the 1999 Lambeth Conference in Britain, where a resounding vote against the liberalization of the Anglican Church took place. Nevertheless, radicalization continues apace, and Bishop Ingham and Reverend Barbara play their parts.

In the case of Reverend Barbara, radicalization takes the form of the labyrinth of St. Paul's, created in January 1997. Modelled on the labyrinth at Grace Cathedral in San Francisco – itself a replica of the labyrinth at Chartres Cathedral in France – the labyrinth at St. Paul's, while modest, still fosters all the symbolism and spiritual potential of its glitzier parents. When you enter the church hall, you are inclined to miss the labyrinth, since, unlike country-fair mazes constructed of hedgerow (purportedly the work of the devil because, unlike a labyrinth, mazes have no centre and no exit), it is merely painted on the floor. More likely, your attention will initially be drawn to the vivid stained-glass medallions around the hall, depicting among other themes the tree of life, the Tetragrammaton, and Lucifer, the fallen angel. When your eyes finally drop to the floor, you spot the labyrinth – forty-two-foot-wide swaths of purple paint in three concentric arcs on each side of the centre. Simple, yet tantalizing.

You enter the beginning of the labyrinth boldly, but are immediately ensnared by a succession of short arcs that return you repeatedly back to the beginning, bedevilling expectations of immediate access to the interior. Then you are invited into a perambulation which transports you right around the centre – the tease – but then instantly you are cast into tightly arced routes which, like life's setbacks, take you progressively farther away from the centre. Then, another flirt to the centre in full confidence of reaching the goal – ever so close – before middle-sized arcs, which act as wrong turns, take you back to the outer periphery though, at one point, nearly returning you to the very beginning. Then a series of very wide swaths of passage, encircling the entire labyrinth and encouraging confident, even bold steps. The arcs diminish, and appear to be taking you back to the beginning again, but, with one last detour, you are cast into the centre and the end. Or maybe the beginning.

Labyrinths are as old as the Greek myth of Theseus and the Minotaur – the Greek myth which tells of Theseus, the son of King Aegeus, who insists on being one of the youths of Athens sacrificed annually as tribute to the monster. But Theseus vows to kill the Minotaur and promises his father that, if successful, he will replace his ship's black sails with white ones. Ariadne, daughter of King Minos, falls in love with Theseus and gives him a magic ball of thread to be dropped at the entrance of the labyrinth. As Theseus makes his way to the Minotaur, he unwinds the thread. Facing the monster, he kills it and follows the thread back to the entrance. The tale, however, ends tragically: On the way home, Theseus forgets to raise the white sails, and King Aegeus – in grief – drowns himself in the sea that will come to be known as the Aegean. A golden plate commemorating Theseus's victory once resided at the centre of Chartres Cathedral's labyrinth. It too had a bad ending – stolen, and probably melted down, during the French Revolution.

Native American Hopis have labyrinths which they see as mother earth. In Catholicism, the church as the mystical body of Christ is the centre of the world. If you can't make the pilgrimage to Jerusalem – a surefire way of obtaining an indulgence – a spiritual labyrinth will do. The labyrinth in Chartres was built after the first Crusade.

Mircea Eliade suggests that the labyrinth is a pictogram of a ritual of ascent. Just as ritual chants or recitation of names may move one from one level of cosmic being to another, so the steps and paths of the labyrinth are a quest for divine being. A labyrinth's various swaths are homologous to the traditional notches on a sacred pillar, suggesting the stages through which one must ascend to the Real. The arcs are also ways to protect the pilgrims from the intensity of the centre, for this is no mere terminus point, but the cosmic centre itself. As such, it is meant to be obscured from the uninitiated, and gaining admission is intended to be a hard process because the move from profane to sacred is arduous. Entry into the centre is intended to institute healing and hence repeat the act of creation.

In mythic life, every aspect of being has its analogies and homologues. The human soul, for example, exactly repeats the pattern of the visible world, which precisely mirrors the nature of God. Designed with analogue and homologue in mind, the labyrinth is a spiritual journey toward the centre of one's own being, which turns out to be the centre of the cosmos, and thus of God. Eliade suggests that the labyrinth is also a cosmogram – a map of our souls, the cosmos, and God. Each cycle of progress is, at the same time, a progressive interiorization. The centre, shaped either as a thirteen-point star or a six-leaf clover, is like a mandala, linking one's physical and spiritual core to the order of the cosmos. In ancient times, many Christians believed that the labyrinth's centre contained the tree of life. It was intended to be inaccessible and hidden, guarded by monsters. Ancient lore also held that the Cross, upon which God as Christ was crucified, was made of the tree of life. That is why the centre of the labyrinth – said to confer youth, life, and immortality – is, in fact, death. It is emptiness and submission, though perhaps also rebirth to new life and, if not quite endless life, then eternal life.

At St. Paul's Episcopal Church, the labyrinth is no longer an object of idle curiosity, though it was when it was first denounced as pagan. It draws lots of women, Jews, Buddhists, and Wiccans. Some are looking for "zippy magic" and other thrills, Reverend Barbara admits. Once, some teens used it to do a sacred rave, and people come to pray for friends and the planet. But mostly it brings the sick, the confused, the bereaved, the wounded. It has become part of the annual British Columbia HIV/AIDS Conference. Some people use it as part of the Alcoholics Anonymous twelve-step program. Some walk the labyrinth before serious surgery. Lots of people walk the labyrinth crying the whole way, but, despite lots of pain, Reverend Barbara relates, they also experience a felt sense of prayer and a sentiment that they are approaching what they are looking for. Some find themselves weeping about a death years ago, not realizing how deeply troubling it had been. Others walk the labyrinth smiling and spaced out. Some carry a rosary, some their journals, others just like to sit in the centre. Some walk around the labyrinth with Walkmans to the sound of the music of twelfth-century mystic Hildegard von Bingen. One young man with secular parents believed himself to be anti-religious, walked the labyrinth, had a profound experience, and knew he believed in God.

Reverend Barbara likes to just walk to the centre. She never wears her clerical collar in the labyrinth – that reminder of being collared to the church, a remembrance of the collar around Christ's neck on the route up to Golgotha. Like many walkers, she strongly feels the energy, and will often create a mantra to take her mind from "the busyness of life, the surface stuff, and move into a lower level." Here, in the labyrinth, she feels the Holy Spirit. There is no judgment and anger, no exclusion, none of the baggage of the church. Chartres Cathedral, Reverend Barbara recollects, was the most primal and feminine of Europe's cathedrals. What struck her in particular was the "earthy humour" of the art. "It is about grounding and being centred. That is why Buddhists and Wiccans come here. Wiccans – that's an inflammatory word, some are respectable. For my tribe, be they Wiccan or Buddhist or Christian, it's a spiritual journey, as opposed to people who acquire more and more stuff." Later, a friend of Reverend Barbara's confirms that one of the tribes Reverend Barbara named was indeed her tribe.

> I got to the point that I had to abandon my intellectual engagement with the Bible. The evangelicals are so focused on the others they denounce, it's just "true believerism": You have to believe what I believe. They're worse than zealots. I'm a liberal theologian – it's about how do you make room for people. The Holy Spirit evokes the sense of movement, of recreating the world continually. People aren't in church because of what happened in the fifties – there was no transformation or experience. At most churches, nothing is happening, it's so boring. And then there's the Lambeth Conference – those fuckers.

The "fuckers" were mostly men, Reverend Barbara has no compunction in mentioning. And many women baby boomers on spiritual walkabout would agree. But then, even today's New Age man probably agrees. While no faith or denomination can any longer ignore the question of gender, it is New Age thinking which in particular calls traditional religious gender stereotyping into question. It is not surprising that the division of the sexes is a perennial theme in religious writing, since the separation of male from female is a reflection of the human alienation from God. Indeed, the height of religious experience is often symbolized as a reunification of male and female, either in divine bisexuality or in androgyny, as image of the whole human being. And New Age, in principle, takes reflection on what a complete humanity is down a path which has the potential of producing a new relationship between men and women that may be significant enough to be a legacy to civilization. For the moment, however, it contributes to a significant widening of the gap between women and men.

The Vatican's Sacred Congregation for the Doctrine of the Faith restated in 1995 that the teaching stipulating that women cannot be ordained is "infallible." While many faiths and denominations hold a more liberal perspective, for many women, the Roman Catholic position is merely the most visible sign of a deep anti-woman mentality pervading many religious traditions. Whether Eve is blamed for the expulsion from Eden, or women's menstruation is a sign of their impurity, or the fact that none of Christ's disciples were women is interpreted as a sign of their inadmissibility to ecclesiastical ministry, or women must hide their "natural lasciviousness" under heavy veils or undergo surgery to mute their sexual desires, a long pedigree of denying women full religious status mars our histories. For many women, the problem lies much deeper than the formal exclusion or inclusion of women in religious life. Overcoming androcentric language is also not sufficient. What is needed, they say, is a fundamental reconceptualization of God. We must, as Elizabeth A. Johnson sums it up, "transform our over-masculinized culture." And, if the mainstream religions will not undertake such reform, New Age provides alternatives.

Until "God" is relieved of His attributes as angry Father in judgment, as radically transcendent deity who is forceful and exclusive, eschewing the processes of nurturing and generating, there can be no end to the derision of women, claim religious feminists and New Agers. The "Sophia movement" is one answer to the need for a new image of God. It has generated a lively literature, pushing Sophia or Gaia, as images fitting a theology which would celebrate the entire planet as a unified organism and recognize the menstrual cycle, childbirth, and caregiving as ways to acknowledge the sacredness of female experience and the empowerment of women.[25] One of the finest works of feminist theology is Elizabeth A. Johnson's study *She Who Is: The Mystery of God in Feminist Theological Discourse.*

*God is dead.* So Nietzsche tells us, and so Martin Heidegger, *the* philosopher of the twentieth century, repeats. In our times, after ages of conquest and militarism, after the corrosion and inanition of our rationalistic ideals, after hierarchies based on fear and arrogance, after

Auschwitz, after generations of discrimination, exclusion, and control – all projects bolstered by the certainty of religious truth – we can no longer sustain the God of the Pentateuch, or the Old Testament, or of childhood memory and actor Charlton Heston's fame – God as King and Father. And, arguably, the old God who demanded our intellectual attention, who insisted on the obedience of our emotions and bodies, and who obliged us to subordinate the earthly to the celestial, now dead, has left us to recover what He had so ruthlessly oppressed. Citing Heidegger's death knell for the God of theism, Johnson writes: "Man can neither pray nor sacrifice to this god. Before the *causa sui*, man can neither fall to his knees in awe nor can he play music and dance before this god."[26]

Women, in particular – in the "context of myriad sufferings resulting from women being demeaned in theory and practice in contradiction to the creative power, dignity and goodness that women appreciate to be intrinsic to their own human identity"[26] – need a God of powerful, compassionate love. Such a God will permit women to focus on the graciousness of divine mystery, relate to the intrinsic relatedness to the world, form alliances with human flourishing, and undertake liberating care for the poor. To speak of God/She, thus generating new contexts for references to the deity, is to appeal to nurturing traits of gentleness and compassion, reverence and care for the weak, sensitivity, the desire not to dominate, and unconditional love.

Men, who share women's wish for a more feminine God, often evoke the image of Mary as mother and virgin, an option Johnson derides as "coming nowhere near summing up the totality of what is possible for women's self-realization."[28] Closer to the mark is recovering the idea of God as breath (*ruah*), not just Father (*abba*), or – as can be found in kabbalistic texts – God as She-Who-Dwells-Within (*shekinah*). Such images, which invoke the experience of divine aliveness gracing all creation, do not mistake God as a static Being or noun (*esse*), but reaffirm God/She as a predicate nominative, "to be."[29] Word and Logos, the old supports rationalizing hierarchy and control, must be replaced by Wisdom and Love. Sophia, alluded to in the first nine chapters of Proverbs, meets the new requirements – a female personification of God's own being, the feminine spirit of wisdom, in creative and saving involvement with the world.

Quite apart from women's need for a religion closer to their own experiences – liberation from lived oppression, openness toward infinite mystery as disclosed in personal intimacy – the old symbols just will not wash today.[30] "The triune symbol and thought to which it gives rise have become unintelligible and religiously irrelevant on a vast scale, appearing as esoteric doctrine that one could well do without."[30] Contemporaneously relevant symbols, like fire and light, must speak of a radiance that flashes out in unexpected ways in the midst of our broken world (*kabod*).

Apart from finding restorative possibilities within our own Western traditions, feminists are also examining alternative options. Susan Starr Sered's book *Priestess, Mother, Sacred Sister: Religions Dominated by Women* roots among the ancestral cults of the Black Caribs in Belize, the zār cult of North Africa, the Sande secret society of Sierra Leone, and Afro-Brazilian religions. These movements, she argues, are akin to women's religions for they do not engage in missionary work, their ceremonies are innovative and personal, demonstrations of emotion are respected, and sympathy and nurturing are central.

Legions away from "ecological spirituality" is the world of Louis Farrakhan, the Nation of Islam, the 1996 Million Man March, and Robert Bly's "men's movement." Yet, ironically, the call to men's self-sufficiency and spiritual worth could be – at a metaphysical level – the kissing cousin of Sophia theology.

Robert Bly's manifesto, *Iron John: A Book About Men,* stems from his assessment that one of the major sources of social disorder is fatherlessness – the absence of strong men as heads of families. In a world where men are invited to be in touch with their feminine side – however "life-preserving" this may be – there is no "energy," no "life-giving" power. "We are living at an important and fruitful moment now," Bly writes, "for it is clear to men that the images of adult manhood given by the popular culture are worn out; a man can no longer depend on them."[32]

Bly distinguishes between two types of men: Savage Man, who damages the earth, the soul, and humankind, and who knows he is wounded but does not examine it, and Wild Man, who examines wounding, and is able to transform himself into Zen priest, shaman, or woodsman, and undertake forceful action. But because our society continually feminizes men toward gentleness – and here Bly points the finger particularly at "the ethical superstructure of Christianity [which] does not support the Wild Man" – Wild Man is suppressed, and one sign of the anguish of soft men is the periodic eruption of acts by Savage Man. Real men, Bly contends, are looking for a Second King – they have a need for father and mentor connections, which help them bring the interior warrior back to life. While the Golden Ball of wholeness and radiant energy, known in childhood, is gone, it lies within the magnetic field of Wild Man to retrieve it. For this to happen, he must learn to worship the animal soul – and voyage to "a time before time." To evoke such a "time," Bly uses fairy tales, medieval myths, and rituals from Hawaii, Mayan culture, and Tibet which, together with ecstatic drumming and primordial chanting, let men express their primitive masculinity.

The "men's movement" aims at restoring wholeness to men, though its modus operandi is often to point an accusing finger at feminists' success in reshaping the image of maleness. To illustrate, Robert Moore suggests that exaggerated attention to feminine identity, or the preoccupation with seeing all male behaviour as patriarchal, has left men at a low level of maturation and in unresolved, bipolar "boyhood" states – either the tyrant or the weakling, the impotent or addicted lover, the high-chair Lord Fauntleroy or Weakling Prince, the Dreamer or Mama's Boy.[33] Only a return to deeply expressive, primordial rituals, ceremonies, and symbols can constitute a sufficient crucible in which authentic King, Warrior, Magician, or Lover can be formed.

Phil, an engineer from Vancouver – burly and strong – has just slipped out of Baba Haridass's afternoon ashtanga yoga session on Salt Spring Island. This visit to the island is a "one-off" for Phil, since he is really only at home with the "poet-bard, the jester – Bly." "Meditation is just a crutch," he editorializes on the last half-hour of physical contortions. "I use it to escape the shit of the world, it's just a bag of tricks."

> This guy [Baba Haridass] has a good retirement plan, but he's just rearranging the deck chairs, and some of the chair legs are broken; it's all drama. But there's also no alternative. All the mainstream religions say to me is something like "One day you're going to die – have a nice day." Bly's right – it's the Wild, Wild West out there. And we can't rely on the past. All our myths need desperately to be

re-examined. Our history is nothing but man's stupidity in chrono-logical order. All the great men of the sixties and seventies – like Lyndon B. Johnson – were terrible. An incredible lie it all was. It was good in the seventies when we raised hell with the old men. We have to be aware of the giants whose shoulders we're standing and piss-ing on. But now we're in need of extreme fundamentals.

Phil is looking for "extreme fundamentals." After his first marriage collapsed, he took the blame upon himself and experimented with monastic life for a year. Immensely depressed, he went into psychotherapy and the therapist taught him to meditate and use yoga as a tool. He was attracted to its exotic medley of sounds and postures. Since then, he has remarried twice, stopped working for a ten-year period, separated from his latest wife and son, and begun participating in a men's group in Vancouver. "Men are emasculated, the survival thing bonds us. We're in search of constructive relations with men, to combat our fear and terror, perpetuated by our mothers. Our ideas of intimacy are a joke, especially marriage – it's just legalized prostitu-tion." Phil's father provided little comfort and no direction – he was an alcoholic and a redneck.

Additional troubles befell Phil. His wife became sick – "I've been giving, giving, giving, with no taking or receiving." Small businesses with which he was involved collapsed. "We've got all these silent part-ners – landlords, insurance companies, power companies, who say they are entitled to 10 per cent profit. We each own one six-billionth of the earth. I don't remember selling my air and oil. Being nobody, going nowhere – that was me, just massively supporting the economy."

His strongest childhood memory was hearing the story of David and Goliath in Sunday School at the age of five. In his impressionable mind at the time, he associated the story with the idea that all big men get killed. He was big and it terrified him. "I thought it would all be angels and fun, and then this thing came down. I left and never went back to church." Baba Haridass became a mentor, a father figure. "My own father just flipped – he was always casting aspersions on Pakis." The guru taught him to endure extended yoga. "I remember once meditat-ing eight hours a day, every day for twelve days. After this, there were tears streaming down my face, suddenly I was back at eight years old, making models." When they met, Baba Haridass would usually ask him, "How's life?" Shortly after Phil's wife became ill, Baba Haridass asked, "How's wife?" and Phil just stood and cried his eyes out. Baba Haridass gave him a *saddhana* – a training exercise in spiritual discipline – and he felt like he was back to the beginning of creation. "We need magic – the Franciscans and the Mormons understand that. It's not about reason and cheap talk. Endorphins show there is a pre-intellective interaction between people. We lost a lot of experience with the displacement of the olfactory sense. You have to have your feet on the ground and your head in the clouds."

Today Phil teaches Tai Chi in Vancouver. He's fighting unwanted thoughts, but finds he can barely cope with society. His thoughts run to the fear of global catastrophe, survivalism, and what he can contribute once rebuilding the world begins. "We've got all these store-houses of energy, and no old-time work ethic. We have to build tribal communities, eighty to a hundred people, maximizing economy of scale with existing technology – self-sustaining, bartering, no taxes." Occasionally, he starts smoking cigars, drinking, prowling the strip clubs, then remembers the space Baba Haridass has created, and the intimacy of his men's group, and stops. He says he wants a team – a home that is protection and safety. Phil explains:

> We're awake in the last eight seconds before midnight. Everybody is on edge – look at the drive-by shooting, the road rage. We're being dissed – no one can handle insult or dishonour without taking extraordinary action. There's no remorse, it's just vanished. Robert Bly explains why we're so removed from remorse, honour. We're all just isolated people – men who can't hug each other.

"The dearth of hardship – that's what people are experiencing in all this spiritual stuff," Phil concludes. "The badge in the future won't be biggest salary, fastest computer, smartest wife. The biggest thing will be spiritual experience – this is all about power and tribe."

Phil's self-analysis is a rich commentary on the heady decades through which he has lived, particularly as registers of the changing roles of the sexes. In December 1970, following two years of public investigation and hearings, the Report of the Royal Commission on the Status of Women was tabled in the House of Commons, capping a decade of intensive politicking by the women's movement to bring about an overdue recognition of women as full equals. Equal pay for work of equal value, access to managerial positions, maternity leave, and educational opportunities – all rightly adopted in recognition of equality of opportunity for all Canadians. It was inconceivable to subscribe to any other notion, least of all that women were passive and dependent, emotional and irrational, or – of all things – sinful, by nature. The women with whom most baby boomers grew up were the exact opposite – mothers who were modern and progressive, sisters with serious occupational ambitions, remarkable women professors, and accomplished wives. It was repugnant to think that anyone could, even residually, hold the undemocratic sentiment that there were gradations of privilege and superiority. If the recognition of women's equality came to focus almost exclusively, and thus narrowly, on equal access to the workplace – in turn engendering the whole new problem of latchkey kids who lacked sufficient family roots – the potential expanding larger civilizational forces was nevertheless indisputably positive. The ascendancy of women's lives, and, in particular, the valorization of their distinct experiences, augured well for the pending reassessment of what a more complete image of a human being could be.

What was more problematic was the vacuum that women's advancement left for the legitimate role of men. In the past, work and war were the traditional venues for the formation of masculinity, but, in the sixties, these became disenfranchised as authentic modes of being. The television series *Father Knows Best,* not to say *Leave It to Beaver,* were already dated when they aired in the late fifties and early sixties. Looking back, their depictions of the proper relation between men and women were simply laughable. The post-Vietnam perspective on war, bared in such gritty, hard-hitting movies as *The Deer Hunter* and *Apocalypse Now,* once and for all destroyed the glamour of battle, that activity which was the natural corollary of men's workaday world. But, in society's headlong transformation of the image of femininity, masculinity remained undefined – other than the vague notion that, like women, men should be caring and nurturing. For some men, however, a process of the feminization of culture had befallen North America, leaving them only two options – men could be either "brutes" or "saps." Men's identity, not to say a renegotiated understanding of the relation between men and women predicated on a need to abandon traditional notions of "manliness," remained unfinished business for the baby boomers, awaiting future resolution, but the delay inflicted a culpable toll on marriages, workplace etiquette, and the care of children in the eighties, as unspent potential percolated.

The need to redefine masculinity, and Phil's difficult search for a resolution, is a symptom of what is transpiring in all the spiritual searches we have examined. Looking for wholeness, and equipped with prodigious self-consciousness about the nature of the axial times in which we live, baby boomers have an opportunity to reconcile the powerful divisions of modern life and stimulate ways of being in the world with a heightened sense of personal life, community, and transcendence. Yet, after abandoning modern ideas of the individual and formal equality before the law in favour of a descent into primordial emotions, many of these searches conclude with the discovery of a clash between the most elementary psychobiological impulses (forcefulness and gentleness, battle whoops and empathy tears). Instead of looking upward to a coincidence of opposites – the most traditional symbol of spiritual transcendence – and encouraging the spiritual fertility which comes from their union, the search for wholeness is played as a zero-sum game, where the differences are just variations in quanta of power. SpiritFest, *The Celestine Prophecy*, A Course in Miracles, the Pathwork, and many of these other diversions of enchantment each in their own way trivialize the opportunity for transcendence by isolating aspects of reality from one another, and seeing any gain of one as a loss to the other.

· · ·

However distinctive each of the spiritual searches of this chapter is, they comprise a set of experiments with a family resemblance that could be labelled "fusion faith." Fusion faith is a medley of traditions, forms of worship, devotional practices, spiritual experiences, and religious beliefs. Like fusion cuisine, it takes the best from each tradition and blends all these prime ingredients into a new concoction, often with a panache that makes the original seem dry and outworn. By necessity, it is antinomian – impatient with custom, adaptable, often brooding and apocalyptic, and rarely does it persist over time. Fusion faith is oblivious to the fact that there are gross contradictions and incompatibilities between its elements, favouring dynamism and drama over coherence and subtlety. Like all the fusion trends in ascendancy throughout popular culture, fusion faith is often aesthetically stylish, seductive, and arousing.

Fusion faith is, in many ways, the apotheosis of baby-boom culture and consciousness, for it accentuates virtually every pure impulse, and harbours every idiosyncrasy: the need to touch the really *real*, accompanied by antinomianism; the hope of renewing creation, driven by the dream of a wholly new creation; the astute realization that modernity's false declaration that "God is dead" led only to making immanent reality the substitute ground of existence, but then led to the total repudiation of the mystery dimension in the everyday; the return to a tradition of worship, compromised by the right to pick and choose; the ascendancy of spiritual experience, as long as it is measured exclusively by personal fulfillment; the longing for covenantal communities, often exhibiting nothing more than the need to be part of something that is happening; the yearning for an indwelling presence of the divine in the world, radicalized to mean a secret self; the noble goal of reunifying the male and female principles, transformed to a hardening of differences; the search for spiritual exaltation, cheaply transmuted into a trigger for the next thrill; the hunger for transformation, imperilled by the wish for instant gratification, like James who, at first prayer, awaits the prospect of a 5,000-volt charge thrashing through his body, or Reverend Barbara, who walks directly to the centre of the labyrinth – illustrations betraying the absence of systematic, self-controlled spiritual discipline.

In some ways, none of these dreams and syndromes are particularly novel. Indeed, so expressive of our times, everything old is being recycled and experienced as new again. Some baby boomers are acting out the Pelagian heresy: We not only deserve grace when we live holy lives, but we actually merit it, and our own natural power is sufficient to achieve our destiny. Others are embracing the old Donatist perspective that ministers and believers must "walk the talk," that only the few within "the community of saints" are chosen. Various baby boomers are like the Essenes (of Dead Sea Scroll renown), renunciating ordinary life, giving up property and wealth, and living in communes to await the miraculous coming. Embracing "voluntary simplicity," or escaping urban decay for recovery in the wilderness, for that matter, goes little further than the renunciation of the Benedictines or the self-denial of the ancient mendicant orders of Franciscans and Dominicans. When baby boomers demand a faith which highlights private conscience and personal fulfillment, it is not so much a repudiation, but an extension, of Martin Luther's declaration, "Here I stand," and his advocacy, on behalf of a conciliar rather than an episcopal faith based on sacerdotal authority, for a "priesthood of the believer." When baby boomers ignore theology and ecclesiology, preferring to attend to practices which purge and purify, they harken back to Wesleyan Methodists, the holiness movement, and the Anabaptists. It was not baby boomers who began a tradition of seeing God in personal experience – the lives of Teresa of Avila, John of the Cross, Catherine of Genoa, and Ignatius of Loyola provide significant evidence of that. Nor is it unique to baby boomers to engage in "cognitive bargaining," to use Peter Berger's term for baby boomers' eclectic choosing of rituals, since forms of worship are never wrought in stone. If Tertullian's statement, "The glory of God is the human fully alive," is to be taken seriously, human creativity is invited to share in God's activity in continually renewing creation.

Often, dismissive judgments about the New Age simply reveal ignorance about the complex historical richness of our religious traditions. In many regards, fusion faith repeats the extraordinary ferment from China to the Mediterranean of a time that Karl Jaspers calls "the axial period" two and a half millennia ago.[34]

What distinguishes fusion faith from each of these distinct theological options, and from earlier periods of experimental syncretism, however, is the distended individualism at its centre. This individualism assertively relegates to itself the authority to use and discard. Its global reach and absence of shame or piety often renders fusion faith simply vulgar. Fusion faith revels in a glut of options, allowing baby boomers to want it all and have it all, for a time, for a spin: eco-feminist spirituality, aboriginal spirituality, men's spirituality, creation spirituality, recovery spirituality, earth-centred spirituality, goddess spirituality, and, for some, a leavening of Tridentine Catholic spirituality, evangelical spirituality, kabbalah, or Eastern spirituality. Rooting around this endlessly tantalizing potpourri, baby boomers are fulfilling Ralph Waldo Emerson's philosophy that we are entitled to an inexhaustible supply of possibilities and satisfactions. It is as if to say, there is a global spiritual heritage out there, there for the reclaiming, and here is a licence to raid tradition after tradition for stimulation. "I will assemble my own high altar as the axis of the cosmos, and if I wish to wear a tallith and doven, or link sweats with Gregorian chants, or be a pagan but enjoy incense, then I am entitled to do so," the baby boomer asserts by his or her actions. Under these circumstances, experiential religion becomes extravaganza religion, and the cluster of ideas becomes a clutter. There is so little sign that the mystery of existence is being deepened.

Fusion faith is unique in its reaching back to the pre-modern era to accelerate civilization into the postmodern era, and, as such, should be a candidate for the benefaction of St. Jude, the patron saint of hopeless cases. Ancient metaphysics were established on, and derived from, an intellectual apprehension of the universal ground of reality. That ground conferred coherence, a hierarchy of priorities, and overarching purpose to existence. Because of a solid foundation, aesthetic delight in playing with forms of worship could be indulged. But resurrecting the beauty and pageantry of the ancient metaphysic, while denying its claim to truth, risks sending the natural playfulness of religious celebration into freefall. Play on the surface is a posture, a style, an affectation, an indulgence. Like fusion cuisine, it is big on ornament and sizzle, little on substance, leaving one hungry for more. Fusion faith is soul candy, but too much of it, like a sugar high, produces zing, but no staying power. It is neither intellectually nor spiritually demanding, giving rise to neither fidelity nor discipline, yet parades as a grimly solemn commentary on modern life. Fusion faith, though arousing, is insipid, incapable of generating real fulfillment because it lacks the rich patina of tradition, integrity, and weight. And it cannot answer to Tolkien's challenge: Can a willing suspension of disbelief make the move from sentimental association to truth, from "what is desirable" to "what is significant"?

Fusion faith covers a spectrum whose poles epitomize what believers in mainstream religions would consider the gravest theological errors. On one end lies the fascination with fetishes, amulets, herbal remedies, and primal elements and incantations, harbouring the error of misplaced concreteness. Here physical objects and spontaneous or stylized gestures are not understood properly as symbolic representations of the divine, but as actual gods and goddesses inhabiting and incarnate in the everyday world of the practitioner. But when the divine is denied its sovereign transcendent status, the religious seeker is potentially deprived of the experience of awe, and the absoluteness of the divine is compromised. Superstition and magic intrude, their presence arousing a false pride in the human power to conjure up the gods, while undermining the humility indispensable to spirituality. Moreover, when crystals equal animal spirits equal humours of the body equal the symmetry of the soul equal the Garden of Eden equal the cosmos equal the divine, the result is a medley of resemblances within which every phenomenon can signify anything at all. Though the chain of poorly developed ideas might exhibit some rudimentary logical consistency, it often has no publicly demonstrable meaning, and constitutes a purely private reason. Combined with a taste for colourful, but highly subjective metaphor, fusion-faith risks derailing into fantasy and madness.

On the other end of the spectrum lies the desire for an unpatented, universal god, expressed in an appeal to "the whole of everything," "Being itself," "the integrating principle in the universe," "the meaningfulness of the cosmos," or the "concern with ultimate concerns" (to use Paul Tillich's term). While such a god offends no one, the generic nature of the divine is so catholic that, like Mary Poppin's medicine, it will answer to every taste. Such a god neither excites righteous anger and commitment, nor connects to the historically situated human community. God is reduced to a vague generalization, an impassive – often stupefying – mere titular authority.

Fusion faith often gravitates to either of these poles, whereas traditional spiritual discipline inhabits the more complex and uncertain middle ground between them. It is not surprising that fusion faith at either of the poles is often transitory and ephemeral, distinguished by repeated alterations and novelty. In the absence of the deepening which occurs through years of work, study, and commitment – often accompanied by tedium and perplexity – fusion-faith often seeks the quick fix to human malaise and boredom. Indeed, what primarily distinguishes the baby boomers' actions at the poles from traditional spiritual disciplines is their search for the magical gimmick which could transmute reality. Often baby boomers' spiritual searches are confined to the "triggers" – incense, chanting, celestial music, ecstasy, and enchanted gestures. Ironically, the arousal accompanying the use of these triggers is often justified by appealing to Abraham Maslow's idea of "peak experience," the suggestion that surprise, aesthetic shock, and first-time experience are essential ingredients of human happiness. Although Maslow argued that a peak experience was a primary index of "self-actualization," he warned of the dangers of being captivated by the gimmick – and especially of the risk of moving into the exotic, the occult, and the cultish. He sensibly advised that, for the sake of verifying the validity of religious illumination, and preventing a derailment into subjective madness, religious practitioners should search for a "dimension of depth" in the everyday.[35]

Baby boomers on either end of the spectrum rarely dwell, however, in the everyday. Habitually, its ambiguities and contradictions – where good and evil are inextricably mixed – are peremptorily dismissed as the site of a home in which gods and goddesses could dwell. The major reason for such a dismissive attitude is baby boomers' residual commitment to perfectibility and the dream of a pure and unadulterated state. Despite the fact that baby boomers practising fusion faith sense they are dabbling in black magic, they often subscribe to a theology of goodness which has no place for evil or the demonic. Yet, incongruously, in recognizing the depths of consciousness – orgiastic, Dionysian, mystical – they reside in the realm where evil and the demonic flourish.

Moreover, fusion faith easily derails into a pathological syndrome that some psychologists call the "ecstasy deficit." In a generation brought up on Abraham Maslow's idea that the apotheosis of human striving is "self-actualization," bagging "peak experiences" became paramount. The ultimate thrill, it seems, is always around the corner. Such seekers want the total gratification of desire, even, for some, to the point of "polymorphous perversity," to use Herbert Marcuse's apt expression.[36] If, traditionally, these experiences were encased in moral, intellectual, and institutional contexts, and required following practices understood as integral to the value of the experience, now the means are only "tools" and "mechanisms," secondary to the experience itself, and easily abandoned when the result is achieved. But ecstasy, as these New Agers discover, is never actually forthcoming. The more it is pursued, the faster "self-actualization" usually recedes, inducing an insatiable search for "the challenge beyond all challenges."[37]

Unrequited longing is, of course, not a failing. Behind the desire for "more and more" is a real hunger for a revivifying encounter with the primal sources of life. If the search for the primordial is at times maudlin, it nonetheless contains a perennial human need to truly experience and reconsecrate life. All worldly forms deteriorate and corrupt, and thus must be re-hallowed by a return to the wellsprings. The ultimate relationship – between "me" and "myself," "me" and the "other," and eventually "me" and "God" – is the object of all longing, and its pursuit both elevates and ennobles it. Martin Buber once wrote, "If I and another 'happen' to one another, the sum does not exactly divide. There is a remainder somewhere, where the souls end and the world has not yet begun."[38] The restless, striving baby boomers have been looking for this remainder all their lives.

Despite the contradictions and dangers (perhaps because of them), fusion faith places immense pressure on modernity. One might suspect that fusion faith is a characteristically modern phenomenon, merely extending its reach with its me-first, where's-the-next-thrill outlook. But cardinal features of modern consciousness are, in fact, being recalled. Baby-boomer consciousness is no longer satisfied with the concepts of the individual person, of history as dynamic progression, of world politics confined to nation-states, and of experience limited to positivistic fact and inferential reasoning. In the disillusionment with the modern idea that transcendence can be contained by temporal forces – current economic, social, political, and moral constructs – baby boomers are pushing for a decisive rewriting of the axioms of modern life. The pressure for covenantal communities and tribes abjures modern notions of the social contract, the myth that society is nothing but the aggregate of everyone's self interest or an ideal of social justice. The indifference to a narrative of history in favour of a desire for "being," or widening of the present moment, erodes the will to act and to have, so characteristic of modern ambition. The appeal to global consciousness, not to say the indwelling divine self, defies borders and insularity, rendering patriotic loyalty, even citizenship, phenomena of the past. The rediscovery of transcendence has muted the grim and resolute moralism of modernity. The longing for sanctification demands dimensions of reality – ceremonies and rites acknowledging divine being – to be publicly recognized which presently are relegated to privacy, such as rites of passage and processes of exaltation and healing. And, although the mutual recriminations of the women's and men's movements threaten to harden gender distinctions, especially to the extent that they build religious experience on the destiny of biology, their push to have women and men expand their experiences of reality may ultimately achieve a state where a higher and fuller idea of humanity is the norm.

Deborah's concluding comment, "To be in the rawness of what one is as a human being," is precisely what makes fusion faith's experiment with multiple faiths, and with the interconnectedness of all things, attractive and frightening: It permits the most widescale re-evaluation of centuries of error and miscalculation, while risking the loss of many of the safeguards accompanying the modern horizon. The gamble is whether its intensity and its power to backtrack creation to its primal origin, to the root of all existence, can generate decent images of humanity. And that question led me to the East and to a community which has turned its back on the West, which nevertheless – in my judgment – is the consummate expression of baby boomers' spiritual searches.

# Turning East

## The Rejection of the Modern West

The fox knows many things. But the hedgehog knows one big thing.

ARCHILOCHUS

The adventure of meeting Swami Shyam begins in misadventure. I am travelling with John Stackhouse, the *Globe and Mail*'s former South Asia correspondent. We are flying over the lower Himalayas in a vintage double-propeller plane. The pilot reports that weather disturbances over the Kullu Valley make it necessary to reroute to Simla, the famed British Raj hill station. Simla's airport is on the peak of a high mountain, offering a minuscule runway onto which the plane drops, skids, and brakes acutely, stopping sharply by the edge of the tarmac, overlooking a thousand-foot drop into the valley below. We are now obliged either to wait out the weather or to find an alternative way to get to Kullu.

We are joined by Jennina, a dental hygienist from Vermont, and her duffle bag, the size of two Afghan dogs. She looks forlorn. She is on her way to be with Swamiji (dearest Swami) and we agree to share a taxi. As we ride the treacherous, slippery roads to Kullu, falling off the road once and collecting innumerable tire punctures – Jennina turning progressive shades of white and green, her teeth resolutely clenched ("First time in India," John and I smirk) – we learn that she met Swamiji in Vancouver, felt his "aura," and was so inspired, she formed her own meditation group in Vermont. How does she know she will be well received in Kullu? "Oh, for years I've been watching the videos of *satsangs* taped in Kullu and sent out to devotees around the world. We all know one another from the videos." She is looking forward to being known by her Sanskrit name, Jotishna, her identity for the next four weeks. And she will enjoy the passage through the four states of mind – sleep, wake, dream, pure consciousness – which Swami's "aura" facilitates.

Kullu Valley is situated in the lower Himalayas in the Indian state of Himalchal Pradesh. Under normal conditions, it is a short, hair-raising one-and-a-half-hour flight from Delhi. Here, too, the plane must literally drop onto the airstrip, an action necessitated by the ridge of mountains tightly circling Kullu, rendering a slow and gradual approach impossible. The runway in Kullu, however, does not end with a cliff.

Graced with an abundance of apple, apricot, and plum trees, oversized red rhododendron bushes, breathtaking views of the snow-capped mountains forming a ring around the valley, and a cool, refreshing climate, Kullu is legions away from the frantic pace and heat of India's cities and roads. The Beas River, holiest of holy rivers for Sikhs living in the adjacent state of Punjab, thunders through the valley – living, restorative water. A single road ribbons through Kullu, connecting it to Chandigarh in the south (designed by the modernist architect Le Corbusier) and the town of Manali – known for its drug addicts and its stunning Kohlang Pass (access to Ladakh) – forty-two kilometres north. Every ten seconds, India's infamous TATA trucks – festooned with marigold garlands and icons of gods to ward off the nearly inevitable deadly accidents these trucks visit on India's roads – careen through the city, blaring their horns.

In between, situated above the river and the road but beneath the mountains, an inconspicuous collection of buildings is splashed up the hill. No sign beckons the visitor. Our welcome is not a warm one, for we have arrived uninvited. The resident guardian, Dikpal, guards the entrance jealously and menacingly – which god does not have a ring of protector-monsters? – and for long moments it is not certain that we will be granted admission. Finally, we are invited to come back at eleven a.m. for the daily *satsang*, or spiritual exercise (literally, "keeping the company of Truth"). Before we depart, another misunderstanding needs to be cleared up. This is not an ashram; it is a scientific laboratory called IMI, the International Meditation Institute, or – more gnomically – "I am I," and "Shyam Space." Ashram means "a place of striving," a wholly inappropriate description of I M I.

Upon our return, a steady troop of Westerners is mounting the stairs into the main building for *satsang*. We are curious about the rumoured 200-strong Canadian élite here making up a who's who of the Canadian establishment. Mulroney, Stanbury, Radley-Walters, Desmarais, Rosenburg: the sons, daughters, nephews, brothers, and sisters of prominent politicians and senators, military generals, business tycoons, and Supreme Court judges. The assembled community, the "Shyams," as they call themselves, looks utterly ordinary, yet – as we learn – in no ashram in India will one find such a concentration of baby-boomer professionals: doctors, biologists, philosophers, physicists, systems analysts, architects, businessmen, lawyers, international relief workers, nurses, psychiatrists, yacht appraisers, filmmakers, and artists. And, thanks to the Swami's own indomitably buoyant spirit, nowhere else is the daily two-hour *satsang* as intense, boisterous, and exhilarating.

Swami Shyam looks like a guru straight from Hollywood's central casting – a venerable, white-haired, beard-stroking mystery man who sits on a dais in front of a wall which has a large black circle painted on it, a dot allowing meditative absorption, nearly total sense withdrawal, and the focusing of consciousness. It recalls the German mystic Jacob Boehme's words:

> Cease from thine own activity, fix thine eye upon one point ….
> Gather in all thy thoughts and by faith press into the Centre ….
> Be silent before the Lord, sitting alone with Him in thy inmost and most hidden cell, thy inward being centrally united in itself, and attending His will in the patience of hope.[1]

Though our own restlessness and curiosity prevent us from enjoying it, we learn that the meditation is an invitation to suspend our sense perception, logical reasoning, and reflective powers – all the aspects of surface consciousness – in favour of a deep peace and silence, so that, in the words of Meister Eckhart, "In the midst of the silence the secret word was spoken to me."[2] John and I, however, are gawking around and, somewhat to our surprise, others gawk at us – word of our arrival has spread like wildfire throughout Kullu.

The *satsang* is a long, rambling, convoluted stream of free association, the sort of babble Don Quixote encountered in his romantic tales of chivalry that brings Cervantes to say, "Of this sort of folderol, the poor gentleman lost his wits." Neither of us could remember a word afterwards, though the devotees hung on Swamiji's every word and gesture. When we pointed this out later to the woman sitting next to us, she retorted sardonically that we were still caught in duality. John and I privately admit to one another that we think we're in the land of the weird. Do they think Swami is *God*? Instead of embodying the classic humanist quest conveyed in the humanly unanswerable question "Who am I?" Swami Shyam says "I am I" – denoting the total self-referentiality and perfection of divine being, the attribute of the God of the Hebrew Bible and Old Testament whose name shall not be pronounced. John, whose father is a minister, is scandalized when I point this out to him.

The devotees are mystically enchanted around the Swami, professedly sustained by the experience of high-oxygenated pure consciousness through daily meditation. Here, we are told, they seek and find metaphysical oneness, the opportunity to touch ontological reality that ordinary Canadian life lacks. Self-professed freedom junkies, some of Canada's finest are in Kullu seeking an utterly unconditioned life – free of bondage of any kind, be it sexual needs, moral judgments, or relations that produce dependency. Ascetics and lovers of peace – all are vegetarians, most have taken vows of celibacy, all exude an indefatigible sweetness – they are, in great part, traditional Eastern mystics. They aspire, they explain, to the absolute space of the sky. Some come for a month – a spiritual refresher course. But most come to stay – some for as long as twenty years now. Inheritances, legacies from family dynasties, a bundle made on a quick stock market flip – one way or another, expenses are met.

Swami Shyam, the magnet to this enchanted retreat, is seventy-four years old, the father of five children, a career civil servant whose own family upbringing was marked by a close relationship to the family guru. At nine, he began to meditate. Possessed of a strong will, he chose to cry with only one eye on an occasion when his father slapped a servant for pleading. Early on, too, he became aware of the experience of oneness; his friend was slapped and Shyam felt the slap and cried; his father then slapped him and his friend cried. There is no record whether this was from one eye or two. Nonetheless, Shyam became a career civil servant, edited the parliamentary Hansard proceedings for the state assemblies of Punjab and Harayana, and one day looked out the window at a mango tree, noted one overripe fruit which refused to fall and risked rotting on the tree, and decided that there is a dead-end futility to worldly careers and he had to do something. Linking up with the followers of Transcendental Meditation, and in the wake of intense religious experiences confirming to himself that he had become a self-realized being, he took his teachings on the road – to Canada. "Only fruit shipped worldwide can have its sweetness and goodness experienced by all those who need it," Swami Shyam explains.

Taken advantage of by a Calgary businessman, and the victim of a Vancouver thief who entered his room in the Silver Hotel while he was in the shower, taking his passport and money and leaving him with nothing but his *dhoti*, Shyam concluded his destiny was to remain in Canada and spread spiritual enlightenment. Destiny's timing was excellent, catching the 1970s fascination with India's holy men and allowing Shyam to take Canada by storm.

Wherever he spoke – Montreal, Ottawa, Vancouver – his new devotees flocked, eventually deserting such prestigious organizations as the Privy Council Office; the Canadian International Development Agency; Ogilvie Flour; York University; the Canadian Broadcasting Corporation; Les Grandes Ballets Canadiens; Skadden, Arps, Slate, Meagher & Flom, LLP; and Ogilvie Renault. Many are the scions of the most powerful families and institutions in Canada – from the Power Corporation of Canada to the Supreme Court. René Lévesque's electoral victory in 1976 was the impetus for exiting Quebec, especially for the Montreal Jewish community. One and all, they threw away their successes and now – childlike – follow Swami Shyam around, much like Jesus' disciples, who parroted the Master's teachings and endearingly related every mundane event of his life as a revelation of Truth. And the proximity of the Shyams to their own Jewish tradition of mysticism is striking. Swami Shyam is their Hasidic saint, and his personality substitutes for religious doctrine.

Our first direct encounter with Swami Shyam occurs in the afternoon over tea, with a small number of other invited devotees. I am invited to pose a question. Having learned how many of the devotees were former international relief aid workers, and struck anew by

India's dire poverty, as evident in Kullu as in the streets of Calcutta, I wonder about Swami's message of "Devote yourself to your Self." I ask how one is to balance our moral obligations to the poor with the task of making ourselves worthy to undertake such a task. The answer is long and circumlocutional.

The poverty of India hides its strengths; the tradition of giving everything – the villager who gives all that he himself needs – has made India impoverished; (more darkly) the invaders who came and stripped India 1,100 years ago (Muslims) and destroyed her great civilization are to blame. "Your focus on the poverty of India blinds you to your poverty" – the busyness of the West, and its dualities of rich and poor, East and West, are the true poverty, for they deny the essential oneness of all things and have enslaved Indians to foreign forces. Nonetheless, Indians will not learn from Swami, for they are fated to the destiny of their caste and thus not open to his invitation for a change in consciousness.

The commentary ends with a call to meditate for one minute, as Swami looks at us and says, "I want to embrace you, I see love in you – intelligence." Two women, like Mary Magdalenes, I think, meekly offer us fruit and nuts. After the meditation – I'm fidgeting, trying to loosen a bit of nut stuck in my teeth, and look up to see John rolling his eyes – we are offered tea, and we all look at one another with beatific calm. Before leaving, we are offered chocolate from a tray being passed around. Swami has just said, "Every person who has realized the self will see every one as his own self and be loved by all." John impishly takes two chocolates and comments to Dikpal that if he and Dikpal are one, surely he can take for both of them, since Dikpal could not possibly feel deprived. Dikpal is not amused.

Dikpal is a self-professed "lifer." He obtained his MBA, went to work as a systems analyst for Michael Pitfield in the Prime Minister's Office, became increasingly dissatisfied with the rare opportunities for experiencing wholeness and peace in the midst of recurring returns to anxiety and restlessness, and began to meditate. Since 1980, he has been a permanent resident at IMI. "We want to get enlightened, we want to get realized. We are trying to de-identify ourselves as individual beings." In his fifties, and possessed of an old beatnik vocabulary, Dikpal still has the enthusiasm and energy of a Club Med greeter, and displays a singular ability to pop up everywhere, especially during my one-on-one interviews, as if to prevent the devotee from straying from the official line.

He missed my conversations with Manorama, however. Her husband had been a senior development officer with the Fogo project started in Newfoundland by Joey Smallwood, and he had died of a stroke in India. She herself abandoned development work, "except for inner development." While once a member of the United Church, when she learned the minister beat his wife, she turned her back on Christianity. From then on, she would accept only someone who lived what he professed. Like others, she is quick to tell me that I M I boasts a physicist, a biologist, a psychologist, a teacher, a Presbyterian minister, a doctor, and the son of a general. Credentials are a big thing at I M I – the university degrees and professional accreditations held by fellow devotees are worn as emblems by every member of the community. Manorama's deceased husband knew Jeff Stirling, the well-known Montreal radio host, in the early 1980s at Memorial University. Together, they watched videos of Swamiji, did drugs, read Ram Dass's *Be Here Now*, and experimented with alternative therapies. They were attempting to start a development institute when her husband died. The death provoked an "out-of-body" experience, which combined with another strange event: She met a relief nurse who claimed she had had an immaculate conception, and an Indian child. Manorama pondered this tale, and a penny dropped. She herself was adopted and had never known her natural mother. Putting the facts together, she realized she must be the Virgin Mary, and that she must have been immaculately conceived (and, presumably, without original sin).

After this inner revelation, a neighbour of her in-laws told her about Kullu, suggesting that she go and look for the nurse's child. Feeling unhappy and unworthy, she departed for Kullu and has been there ever since. Her strongest memory of childhood is of a stained-glass window of Jesus, standing on railroad tracks holding a lamb and a lantern. I often observe Manorama alone at the river, looking intense and lost. She confesses to being anxious that she was not invited to the tea John and I attended with Swamiji: "I am not included in this tea, that meeting. I need to be around Swami."

There are concentric circles around Swami – competing. Fights and bouts of self-doubt, I learn, are not uncommon – Swami deals his favours out selectively and, in the midst of oneness, jealousy has obviously not been vanquished. "Mary is simply your name," Swami admonishes. "It is not you. When you know yourself as You and not as Mine – not skin, not body, not senses – you realize yourself and are totally free." But Mary remains Mary.

The achievement of the state of oneness, and the practices which will lead to a renunciation of ourselves as separate, self-contained, acquisitive, and competitive units, is, however, precisely what Absolute Bliss Consciousness is meant to achieve. The aim of hatha yoga, and the *saadhana* (spiritual practices) integral to it, is to release the cosmic Self, the source of Life, to experience *Sat Chit Aanand*, Pure Existence, or, as the "Shyams" say, Pure Sky Space. "Pure Space," Swami comments, "is one without a second and indivisible. It is infinite knowledge, the eternal Knower, which has no boundary. I call it *amaram*, or immortal, because it is undying and never ceases to exist, and *madhuram*, or perfectly blissful, because it is the supreme attraction of the mind. If one can grasp Pure Space as the background of all forms and realize that it is immortal and blissful, then no matter what form one may have, he is immortal and blissful. Everyone can say '*Amaram Hum Madhuram Hum*, I am immortal, I am blissful,' and over time come to know the knower."[3] "Pain and suffering," which have driven so many into the search for spiritual enlightenment, "are caused by people's lack of knowledge of their own immortal nature."[4]

Pain and suffering, and the Swami's uncanny capacity to see the "mechanism" that is their source, and then shape his teaching precisely to an individual's need, are prime concerns at IMI. Pure consciousness has taken on the form of the human body at birth, and forgets its nature as infinite Being. It becomes body and mind, and the craving ego takes the previously single identity down a never-ending spiral of mutual contention. The task, through yogic meditation and analysis of the limits we ourselves place on human consciousness, is to become one again with the source. But it needs a representative of the Self, a guru, to diagnose the blockage or mechanism preventing the return to oneness. "The guru is one who knows you; he draws you, which is to say, he draws himself. He sees the knots, the blockages." Robert Eaton, the author of the self-published book *Genesis Dawn: I Meet Myself* on his experiences in the early years of IMI, relates that the Swami, as a self-realized master, can perceive – often at a flash – the cause of a Shyam's suffering, waywardness, ignorance, sense of alienation, and smallness, and, unlike anyone else – parent, rabbi, colleague – can tell each of them "who they really are."

Daily *satsangs* bear out the claim of Swami's adeptness in cutting to the chase, reading souls, and swiftly dispatching malarkey. One day, Robin Tweig, the British founder of the Open University, is invited up to the dais. He has spent an intense but regenerating month at I M I, it is his last day, and his final statement is a gift to Swami. Characteristically English, the talk is witty and self-deprecating, about how seriously he had once taken the study of history, how it gave him a sense of purpose, and how it provided him with a sense of the meaning of pain and suffering. But now, and especially after this last stay at I M I, he realizes how meaningless all historical acts are – "Look at the futility of Ashoka's little columns. Everything just comes to dust." He concludes with a sweet tribute to Swami in gratitude for the month of meditation, *satsangs*, and private sessions – "Swami knows what he's talking about, he can use anything as the basis of teaching, a cow can walk in, he uses it, he teaches with ease and lightness, he loves and cares, this is *bhakti* with intelligence."

There is a moment's silence as Robin finishes, and then Swami breaks into a harangue, berating him for having learnt nothing in the last month, and advising him – in as arch a tone as conceivable – that detachment is too easy, that enlightenment means being at a level that embraces all life, that renouncing and detaching oneself is just another dualism. Visibly shaken by the stern tone, and humbled, Robin slinks back to his chair, the final goodbye crumbled to dust.

Yet, only one day earlier, Swami had praised detachment and derided the historical busyness of the West. Sukhindra, a Montreal lawyer who walked out of New York's largest law firm – Skadden, Arps, Slate, Meagher & Flom, L L P – offers an explanation for Swami's behaviour:

What he says depends on the constituency in front of him. Intellectually he is a genius. He says everything and nothing. Neither paradox nor logic are strange to him. Swami does not destroy everyone on the hot seat, but he is omniscient and articulates himself differently. You're not supposed to make sense of it, but to be. And, afterwards, the individual will work away at it. A willingness to have him strip you is a sign of your maturity, seeing the particularity of yourself not as the extent of yourself. Once the ego is surrendered, the public stripping is not felt as such. He has a force, whatever he's manifesting is beyond what you think perfection is.

Swami's ability to spy out each Shyam's distinctive weakness, depravity, and hidden secrets is institutionalized in a way that a visitor does not at first appreciate. All the devotees acquire a Sanskrit name, devised by Swami Shyam. A new name, appropriate to the shedding of an old life and transition to a new community, confers a new identity. But a name is not randomly generated. It is the essence of the soul. It is almost Swami's little joke. The name, worn like a lapel badge, identifies to the world the ego mechanism which has defined each Shyam's actions in life and which has blocked her or his access to pure consciousness ("As is his name, so is he," 1 Sam. 25:25). The names have a double meaning – they are both the faulty ego mechanism and, at the same time, the ideal to which the particular Shyam must live up, thus both descriptive and prophetic. A girl who exhibits a general fear of things – good reason, with India's snakes, scorpions, and germs – is called the fearless one. Another has all her life looked for power in the achievement of an ever-receding goal – her name means power that is nearest to you. A boy used to be a lover of wealth. His name evokes the recognition of the wealth of love. The casual visitor who drops in probably would just as soon not know the intimate secret of the name. Yet nearly all divulge – with a certain glee. In a community of oneness, there is a panoptic visibility to all things, and nothing remains secret. "All the ignorance and conditioning is focused on one point," Savindra acknowledges. "We all see everyone's blind spots, because we keep coming back with the same problem."

We are born of the free infinite Being, Swami says. We are not meant to fulfill other's expectations. Jaishri comes from a family of non-practising Jews. Her father is an English professor at McGill University, and Allan Gold, the judge, is her uncle. At eighteen, she began to meditate, and experienced herself as a channel. Meditation offered her an ecstasy which daily routine lacked. One path lay before her – marriage and family – though, at the death of her grandfather, the rabbi coldly admonished the family, "It takes an event like this to bring a family together?" and she recoiled in offense, feeling already the stifling dependence that "marriage and family," not to say Judaism, would bring.

Love did not offer a greater reward. She experienced the intoxication and infatuation of love, but this too led to disappointment and a false exclusivity.

The first sign of freedom came from a grandfather's legacy. She began to study Jewish mysticism, but it was study, not a living tradition. The search for freedom, specifically release from duality, preoccupied her, and meditation's purification of the mind was the key. Swami offered her the light, joy, inspiration which has transformed her consciousness. "Today, I am a thousand times freer than last year." It's alchemy, she confesses, and the ether is "Space." "Freedom doesn't start in bondage," Swami tells her, and IMI allows her to "keep on expanding," without ties or interests, and be liberated from the causes of affliction.

Contrary to the premature conclusion that IMI is insular and its members exclusively inward-looking, all the world, in all its aspects, is, in fact, paraded before them. The famed Sir David Frost, BBC's anchor in Israel, came to see why so many Jews and Israelis came to Kullu. Indian generals, Norwegian philosophers, Moroccan Jews, German psychologists, English missionaries – all drift through IMI. A Swedish fireman with a badly burned face visits Swami Shyam, who immediately confronts the fact of his burns for all the group to hear. While the Shyams complain (or boast) they have lost a sense of time, the Swami is up on world news – the first, for example, to know about Pol Pot's cremation. One day he announces that he dreamt he was on *Larry King Live* and was asked to encapsulate his thought in six seconds. And while his devotees spill out their guts sitting on the dais, he reads a voluminous correspondence from politicians and yogis worldwide, never missing a beat, and noticing even so slight an occurrence as a grimace on the face of a devotee a hundred feet away, distracted from Swami's words by a chirping bird.

*The Contributions of Swami Shyam to the Development of Society* is a publication evidently necessitated by the persistent question of what good the ashram really does for the larger world, and to answer the charge that IMI is a product of Western self-indulgence. The authors point to the fact that local homeowners make two lakh rupees per month from residents' rent. There are other modest contributions, though some – like pressuring the Himalchal Pradesh government to install a sophisticated satellite dish in Kullu – seem more obviously associated with the needs of Western residents. Be that as it may, in great part, the pamphlet continues, the contribution is "spiritual" and a gift for the future:

> Swami Shyam has recognized that what is missing in today's world are enlightened leaders. Therefore, he has created a unique laboratory where spiritually and intellectually evolved people are preparing themselves to take this essential work. Not only is Swami Shyam assisting these people in the unfoldment of their realization of the vision of oneness, but he is also personally training them in the clear and precise communication of this knowledge.[5]

But while *samadhi* (perfect union with God) may bestow a good on all the world, a comment by Robert Eaton, one of the charter Shyams, is equally telling: "He wants to help the healthy, bright, and unconfused people of the world since there are already so many institutions dedicated to helping the poor and unhealthy."[6] Not surprisingly, the Shyams have little contact with the Hindu community around them, whose devotion is seen as fetishism and magic, in contradistinction to their own inward epiphany of a primordial Being.

So, apart from the promise of a future, enlightened leadership (for what, one asks?), how does IMI make a concrete difference to the world? The answer is astonishing, though one I would hear often, in many forms, on my travels through the world of the baby boomers. In this case, it is Davindra who enlightens me.

Davindra graduated from Carleton University with a degree in psychology. One of his professors experimented with terminal food-deprivation in rats, which provoked Davindra to ask, Why not study the fulfillment of man? He turned to Ram Dass and Aldous Huxley, and one day picked up a piece of chamois and wrote out on it, "I know I'll never die." He placed the chamois in a box, and said to himself, "I know I was put on earth for a reason, my life is a railroad track." He embarked on experimental classes in sensitivity training, went to India and interrogated enlightened teachers, met Swami and was struck by his purity of thought and dignity. Davindra then began to teach meditation and yoga, and left his wife (the daughter of a distinguished Carleton historian). A year later, he tried the "Western" way again in Montreal by working with delinquent teenagers from prisons and asylums, and running a newspaper for Ogilvie Flour, but finally, with the interest from investments left to him by uncles and his mother, he went to "the master of consciousness," Swami – "a guy on the path for me." What attracted Davindra to Swami's teaching was the prospect of pure consciousness, where you "hit the zone, the wall – a state where everything is just happening, like Michael Jordan, who just knows he'll hit the basket, or being a member of The Club (car accident survivors who report out-of-body experiences)."

And everything *is* "just happening." Davindra confides just how scientific the IMI laboratory really is. Many of the more scientific devotees, he reveals, subscribe to the theory of a morphogenetic field, first theorized when Harvard University zoologists observed that a group of monkeys on one island began washing their food soon after another group of monkeys on an adjacent island began washing theirs. The IMI community believes that its laboratory experiments on itself and the achievement of pure consciousness and peace will have a similar effect elsewhere. Strict cause and effect are not sufficient to explain how this will happen. "Things resonate," Davindra says. Davindra has even written to CBC anchorman Peter Mansbridge about the wonder that is IMI. Mansbridge replied that he would like to go there. "Proof," according to Davindra, "that morphic resonance is working." Or not.

Another devotee muses over breakfast that, as order accumulated in the scientific laboratory at Kullu, the overall world's order was decreasing, consistent with the compensatory entropy hypothesis operative in thermodynamics. Kullu's negative entropy, he informs me, is paid for by the world's growing entropy. Indeed, he whispers *sotto voce*, the world has nearly reached maximum entropy. And IMI is also confirming Ilya Prigogine's hypothesis of "dissipative structures" – at the point of maximum disequilibrium, spontaneous organization occurs.

Swami Shyam, and many of the other devotees, tend to be more down-to-earth. While his name, Shyam, means space – the infinite space, the vision of oneness, the wholly liberated state of consciousness, which is realized in him – his psychology is often homespun and spontaneously humorous. "I am suffering from this thought," admits one devotee on the stage. "You should drink two glasses of water," counters Swami.

He comments on their personal hygiene. Archana (whose father was private secretary to Lester B. Pearson) shows up at Kullu wearing a low-slung dress – a refugee from Rajneesh's ashram at Pune, and the life of free love and drugs there, child in tow. Swami takes her aside, scolds her for her lack of commitment to *brahmacharya* (abstinence, celibacy), and says he is appalled by her lack of understanding of enlightenment. "You haven't thought about any of these things for yourself. They have been trying to kill your mind. I don't want disciples. Anyone who takes away your intelligence is an enemy." Morally admonished and penitent, she conforms to the new life.

One day, Swami hears rumours that some devotees are smoking pot (untrue, as it turns out). Nonetheless, a note appeared on the wall: "Those who smoke and buy *charas* from anyone should not stay here. I will be sending their names to responsible quarters. Either you collectively manage the affairs, or I will not attend your *satsang*, rather dismantle the whole scene."

Often Swami's displeasure is more subtle. One morning, John wanders around and up the dais snapping photographs during *satsang*. Wrong. A day later Swami, amid a long meandering talk, digresses and makes a sharp comment about those who think they can capture the Self in a static photograph.

One night, I am invited to meditate with Savita, an architect, her husband, Daya Narayan, the director of communications for a United Kingdom satellite consortium, and Dikpal. We sit cross-legged on couches and close our eyes. "Watch the space you perceive, whether it is thoughts, impressions, or visual images," Dikpal offers. "If you wish, repeat the mantra *Amaram Hum Madhuram Hum*, 'I am immortal. I am blissful,' and let the soothing repetition take you to the space from which consciousness flows." *Amaram Hum Madhuram Hum, Amaram Hum Madhuram Hum, Amaram Hum Madhuram Hum* – I start to feel like a lopsided wheel on a bicycle. More quietly, Dikpal whispers, "Watch the waves of experience enter and fill the infinite space of the mind, begin to watch the process of watching itself." *Amaram Hum Madhuram Hum, Amaram Hum Madhuram Hum, Amaram Hum Madhuram Hum*. At this point, an enormous calm enters my mind, and I actually start visualizing – patterns of sails, fibres in Japanese printing paper, peacock tails, waves. Suddenly, the meditation is over. Savita tells us to rub our palms and brush them over our eyes, facilitating the transition from deep meditation to waking.

In Hinduism, the deities lie in wait in one's "subtle" body. A mantra, properly understood, is a sacred sound, and all the mantras invoking the deities are already vibrating in one's being. If one can harness the power, or *shakti,* of the mantra sufficiently, thus raising its vibration, one will achieve attunement to divine being. Often, a mantra is deliberate gibberish, meant to circumvent ordinary logic and reason, thus making liberation, *moksha,* possible. But raising the vibration of a mantra is not a mind exercise alone. It also calls for celibacy – the conservation and sublimation of sexual energy leads to the induction of psychosomatic heat necessary to acquire spiritual discernment – eating pure foods, and having pure intentions.

Another night, a larger group meets for dinner and song. Swami Shyam is a gifted poet and his Canadian devotees have put his poems to song. Sometimes, they spend evenings together, strumming their guitars, singing, "I'm the Creator,/I am the Sustainer/I'm the Dissolver, And the Power of them all/I am the 'I', the 'I' of all beings/In all beings, My story is told." Abiba, a Moroccan Jew from Montreal, is doe-eyed, her head and hand motions precious and affected, though her voice is lovely. Later, she admits she tends to excessive sentimentality and acts too much like a Jewish mother. There is something maudlin and gushy about the mood in the room, and I feel terribly uncomfortable. But soon the evening turns to talk, and particularly to the authors they like to read. In addition to the early Vedic writings, they like Patanjali and Krishnamurti.

At the core of the Vedas is the teaching *advaita vedanta* – the complete identity of the inmost soul and the impersonal, ultimate God Brahman. But, simultaneously, the Vedas teach that while "All the world is Brahman" (Mandookya Upanishad), yet Brahman cannot be defined or classified. As Shankara, the master of Vedanta Hinduism writes, Brahman is "before whom words recoil." Brahman is ineffable, unspeakable, beyond words, logic, and symbols. No attributes can be predicated of what is Absolute, "One without a second," reads the Chandogya Upanishad. Indeed, Brahman is an unimaginable abyss. And to be one with Brahman is to identify with the void: "Who says that Spirit is not known, knows; who claims that he knows, knows nothing." *Neti, neti* – not this, not this – but *Tat Tvam Asi* – "Thou art That."

Vedantic Hinduism, like Judaism, is not a religion of the Book, or text, but of the Word. The major Hindu texts – the Vedas, Upanishads, Brahmanas, Aranyakas – are called *sruti* (what is heard). Hence, they must be orally recited, inviting the believer into responding to the primal experiences and forms which emerge from the sound of the language. Sanskrit is God's language. The same is obviously true of the primordial language of Hebrew, especially for the kabbalist. Neither Hinduism nor Judaism is, of course, exclusively a religion of the Word. Just as the oral Torah is systematized in the Mishnah and Talmud, so the Ramayana and the Mahabharata, the Dharma Sutras and the Puranas, are the *smrti* – what is remembered, what has been written down. In Kullu, where the Shyams study Sanskrit to hear the Vedas, it is the living tradition of an oral religion – so attractive to those opposed to the sclerosis which sets in once a religion becomes scribal, rabbinical, and scholastic – which fulfills Jaishri, Abiba, Sasmiti, Sharda, Satyam, and the other Jews. But the Brahman of practised Hinduism incarnates himself in many aspects – as Shiva, Vishnu, Kali, Durga, Krishna – and invites devotees into a genuinely sacramental religion. For the mystic, this is idolatry. The Shyams shun the idolatrous Hinduism on the streets beyond their gates.

The "God" the Shyams seek is the God of the "apophatic" tradition, the *via negativa* followed also by St. John of the Cross, Teresa of Avila, and Nicholas of Cusa, not to mention the Jewish Kabbalah. It begins in the most profound piety. As Carl Jung once wrote, "Every statement about the transcendental ought to be avoided because it is a laughable presumption on the part of the human mind, unconscious of its limitations."[7] It is only given to us, writes St. John of the Cross, to encounter the "Dark Silence," the "Wayless Way," and "Nakedness," for the Absolute cannot be conceived by humans in their present condition. Finite beings cannot know the Infinite. With our organs of perception and understanding, we can only understand the Infinite relatively. Such a God is not grasped by thought, analysis, and classification, and this God cannot satisfy the logician's demand for non-contradiction, for in this God lies a coincidence of opposites. "The place wherein Thou dost abide is girt round with the coincidence of contradictories," writes Nicholas of Cusa. "'Tis beyond the coincidence of contradictories Thou mayest be seen and nowhere this side therefore."[8] The "beyond" is where thought ceases to be dualistic – personal/impersonal, transcendence/immanence, unity and multiplicity, light/dark – and where contraries coexist.

What has drawn believers to the apophatic tradition is the credible conclusion that if God is truly transcendent – the principle of all that is –

then He cannot be a God restricted to natural epiphanies like beauty, order, harmony, and logic. For then he would be limited. The theistic God, uncompromised by human needs or earthly regularities, is a Void – not emptiness, but a plenum where void and fullness are one. A God of paradox provides little consolation. To the old chestnut, "Why must I suffer so?" the Book of Job, for example, provides no answer. As various associates of Job seek an explanation for Job's wretched lot – maybe it is "just desserts," maybe Job doesn't subscribe to the right beliefs (Job hopes God will reciprocate and turn his fortunes), his case just keeps deteriorating. God will not be confined by human need. Job's God is the utterly transcendental, mysterious, awesome God who does not deign to barter with man.

One of the Western world's greatest mystics, Dionysius the Areopagite, understood the iconoclastic desire to preserve the uncompromising transcendence of God by refusing to represent Him when he wrote, "Refuse being insofar as its obscures nonbeing, find the darkness beyond the light," and thus to unite "to Him Who is wholly unknowable; thus by knowing nothing he knows that which is beyond his knowledge."[9] St. John of the Cross offers a no less enigmatic teaching:

> In order to arrive at being everything, desire to be nothing. In order to arrive at knowing everything, desire to know nothing. When the mind dwells upon anything, thou art ceasing to cast thyself upon the All. For, in order to pass from the all to the All, thought has to deny the self wholly in all.[10]

St. John of the Cross leaves, too, the haunting testimony of the austere, mystical path of purgation. There are two nights, he writes, through which the mystic must pass. The first is the "dark night" where the senses are purged, perception abandoned, and images renounced, though thought is perdurable. The second night is the "dim or dark contemplation," where darkness overtakes concepts, knowledge, and understanding:

> The higher part of contemplation, as it may be had here, hangeth all wholly in this darkness and in this cloud of unknowing; with a loving stirring and a blind beholding of the naked being of God Himself only.[11]

So unworldly, isolating, and enigmatic is his description of the moment where darkness and light, deprivation and attainment, and emptiness and fullness coexist – and the conditions of ordinary existence evaporate – that St. John's words need to be read in full:

> It is secret wisdom, and happens secretly and in darkness, so as to be hidden from the world of the understanding and of other faculties ....
>
> It is secret not only in the darkness and afflictions of purgation, when the wisdom of love purges the soul, and the soul is unable to speak of it, but equally so afterwards in illumination, when this wisdom is communicated to it most clearly. Even then it is still so secret that the soul cannot speak of it and give it a name whereby it may be called; for, apart from the fact that the soul has no desire to speak of it, it can find no suitable way or manner or similitude by which it may be able to describe such lofty understanding and such delicate spiritual feeling ....
>
> This mystical knowledge has the property of hiding the soul within itself ... so that it considers itself as having been placed in a most profound and vast retreat, to which no human creature can attain, such as an immense desert, which nowhere has any boundary, a desert the most delectable, pleasant and lovely for its scenery, vastness and solitude, wherein the most the soul has been raised up above all temporal creatures, the more deeply does it find itself hidden.

An equally sublime mysticism is found in Vedantic Hinduism. Ultimate reality is Brahman – the Absolute "One without a second," the unimaginable abyss, "before whom all words recoil."[12] The material universe, by contrast, is an unconscious emanation of Brahman, without beginning or end, and unreal. Human salvation lies in the inmost soul's identity with Brahman. But for an individual, the living personality is not this inmost soul, *atman*, but an illusory phenomenal ego. To recover one's *atman* requires extracting oneself from the mere transient ego and extinguishing the multiplicity of relations with objects and actions, through a yoga which reveals the insubstantiality of perception, knowledge, and thought. As the Isa Upanishad reads: "Into deep darkness fall those who follow the immanent. Into deeper darkness fall those who follow the transcendent."[13] Union with Brahman, like St. John's of the Cross "dim or dark contemplation," is the realization that "Who says that Spirit is not known, knows; who claims that he knows, knows nothing." Brahman, or the *realissimus*, is *neti, neti* – not this, not this – but *Tat Tvam Asi* – "Thou art That." Here, divine truth is experienced as *Nada* – the soundless Sound.

Hatha yoga, like the mystical *via negativa*, is a path of stripping away the determinations that incline us to domesticate God (soliciting God's attention to cure an earache, thanking God for good fortune), and thus limit Him by our all-too-human perspective. And, if we are to unite with this God, we too must be emptied of all the conventional attributes which determine and individualize us. As Georg Feuerstein points out in his anthology of Patañjali's aphorisms, "Classical Yoga is entirely a process of negation of everything that is ordinarily considered as typically human."[14] Swami Shyam, true to the apophatic tradition, is like a psychopomp who takes his devotees to the kingdom of the dead, and then re-initiates them to the light. The passage from life to absolute reality is a radical purification of their humanity.

Patañjali wrote the first codified tract on yoga, the Royal Yoga, and his aphorisms comprise the Yoga Sūtra. In yoga meditation, God is a hypothesis or useful focus of attention, as the eight limbs of yoga – moral observance, self-discipline, posture, breath regulation, sensory withdrawal, concentration, meditation, and *samadhi* – are exercised to act on the fluctuations of consciousness, and the devotee reaches the inner peace which comes through purification of body and mind.

Krishnamurti is today's leading philosopher of Vedantic Hinduism. "The shoddy little mind, the second-hand little mind," he writes, "is always occupied about knowledge, about becoming something or other, enquiring, discussing, arguing, never quiet, never a free unoccupied mind."[15] "The essence of meditation," he explains, "is to enquire into the abnegation of the self" – to achieve a mind free of conditioning and control.[16] In silence, there is space – the "energy of the universe." Meditation teaches us to overcome division, by refusing to name and control the phenomena around us. "You are that – there must be no division. When there is no division you remain entirely with it."[17]

Thought is always divisive, separative, fragmentary, and knowledge is never complete, about anything ... is always divisive, because it is

derived from memory …. Thought, whether of the greatest genius,
of the great painters, musicians, scientists, or our petty daily activity
of thought, is always limited, fragmentary, divisive. Any action born
out of that thought must bring about conflict.[18]

Krishnamurti's view of the "self" is grim: We must escape attachment
from the "me" – "this sense of deep inward loneliness …. The 'me' with
all the accumulations that it has gathered in this life, all the pain, the
loneliness, the despair, the tears, the laughter, the suffering."[19]

We must examine why, after millennia upon millennia, we are living
in constant conflict and misery and why religions have totally lost
their meaning …. We are going to observe together and see if it is
possible to be radically free of all this torture of life, with its occasional joy.[20]

"Meditation is to discover the relationship of thought and silence ….
As long as one has an image about oneself, one is going to get hurt,"[21]
and, "We have seen the enemy and the enemy is ourselves."[22] Individualism and personhood are an illusion, and we are wrongfully hurt by
the comparisons and competition they produce.

"Beauty is where 'you' are not. The essence of beauty is the absence
of the self. To be able to look and see without images intruding." "The
explanation is not the actuality. The word is not the thing."[23] And he
concludes with a pointed story:

A religious teacher had several disciples and used to talk to them
every morning about the nature of goodness, beauty, and love. And
one morning, just as he is about to begin talking, a bird comes on to
the windowsill and begins to sing, to chant. It sings for a while and
disappears. The teacher says: "The talk for this morning is over."[24]

Concretely, what perspective on life do these thoughts sanction?
Sasmiti, who explains that her name means "God smiled on my lips," is
married. Like most couples at IMI who are devoted to freedom without bondage, they are celibate and live in separate chalets – "It's not
economic in the West to live separately." Sasmiti studied design at
Dawson College and became a commercial designer in the rock and

roll business, working for Donald K. Donald at Polygram. She started her own company, and soon the contracts poured in. But she felt "alienated from the system, a stranger from friends." Years earlier, she looked out the window and had a conscious vision of something immense. She swallowed and the immensity was localized. She realized that her friend next door also had a mouth and swallowed and could have this same experience. Out of this experience developed a burning desire for unity, combined with a perpetual sense of being unfulfilled. While she sang in a Catholic choir, she would watch the church drama and nothing corresponded to her own experiences. From this, she concluded, "You don't have to go anywhere they call the home of God; the home of God is within you." Her Israeli parents were burnt-out kibbutzniks who became disillusioned by Zionist nationalism, concluding that the purpose of the cause – freedom – couldn't be maintained once independence occurred. Nevertheless, they residually held the view that dialogue would bring fulfillment and oneness. But, Sasmiti wryly comments, family dialogue always derailed into debate, and the process of debate only empowered the sense of self of each family member, dividing the family over and over. Her gay brother and lesbian sister were also defining themselves as separate and divided, "negating life." Sasmiti started to feel that she had become a sum of partial thinking. She approached Swami with caution, fearful of having the carpet pulled out from under her. Yet, she watched the relations of people at IMI, and concluded that something else than her own life was possible, and it was here, a part of what she was living. She realized that what was at war in her was an interfering personality which observed, categorized, and judged, contracting the child as pure potential which knows not to be confined. "By spending longer here, you end up redefining the categories. I've learned the only attachment should be the continual process of living."

Filtering through Sasmiti's life experience – the genuine anguish and authenticity, the elevation of banal experiences to self-inferred profound spiritual insights, the lack of any idiom that doesn't end up sounding utterly flaky – is the indomitable spirit of the sixties: the Age of Aquarius, the cynicism about corporations and all institutions, the need to feel the really *real*, the desire for a freedom without responsibility and consequence, the need to have the special child within indulged just a little longer. And Swami's "Pure Space" both reinforces and fulfills the highs and the lows of that spirit. Antinomian, anti-speech, anti-reason, anti-creation: What draws this group of Canadians to a religion which stands in such obvious contradistinction to the formidable momentum and dynamic of the Western world? The answer is certainly not lack of intelligence, nor education, nor record of achievement.

Take Sasmiti's husband: Sukhindra is a Montreal Jew, but, like most liberal Jews, carried only the marks of ethnic Judaism, and then mostly for outward appearances ("kosher out of home, but not in"). He was admitted to Brandeis University at age sixteen. There he studied philosophy and wrote an honours essay on Nietzsche and the pre-Socratics. He went on to a Ph.D. program in literature at the University of Toronto, spent a year at Columbia, and acquired a law degree at Yale. The New York mega law firm Skadden, Arps, Slate, Meagher & Flom, LLP hired him to do international mergers and acquisitions. For leisure, he threw himself into solo high-altitude hiking and skiing, and modelled for ski magazines. Four years later, he went to Kullu, studied the classic Kullu mountain home, and built himself a stunning chalet, replete with bay windows, cathedral ceilings, and a loft. His bookshelves are filled with the Upanishads, and the works of Heidegger, Aristotle, and Marcuse, and he spends part of each day writing poetry. At first, he applied standard psychological control tests to his experiences in the presence of Swami. In the end, skepticism and doubt were replaced by faith – "as much faith as David Hume says we need to see the sun rising every morning, I have that faith in Swami."

"Swami is the Jimi Hendrix of the mind, a virtuoso. He sees the contraction, the burning desire to be liberated." I ask, "Isn't there a perverse voyeurism to the performance on the hot seat, a cruel pleasure enjoyed by both Swami and the rest of you?" "It is fun to be a spectator [watching] different minds who are sure their separateness is certain. But Swami is ruthless only in the pursuit of perfection in us. He has no vested interest, but a ruthless effort to liberate. Here at IMI, you're listening to revelation, to live scripture. He says everything and nothing. Everything is not true, or it is all true." Looking around at his attractively appointed chalet, Sukhindra concludes, "I can talk about having a great lifestyle here. I agree with Zarathustra's injunction: Make your world."

Tripura Shakti has just given up drinking espressos. When I hear her life story, I conclude that the sacrifice was a great one, for, in a past life, she must have mainlined caffeine. Of Jewish parents who refused to let the family follow Jewish practice in Montreal because it was superstition, Tripura rebelled and at age seventeen moved to Israel to experiment with Orthodox Judaism. She had already vowed to be a vegetarian, not wanting to be confined or conditioned, and the move to a kibbutz continued the search for an experiment not dependent on circumstances. On her return to Canada, she completed an undergraduate degree in Middle Eastern studies at McGill University, began law school in Israel, and then returned to McGill, to graduate in two years and receive eight awards, distinctions, and scholarships. After her first year, the law firm Ogilvy Renault hired her and, when she was admitted to the Sorbonne on scholarship to study French private law and jurisprudence, agreed to keep her on full salary as a student in Paris. The summer before leaving for Paris, she went to Kullu for the first time to visit her brother, who had met Swami during a trip to India. Planning to stay only a week, she stayed for six, and was joined by her mother, who also took up meditation classes. In the fall, she went to Paris and persuaded university officials to switch her from law to a doctorate in philosophy, even though she had no background in the discipline.

"It was always," she admits, " a search for the challenge beyond all challenges," and she threw herself wholesale into reading Leibniz, Perlmann, and Heidegger – "I couldn't allow myself to fail in a Sorbonne doctorate." But something happened in Kullu. "I realized that all these challenges were going nowhere and they were artificially self-imposed." She returned to Kullu briefly to acquire some distance, and realized she no longer wanted to be bound by "pre-programmed functioning." The Kullu visit awakened the recognition that she was following a pattern, driven by a low boredom threshhold. Nonetheless, she went back to Ottawa, completed a common-law degree at the University of Ottawa, and concurrently studied for the Quebec bar. She placed first in common law, and went back to Kullu for one last time to consider her options. While there, she spent three months in a Buddhist monastery in Thailand, and – "always upping the ante" – learned the script and the language. But in Kullu she found what she wanted – an awareness of falling away from limitations, a change from the "freedom from" to a "freedom to."

It's wonderful not to be bound, to find something that is not binding. Swami lets me work with my mechanism and go beyond it. He
takes my mental blocks and lets me work with them. Everything
here defies categorization. He just knows my mind completely.
Now, nothing feels personal to me – it's just ceased to be relevant.

"Will you ever marry?" I ask. "No, because it would become boring.
Parameters limit." What would happen if she ever went back to an
office? "I'd probably have to form my own little fiefdom. But when I
was involved with those kinds of political enterprises, I thought they
were useless." After a pause, Tripura sums it all up epigrammatically,
"Needless to say, my résumé is no longer updated."

There should be a sign over IMI that reads, "Only supermen and
superwomen need apply." Archana worked for Mother Teresa in
Calcutta, transferred to Malcolm Muggeridge's home for the dying
(Something Beautiful for God), and finally ended up in a soup kitchen
run by Mussolini's granddaughter. Sandesh danced ballet for Les
Grandes Ballets Canadiens. Veena completed degrees in the academies
of fine arts in Munich and Nuremberg, and her artwork was bought by
the Waddington Gallery. Divia Sarita ran a highly successful international entertainment business, working with Jim Hudson, in produc-
tions from Idaho to London. Dayal studied with Margaret Laurence,
got in at the ground level when information technology was developing, and built the information system QuickIndex. Savita Piskapo was
the project manager for one of the large government complexes in
Hull, Quebec, housing the Department of Transport. With unprecedented economy, the project was completed $5 million under budget
and she was awarded a major citation.

From one point of view, every one of them has thrown away success.
Walking out of careers and retirement-savings-plan tracks, spending
precious inheritances, risking the ridicule and incredulity of friends –
this makes the exit to Kullu at once the greatest risk, but also transforms it into rich opportunity. Leftover flower children from the
sixties, or guardians of its most precious treasures, it is hard to distinguish what is flake from what is profound.

When all is said and done, however, there is little question – in my
estimation – that genuine religious need, and the good fortune of early
theophanic experiences, underlies why most of the Shyams are in

Kullu. To be sure, there are unsettling psychological syndromes evident among them. Nearly all have unresolved or unresolvable tensions with their fathers – abusive fathers, domineering fathers, layabout fathers, driven fathers, "tough bugger" fathers – and this inevitably comes up in conversation. Virtually all had disappointing love relationships, even to the point of grief – explaining perhaps why so many of them are willing to forsake exclusive love. Most of them, at one point or another, have come up against, and rebelled against, authority and limit, and been made to "feel small by the system." A hackneyed sixties vocabulary – "the Swami's really ripping today," "We've done the trip" – drags down the generally elevated tone. A pervasive huggy-feely sentiment betrays an overweening need to belong. And, exhibiting the credulity of cultists, some say, rather portentously, that they would do anything Swami says; all admit they adore him. Having walked out of the churches and synagogues years ago, many rebelling against doctrine and dogma, and forsaking all ornament or icon, they nonetheless all have adorned their homes with multiple pictures of Swamiji.

There is at I M I a kind of nuttiness too, which follows from the baby-boomer axiom, "It must be important because I am doing it." For example, the Shyams are in possession of over 20,000 hours of video-taped *satsangs* (first the experience, now the movie) – produced, it goes without saying, on state-of-the-art Canadian equipment. In the evenings, the devotees sit around analyzing (with great levity) that day's *satsang* "victim" – the devotee called forward to submit to Swami's deliciously wicked psychoanalytic penetration. While the general enterprise of taping all sessions seems aimed at overcoming the awkward question of what will happen when the Swami dies – at another well-known ashram, since the death of its guru Osho, his devotees meet daily and adulate his chair – it also smacks of narcissism and gullible veneration.

Here a pending Oedipal resolution; there a thwarted and misdi-rected desire. In one, evidence of overreaction to remonstration or a soured love affair. In another, exaggerated adulation. Here and there a little self-contradiction. But none of these silly and boring reductionist psychological explanations, and the garden-variety syndromes and afflictions to which they reduce the Shyams, goes very far in explaining the attraction to Swami Shyam.

The reality is that these psychological explanations cannot address the genuine existential need the Shyams exhibit, nor do they adequately explain the rich and imaginative religious experiences the Shyams enjoy. Unlike some activists in the counterculture of the 1960s, very few of these particular Canadians bottomed out. They are longing, in that extraordinary yet all-too-human way, to achieve an experience that is everlasting. Like a caring rebbe, spiritual director, or guru (literally, a remover of darkness), Swami Shyam seeds further their natural receptivity to the eternal.

It is true that the Shyams love the hand that feeds them. Yet the relation Swami has with his followers – so strange and fearful to many of us – is often merely like the relation a psychiatrist has to a patient. In a classic process of transference and counter-transference, the devotees refract their love to him, and he exploits this for therapeutic ends. Granted, Swami Shyam has no accreditation and is, consequently, unimpeachable. Needless to say, the analysis he engages in is only the first step, and the real spiritualization is still to follow. And many signs indicate that Swami does not want control and does not want disciples. His techniques of meditation and the way he conducts *satsang* are remarkably cerebral – a few harangues and occasional head-shaking babble aside – and he shuns adulation. He encourages the Shyams' intellectual and cultural pursuits. He keeps reminding them that "knowing" is not remembering his teachings; the "me" they must capture is not him, but the Space they are themselves (yet, too, "Yourself is not yourself"). The teaching is intended to eclipse the teacher, as any true guru-disciple relationship should. For years, Swami Shyam returned to Canada and went out of his way to meet the parents and relatives of his devotees, intent on dispelling any idea that his institute is a cult. The result of Swami's annual junkets of assurance was that, contrary to their initial misgivings, brothers, sisters, mothers, and fathers have themselves left Canada and joined IMI.

He refuses, however, to let his Canadians mouth the simple formula "West = material; East = spiritual," and sees no incongruity between his followers' search for the eternal and the small signs of their lingering attachment to the profane world of the West – here and there, a Mont Blanc pen, a cappuccino maker, the *Globe and Mail*, a Ralph Lauren polo shirt, a breadmaker in which tomato-pesto bread is baked, even a Victoria's Secret catalogue. He indulges their occasional trips to Manali, where they enjoy the Jacuzzis of the new Holiday Inn. Spiritual guidance is not obeisance. During the day, they sit around, reading and discussing Yeats, Blake, Nietzsche, and Heidegger – heavily weighted toward the Romantic tradition – while mastering Hindi, Sanskrit, and Urdu to read the Gita, the Upanishads, and the Mahabarata in the original. Daily life in IMI is, in some ways, an extended graduate seminar.

Is Swami everything they say he is? He gives many evident signs of being a man of apparently limitless love.[25] He has a prodigious memory. He has the remarkable ability to draw people to their interior cores, mostly by his sheer presence alone, a power understood in the Tantric tradition as that of *shaktipat*. He gives each one of them, and the visitors that follow, tailor-made attention. Sometimes he hectors, loses his patience, uses a sharp tone, but his admonishments are those of a caring father. Indeed, it seems that for many of the Shyams, this is their first encounter with a father who discharges the parental function of admonition and guidance. But equally the Swami is Mother – evoking a mystic oneness, the communion of all existence – a mother who is infinitely good, nurturing, and forgiving. In Swami Shyam, there is a mysterious complementarity of male and female. Later, when I return to Canada and contact ex-Shyams, I hear of sexual escapades, inheritances oddly vanishing, minds poisoned, though the details are always sketchy, and seem, on balance, a product of envy, malice, or misunderstanding. Exclusivity often invites unwarranted suspicion, and wherever virtue exists to an eminent degree, it is often ridiculed or persecuted. Overall, in my opinion, he captivates them, in part because his virtues are genuine, in part because the spectacle he offers them of themselves is entrancing and amusing, in part because he indisputably makes them transparent to the transcendent, and in part because, like a saint, he is – palpably – an augmenter of goodness. He may even serve as a catalyst for grace.

Christ never laughs in the Gospels. One need only look at Christian statuary to see how unswervingly Christianity invites the believer down the *via dolorosa*. I know of no reports of Muhammad laughing, though I met some wonderfully witty Muslims on my travels, notwithstanding that prayer in the mosque was always under an ominous and foreboding sign. Moses, Abraham, and Jacob seem, on balance, a dour group. The Buddha laughs. Swami Shyam laughs, and the Shyams laugh with him. ("And you shall rejoice before the Lord your God.") The Swami is clever: When I tell him about the Kumbh Mela that John Stackhouse and I observed, and how the dip into the Ganges promised liberation, he announces to his devotees that while they can't all go to the Ganges, he is their Ganges. The father of Gugan, a retired Canadian brigadier-general, came away from his meeting with Swami, having learned that many of India's army generals pay regular homage, to announce that Swami was a "general of generals." On his retirement, the brigadier-general was presented with a tank by his Canadian Forces colleagues. It is parked outside his Gatineau cottage. A few years ago, Swami Shyam came to Canada, met the general and, with his characteristic humour, gave an impromptu sermon on peace, seated atop the tank's gun barrel. The gaiety has spread to the Shyams. While they are in, but not of, Kullu, there is humour and openness to what they see – the local milkman is gay, and they call him the Dairy Queen. The chai wallah fronts as a tea seller, but is in fact a bootlegger and owns large tracts of real estate, though he looks like he is counting his last paise. They're in on the ruse. The grand satellite station, hovering over the town's maidan and promising instant communication with the world, is a bust. In past years, they used to go on road trips around India, strumming and singing – shades of *The Partridge Family* come to mind – but the irony of it all (representing the "genuine thing" back to Indian Hindus) is not lost on them. It's all funny, but none of it is pathos. Sometimes solemnity and gravity are masks for a lack of seriousness. It is not a lack one finds in the boisterous laughter of the Shyams.

Now, to be sure, in the broad spectrum of religious possibilities, Swami Shyam's "experiment" is not above judgment or reproach. One day, during tea, I proposed to Swami that his thinking was compatible with the best traditions of the West which put a premium on the self's dialogue with itself, for he – like so many prophets, wisdom teachers, and saints – devotes himself to dialogues with himself.

I couldn't have been more wrong. Swami replied tersely, "I am not divided, I am one. I have no dialogue with myself." To aim at Swami's self-realized state is to seek to overcome the two-in-one, the soul's eternal dialogue with itself.

Michelangelo's famous central panel in the Sistine Chapel in Rome depicts God and Adam, each in a distinct sphere, but with arms outreached, and their forefingers nearly but never quite touching. Michelangelo works within a traditional paradigm – Adam's proximity to God's outstretched hand symbolizes both that creation manifests something of the divine being and that this creation is the privileged object of God's attention, yet God is transcendent, and thus is not compromised by His fallen creation. Only God is absolutely free and whole ("I am that I am"), while humans are irremediably determined and differentiated. Swami says "I Am I," aligning himself with God.

Swami says that his technique and teaching is applicable to any faith, but this is already a decision in favour of Eastern thought, which seeks to overcome the polarities of consciousness and to void the mind, and from which perspective all religious practices and beliefs are mere "tools," to be used and discarded. At a superficial metaphysical level, there is a resemblance between Swami's vision of oneness and Jewish and Christian reflection on Y H W H and God the Father. But, at a more profound level, it is impossible to see any equivalence with Western monotheism at all. Indeed, Swami's vision of oneness potentially corrupts Christianity and Judaism. The God of Judaism and Christianity is not an eternal, impassive, and quiescent God, but a dynamic and moving God, acting in history, moving forward in time, and backward from salvation, animating discrete persons with purpose and design, and promising human beatitude only at the end of history and time. By focusing spirituality on the One exclusively, Swami can mislead his devotees into believing that what they are learning is not incompatible with their own religious traditions. But, as the adage goes, God is in the details, and, for the Western monotheistic religions, the details are in historical revelation and providence, and in the unique way that the Western God's entry into history gave meaning to human struggle and action, morality and politics, and sacramental rites. The Western God acts in time, making judgments, expecting man to heed the events by which His anger and justice are manifest, and requiring man's timely response. The drama of God's way with the world holds out a redemptive promise – all of reality is moving in such a way that desolation and suffering will be overcome in the future. Our present woes will be transfigured into future joy. This means that the finite conditions of existence – our determined, dependent, and differentiated condition – will disappear only after our death. The life of beatitude, the union of God in the beatific vision, is deferred until the end of time. Until then, we are a body and soul, and the conjunction creates the unique form of a "person."

The gap between God's and Adam's fingers in Michelangelo's painting is the very space which Swami Shyam's teaching seeks to close. By contrast, this is the space in which the substance of Western monotheism is formed. For Judaism and Christianity, God revealed Himself in the Torah, or in Jesus Christ, and He does not need to supplement His revelation with an interior mystical consciousness. Swami Shyam offers a technique to short-circuit the Christian and Jewish God's divine plan, and, in the process, Swami's teaching erodes historical responsibility in favour of quietude.

"Ashram" means, literally, a life of striving. Thus, Dikpal was right when he corrected my opinion that IMI is an ashram, for, strictly speaking, Swami Shyam's "Space" is not an ashram. At IMI, one's personal characteristics, and the active striving through time and history, are illusions, impeding the ultimate unity of the deepest reality of the human soul (*atman*) with the divine essence of the universe (Brahman) – you are that. The whole middle world of individuality and personality, judgment, morality, historical meaning, and politics falls to the wayside, in favour of a deep interiority which is, at the same time, ultimate reality itself. To practise the teaching of Absolute Bliss Consciousness means to recover the primordial reality, passive and quiescent, that existed before the dawn of the cosmos and history. The Shyams seek freedom from conditioned existence, from "consciousness of," from the subject-object division, and from the social, political, and cultural mechanisms which reinforce these fatal errors. The *atman*, or true self, is no longer (as in the West) commensurate with, or an analogue of, all cosmic modes of being.

Now, as we have seen, the mystical apophatic tradition in the West has a long and distinguished pedigree. St. John of the Cross speaks of dark contemplation in the "cloud of unknowing." Dionysius the Areopagite refers to a union "to Him Who is wholly unknowable." Meister Eckhart and Jacob Boehme both write of the fading away or dissolution of the self in mystical experience. And *samadhi* – passing out of conscious life to a state where knower and known are one, where self and God fuse – is an experience attested to by all the great Western mystics. However, in none of these Western mystical writers does one find quite the same imagery of passivity and quietude, nor the repudiation of a personal and transcendent God. Western mysticism sees no permanent change in the condition of humanity, but seeks to reconcile the difficult dualities or polarities of experience. And, at the end of the day, even the mystic strives. Hildegard von Bingen's and St. John of the Cross's writings are resplendent with a highly erotic imagery ("ravishment" by Christ, a "spiritual marriage"), the most sublime form of striving, and each describes the mystical experience of God as an active ascent to knowledge, albeit spiritual knowledge.

Western mysticism, consonant with the theology which is its foundation, accents reconciliation – recognizing the mystery dimension of the ordinary, recovering the sacramentality of creation, refining the organs of perception and knowledge to shift back and forth between the sensual and divine realms. Even in the most mystical Western spirituality – the Sufi Qadiryah order – duality (as experience of the sense of distance intensifying the love of God) is the wellspring of resonance with God.

Yet, this striving and work of reconciliation is precisely what the Shyams seek to overcome, and in Swami Shyam – purportedly – they are overcome. While it is credible to believe that striving understood as desire for more and more – wealth, glory, and recognition (and the injustices which inevitably ensue) – is the primary source of so much human misery, the Shyams appear to see only one part of what an active life can be. By focusing on being (One), all activity appears to them homogeneously deformed. But doing, having, knowing, and thinking are also forms of striving, and, depending on their expression, are the ways in which humans distinguish and perfect themselves. Morality, art, music, and thought are dynamic ways of striving. And at least one line of argument would suggest that the moral and political traditions we hold in such high estimation (tolerance and compassion, liberal democracy, and recognition of the individual), paradoxically thrive in, and arise out of, the most vulgar form of striving – competing, acquiring, dominating. And, at least in practised Hinduism with its profusion of gods and goddesses, in the tales of Radha's love for Krishna, and in *bhakti* devotion, there is a symbolic attempt – as in the Christian Trinity – to hold plurality and unity, concreteness and transcendence, together. At I M I, this complexity is dismissed as primitive magic.

The Shyams say that they think and do, but what they mean by this is that they think and do to end all thinking and doing as it is conventionally understood. To think, to act, and to do means to delimit, exclude, and negate. Reasoning is striving, engaging, and re-engaging perplexity and doubt. Acting and doing is striving – differentiating, overcoming, starting every day anew while recognizing the contours of tradition. Consciousness implies polarity – to be conscious is to be self-distinctive. Western literature is strewn with derision and warning about abandoning the life of activity and the distinctions appropriate to it. Immanuel Kant wrote dismissively of the pastoral enchantment of the "Arcadian shepherd," a nostalgia for an easy paradise where we are free from our historical, embodied existence. The expression "lotus-eater" signifies a life of indulgence where even breath and gesture are enchanting, because, without any former association, they are perpetually experienced as new and novel. Perhaps the greatest satire on unworldliness is Jonathan Swift's *Gulliver's Travels*. His description of the Laputans – who have one eye inward and the other up to the zenith – is poignantly applicable to the Shyams, who have lost a sense of the middle world, and, perhaps like the Laputans, need "flappers" to rouse memories of their human condition. They are also a little like Swift's Houyhnhnms, whom Gulliver visits last of all and in whom he believes perfection resides, but who lack eros, and enjoy perfection without change. It is not insignificant that it is among the Houyhnhnms that Gulliver finally loses his humanity. IMI is a pastoral Arcadia, yet all paradises are meant to be lost, for that is precisely how we become human. The term of encounter for Jews is "shalom," signifying peace – not as inactivity, but as a dynamic bid to grow to wholeness. When they toast *l'chayim* – to life – it is an injunction to enjoy oneself and thus to honour creation by taking pleasure in the good things of life. At IMI, peace-loving has become reduction to quietude, and life risks becoming mortification in place of joy.

Without attention to particularity, the Shyams risk being blind to the real virtues and humanity of those outside IMI. When Manorama turns away from international development or relief work, toward an immoderate love of the universal, she echoes Cain: "What, am I the keeper of my brother?" In some, indifference to others risks turning into hating or despising the particular. To be disappointed in the manifold and in diversity, as so many Shyams are, because of the implicit dualism, seems extreme – nearly misanthropic – in contrast to the moderate view put forward by Thomas Aquinas, that the diversity of beings reflects the range of perfections characterizing existence.

But the Shyams are not moderate. Take, for example, their "Donatism." Why are the Shyams at IMI, rather than in churches and synagogues? They say – almost to a person – that as church and synagogue attenders, they observed hypocrisy among priests and rabbis. After that, they walked out. The sentiment is not unique to the Shyams, nor unintelligible, but it is simplistic. In the fifth century, Augustine battled the Donatist sect, which called for a pure church, unblemished by fallen members. Augustine's response was at once more realistic and more charitable: We are all fallen, and it is not given to us to know who is to be damned and who is to be saved. It is precisely this humility which underscores the capacity for forgiveness. I found a comment by one of the devotees of Swami Shyam to be telling in this regard. Archana studied philosophy at Trent University and said she had always been struck by Sartre's comment that hell is other people. Shyam Space offers a solution: a state of consciousness where there are no others.

To desire to overcome all limitation and separation is, finally, perhaps to desire to stop being human. In Plato's dialogue *The Symposium*, in which Socrates attempts to learn what the essence of love is, one of the lovers suggests that all is one. No one in the dialogue can relate this to their own experience, for love is difference. It is only because of absence, need, and separation that humans love. If there were no barrier of individuality or uniqueness distinguishing us from one another, or humans from the world, would we act, love, admire, or engage anything? It would only be a mirror of ourselves. If there were no difference, could we be astonished? If all were one, our lives would be boring and senseless. "Oneness" love is sentimental, whereas human love is turbulent, divisive, and profound. Gentleness without passion is sterile. Perhaps this is why, in the same dialogue, Plato uses the metaphor of the hunt to describe the highest form of love, the love of wisdom. Hunting is not boring – it is adventure, pursuit, danger, daring, and cunning. It is about discriminating between "them and us," friends and enemies, hunter and hunted. Hunters do not have one eye inward and the other up to the zenith – they would risk their lives if they did. The Shyams, by contrast, are vegetarians, celibate, and lovers of peace. And, maybe, not quite engaged enough with the rest of humanity.

In Shyam Space, there is no speech, only silence. The foundation of the Western world, by contrast, is the religion of the Word. While it is true that in Ecclesiastes one finds an admonition against speech, "God is in heaven, and thou upon earth: therefore let thy words be few," this is an injunction against foolish talk. The Western God creates by speech. His speech is that of division and separation – partitioning out the heavens from the earth, one species from another species, male from female, and so on. Humanity, under the Western God, is the privileged being, for in being addressed, hearing, and responding, he has communion with God, which other beings lack. To the extent that Man is the heir of the language of God and can co-create with God, he too continues to separate out and distinguish in speech. He has the gift, for example, of using symbol, thus speaking in time but opening up a higher level of reality. Symbolic language is the medium in which Man experiences the divine. The creature with time in him speaks with the eternal, but the condition of that speech is the separation of God and man. The Biblical story of the Tower of Babel is an admonishment against seeking one eternal language – and thus making oneself God – in favour of a heterogeneity of human languages. The Shyams, by contrast, having been sated on information and abstractions in the West, now live in a world without words, and, for fear that words will be inauthentic and distort reality, prefer a silent union with God in the East. "When a man is speaking, he cannot be breathing … and when a man is breathing he cannot be speaking," reads the Kaushitake Upanishad.[26]

Finally, one is brought to speculate on the institutional, or moral and political, expression of Shyam Space. True, institutionalization is what the Shyams abjure, though at Swami's death, the problem of structure and continuity will emerge front and centre. There is no "pure" metaphysics – lurking in every metaphysic are moral and political consequences, and, at some point, these consequences have to be rigorously examined and not left hidden under platitudes. Shyam Space begs for political analysis. Recall Tripura, who said that if she ever went back to work in any organization, she would have to create her own fiefdom. Think of Dikpal, who closely monitors contact with outsiders. Consider Sukhindra, who has lost his inhibitions of public disclosure and making himself nakedly transparent. And remember that Swami Shyam is "I am I." Whatever else these disparate tendencies suggest, one thing is certain – the Shyams' extreme repudiation of Western ideas of happiness and scientific enlightenment render them politically suspect.

The Shyams are certainly not democrats, having instead fallen prey to the mysticism to which Alexis de Tocqueville feared democracies were so prone. Commenting on the dangers of excessive materialism in democracies, Tocqueville commented:

> If ever the thoughts of the great majority came to be concentrated solely on the search for material blessings, one can anticipate that there would be a colossal reaction in the souls of men. They would distractedly launch out into the world of spirits for fear of being held too tightly bound by the body's fetters. It is therefore no cause for astonishment that in a society thinking about nothing but the world a few individuals should want to look at nothing but heaven. I should be surprised if, among a people uniquely preoccupied with prosperity, mysticism did not soon make progress.[27]

Resonating uncannily with the life of the Shyams, Tocqueville's description is particularly noteworthy for its warning. It is a plea wholly unheeded by the Shyams. He wrote:

> [In democracies,] the concept of unity becomes an obsession. Man looks for it everywhere, and when he thinks he has found it, he gladly reposes in that belief. Not content with the discovery that there is nothing in the world but one creation and one Creator, he is still embarrassed by this primary division of things and seeks to expand and simplify his conception by including God and the universe in one great whole. If one finds a philosophical system which teaches that all things material and immaterial, visible and invisible, which the world contains are only to be considered as the several parts of an immense Being who alone remains eternal in the midst of the continual flux and transformation of all that composes Him, one may be sure that such a system, although it destroys human individuality, or rather just because it destroys it, will have the secret charms for men living under democracies. All their habits of mind prepare them to conceive it and put them on the way toward adopting it. It naturally attracts their imagination and holds it fixed. It fosters the

pride and soothes the laziness of their minds. Of all the different philosophical systems used to explain the universe, I believe that pantheism is one of those most fitted to seduce the mind in democratic ages. All those who still appreciate the true nature of man's greatness should combine in the struggle against it.[28]

What is most at stake at I M I is the idea of a free and rational person. Swami's philosophy extinguishes the idea and experience of a unique person, and simultaneously that of a plurality of individuals. There is neither privacy, nor a public world. Is it accidental that the Swami exercises, in the language of some dissenters, a tyrannical hold on his subjects? Without a me and them, and a me and what is different, how could there be any limit on the power of Swami? The religion of silence has neither room for dissent, nor for rich, multi-textured and diverse debate, though the variations on oneness are, undeniably, richly creative. A sentimental intimacy without desire may be calm and peaceful. Unfortunately, that is not enough for liberal democracy nor is it sufficient to support a doctrine of moral rights and obligations. Political watchfulness is not compatible with "the god indwelling." Only the idea of a transcendent God prevents complacency and credulity. Where the highest state, and most defining moment, is *samadhi* (sensation without recognition or evaluation), discrimination and preference slip between the cracks. With the abandonment of particular consciousness, Shyam Space interiorizes each Shyam to the point where, rather like an onion, at the very centre is nothing. And the weakest have the most to lose.

All these puzzling tendencies in the Shyams lead me to a more contentious judgment. One of the great dangers of iconoclasm and apophatic religious experience is that for fear of compromising too dearly with the world, the seeker ends by exhibiting an extreme hatred of body, earth, and time. The most extreme expression of these dangers is found in Gnosticism, a heresy denounced by the early Christian church though, like most "heresies," it also contains aspects with the potential to heighten and purify the forms of spiritualization. The patristic Christian fathers Irenaeus, Hippolytus, Tertullian, and Clement of Alexandria, however, found only dangerous error. And the Shyams unabashedly live the dream of this error.

Paul writes in his Letter to the Hebrews that faith is "the substance of things hoped for, the evidence of things not seen" (Heb. 11:1), and elaborates in his Letter to the Corinthians that in this world "we see in a mirror, dimly ... [and] know only in part," though, at the end of human history, "we will see face to face ... [and] know fully" (Cor. 1:13). The Gnostic, by contrast, asks, "From where am I coming and where am I going?" and is confident that mere faith can be replaced by knowledge of the answer, *gnosis* – if only for a privileged few of the spiritually adept. And in that confidence lies Gnosticism's subversive stance to orthodoxy.

Self-renunciation and asceticism are by long-standing tradition means of access to the divine, or to sanctification, and history is strewn with examples of Christian stylites who lived on the tops of pillars, had themselves buried in cisterns, locked behind hermitage walls, and suspended in cages to mortify the flesh so as to move toward pure spirit, and thus an encounter with the divine.[29] Ramadan's demanding schedule of fasting is meant to move the pious Muslim closer to Allah, as Yom Kippur's restrictions on devout Jews is intended to stimulate charity. Intense suspicion of the flesh, from Augustine through St. Francis to Luther, would reiterate, "I am dust and ashes and full of sin." But Gnostics take this renunciation and austerity one step further.

For Gnostics, matter is wholly alien to God, and thus earth, body, and time are mere darkness. Indeed, the common Gnostic myth posits that the created, natural order, within which manifests all empirical and psychic reality, and which is the object of human contemplation and affirmation, is in fact the product of an evil demiurge who gave the world its orderly completeness, not as a means of recollecting and knowing the divine source, but precisely to prevent such comprehension. The creator god of this world (YHWH in the Hebrew Bible) is a false god, continually reinforcing the fullness and completeness of this cosmic prison, while preventing humans from seeing their truly alienated and exiled condition. Caught in the world and held within its forces, humans must be awakened by a redeemer who leads them to discover a remnant of themselves – a divine spark (*pneuma*) – that will disclose to them that the orderly inferences from natural perception and cognition (*psyche*) constituting everyday reality are just so much noise and obfuscation. The world will then become an object of abhorrence, a place of homesickness and exile, release from which can only occur in the freedom and knowledge that truth lies only in the unknown God, whose abode is the abyss of silence. *Gnosis,* the object of spiritual practice, is not faith or intellectual intuition, but a secret, even occult, knowledge of this ultimate truth. The Gnostic "pneumatic" anticipates a radical change in the nature of the human, in the conditions of existence, and the structure of being, and, until the final breakthrough occurs, either extreme asceticism (which extinguishes complicity with the world) or utter profligacy (which transgresses and finally exhausts the laws of nature) are the sole authentic modalities of spiritual life.[30]

Gnosticism may be an answer to a church deeply compromised by entanglement with worldly power, for its wholly transcendent God humbles spiritual understanding. It may also be a more reverent understanding of what it means to subscribe to the idea of an absolute God – certainly more pious than the deistic belief that the rational and universal laws of nature discovered by humans, using the faculties endowed them by God, are laws which no being can suspend, not even God, who is also bound by them. And Gnosticism may provide a more consoling answer to the "Why?" of human affliction and suffering. But its intense contramundane posture and radical dualistic separation of body and spirit, reason and truth, the world and the sacred as contending principles may derail simplistically into irrationalism and superstition in the hands of the inexperienced and credulous. Gnosticism is the dangerous extremity into which mysticism may fall. Though implicit in virtually all of the religious phenomena I've examined in this study (consider again Jean Vanier's *The Broken Body*), gnosticism is most acute here at IMI.

There are many aspects of the Shyams' understanding and experience of spiritual wholeness which play out the ancient Gnostic religion, proscribed by all three Western monotheisms. First, as the Shyams are quick to say, they are not "mystics" – meaning irrational or fantastic in their beliefs and practices – but knowers, consonant with the ancient Gnostics' belief that they possessed *gnosis* (wisdom) and not mere faith or piety. At IMI, there is a concerted effort to make a visitor know that he or she is not visiting an ashram, or a religious community *per se*, but a "scientific laboratory." Sufficient numbers of the devotees went to university during the post-behaviouralist, post-positivistic phase in the academic world, and have taken to heart one of its strongest messages – that the study of humans means putting to the test not only the "objective" and quantifiable regularities of behaviour, but also the "I" or subject who does the scientific investigation. As the Shyams like to say, they are experimenting on themselves, and the "empirical" phenomena they are studying include their own experiences. But knowing the highest things (our origin, our salvation, and our destination) is, for Western monotheisms, apostasy – unless one is God. Humans may know many things, but only God knows the one big thing – "the substance of things hoped for, the evidence of things not seen." Unless one is a Gnostic.

The ancient Gnostics of the first and second century in the common era experienced the world as divided into light and darkness. They saw the created order around them, not as something beautiful and knowable, but as a false order which imprisoned them, as if in a tomb. God, the creator, was not, however, the true God, but a false god who fashioned the cosmos as an intelligible whole to deceive us and prevent us from discovering the true God. The unknown God sends a messenger to tell us that we are imprisoned in a world of darkness, that we must "Awake!" to discover that the world – once so familiar and reassuring – is nothing but "noise," and return to our source. Since our bodies, our souls, our families, our political states, are all against us – their very design a sign of their falsity – we must shrink ourselves to a minimal self, a *pneuma*, which, unlike our souls, is not implicated in this world of purpose and order. We will be lonely – after all, the cosmic order and the creator God, and all his creatures, are against us – but we may be fortunate to link up with a few other "pneumatics" who have also become knowers of the esoteric answer to the question, "From where am I coming and where am I going?" and who are akin to one another in no other way than their relation to the a-cosmic God.[31] But therein lies redemption and salvation.

The Shyams are Gnostics, pure and simple. They disavow their embodied selves in favour of a *pneuma*, or true self, which is emptiness. They have constructed for themselves a community of solitudes, where the only thing that is common is what is unseen, unspeakable, and unverifiable. Everything turns out to be nothing. The One is contramundane, and unknowable by natural means, unless one understands the progressive closing down of the ordinary organs of perception and

engagement as itself "natural." The Shyams see archetypes of consciousness, human practices, cognitive instruments, and emotional patterns
as mere "mechanisms" to be used and discarded. Swami Shyam's
"message" is devilishly simple: Realize your Self. Swami Shyam is, in
fact, only themselves, their Self reborn. He may rule like a potentate, but
– as the Shyams say – Swami is only them ruling themselves.

Two features bear further comment. First, the Shyams' very unerotic
mysticism is premised on the fallenness, and even hatred, of the body.
The vow of celibacy may conserve and sublimate sexual energy, but it
seems more evidently an expression of the unwillingness to perpetuate
what they believe is the kingdom of darkness. The Shyams are arrest-
ing the flow of divine substance from generation to generation
(*toldoth*), enjoined by the biblical *toroth*, "Go forth and multiply."
Especially the Shyams who are Jewish forget that their faith does not
permit them to choose to remain without children. But, like Nazirites –
Jews who sought closer union with God through extreme renunciation
of human ways – the Shyams have separated from the world. And,
unlike Christian asceticism and monasticism, there is no attempt to
reconcile the sensual and spiritual realms, as in the doctrine of the
"resurrected body," for the full person is disregarded. The Shyams shun
maternal and paternal love, carnal love, the love between husband and
wife, and filial love because each is a constraint on the free disposal of
the self. To avoid perpetuating the kingdom of darkness, involvement
with the darkness must end. Some might see the Shyams as exhibiting
a strange unwillingness to live, for, having run away from the complex
entanglements of true human relationships into non-possessive love
and love for all, the Shyams seem just to be escaping commitment and
responsibility.[32]

Second, the Shyams exhibit a dangerous, even sophomoric taste for
an unmediated experience of oneness which incorporates an uncompromising refusal to consent to existence. Plato's legacy to the Western
world is the idea that the relationship of the human soul to the cosmos
is one of microcosm to macrocosm – the structure of human nature
repeats a structure within the cosmos as a whole. The "whole" is a
cosmos – an intelligible whole – and we are at home in the cosmos
because we are consubstantial with it. The *berith*, or covenant, in
Judaism attests to a similar identity between human existence and
divine providence. A similar idea lies at the heart of Christianity in the

idea of "sacramentalism" – an action in which, mysteriously, the divine reveals itself in the human world, or where the eternal descends into the concrete. Uniting all three accounts is the conclusion that the natural order is not opposed to our highest aspirations – the ascent to the divine – but is the conduit for them. And, equally important, each tradition offers a strong warning that an unmediated vision of the One blinds. Each account prescribes that the One is only to be observed reflected in worldly forms, just as the sun is best seen reflected in water and things.

The Shyams, by contrast, find the world's forms alien and hostile, and are swept up in a vortex of never-ending self-cancellation and negation. The interminable exodus – from the land of slavery, from the Baals and Ashtarts, from the land of Canaan, from the new covenant foretold by the prophets, even the spirit from itself – is for the Shyams a spiritual event re-enacted each and every day at I M I in an exit strategy from modernity. And, in the process, they have blinded themselves to the diverse human presence in the world, to each and every person's fragile, though ennobling, potential for virtue and goodness. Even oneness seems to evade the Shyams, for in the preoccupation with overcoming duality, duality seems to be at the centre of all they think and do. The more they obsess on oneness, the more it appears to recede.

Northrop Frye wrote:

> These cults ... seem to me to be an aspect, even if a minor one, of a general weariness with history, with being bullied and badgered by all the pan-historical fantasies of the nineteenth century, of Hegel and Marx and Newman and Comte, who keep insisting that by history alone we can be saved, or rather by putting some kind of construct on history that will give it a specious direction or meaning.[34]

Refugees from the fantasies of progress, from violence sanctioned by the historical epiphany of "truth," and from the unrelenting drive for bigger, better, and more, the Shyams represent the ultimate stage of baby boomers' alienation from the world, ecstasy deficit, desire for total transcendence, wish to be at primordial point zero, insistence on an indiscriminate inclusivity, belief in the power to reconstruct reality, and ambition to be destiny. In opposition to the historical dynamism and its incumbent historical responsibilities, which was inherited by many of them from their Jewish origins, and which formed the core of their modernity, the Shyams so evidently bear the mark of the baby boomers' desire just "to be." While that desire is carried forward by the extravagant dream of escape from self-limitation (from the body, earth, and history), and reveals itself as an unrequitable nomadism, and inability to compromise and accommodate – syndromes which are rightfully reproached – it does not differ qualitatively from the apprehensions and ambitions we have observed all along among the baby boomers undertaking spiritual searches. At I M I, one finds merely the most acute critique of the modern West.

One encounters among the Shyams again and again baby-boomer loneliness, a need to belong, and a need for commitment. There is a cry here for healing and reconciliation, and a yearning to return to the experiential source of the human-divine encounter. The plaint against the contractions that the world imposes on the human spirit contains a genuine longing for an uncompromised spirituality. In the hands of the Shyams, the denunciation of modernity and the dream of release is extreme, but – in my judgment – it resonates deeply for all baby boomers. Having walked away from the satisfactions and temptations offered by modernity, the Shyams' lives testify to serious lacunae in modern life – to the absence of true community, to the eclipse of opportunities for genuinely transcendent experiences other than poetry and art, to the poverty of a psychology centred on power and self-realization, to the obscenity of excessive material consumption, and to the privations of a life driven by the demand for reciprocity and compensation.

The Shyams' "fifty-monkey thing" will not, of course, be the lever of world change – as ardently as some of the Shyams might wish – but their articulation of a viable alternative world sharpens the idiom of protest against modernity's reductions and displacements of spiritual longing. The Shyams, like so many of their contemporaries, wish too much and perhaps achieve too little, but they flush out what often remains inchoate among the traditionalists, secular moralists, and New Agers.

In all honesty, the categories of judgment and reproach I have used in discussing the Shyams and Shyam Space – and which I have urged my reader to adopt as her or his own, both in thinking about the

Shyams and the baby boomers' spiritual searches more generally – are meaningless from the viewpoint of the East. At the end of the day, once all the simple comparisons and general divergences are noted, East is still East, and West is still West, and ne'er the twain shall meet. To go to the East, as have the Shyams, is to leave the West behind. Their retreat, however, is a warning to a civilization whose traditional religious forms, intellectual coordinates, and political and social formulations have become – for this articulate, self-conscious generation – lifeless and empty.

# Conclusion

## Suspending Disbelief and the Growth of Sensibility

F or a long time, baby boomers were willing to accept surrogates and counterfeits to their spiritual longings, as answers to human predicaments. Then, as a consequence of age, personal crisis, a heightened sense of responsibility, or a natural (perhaps even supernatural) development in their lives, baby boomers began to suspect something was missing from their lives. It is possible that these children of the sixties are still looking for a home, and this refuge in spiritual discovery is merely the latest expression of that search. More likely, in my mind, are the odds that baby boomers are carriers of a profound civilizational paroxysm which is sounding the death knell for cardinal aspects of modernity. To be sure, many baby boomers are undertaking religious pilgrimages as a kind of spiritual insurance, which would not make their generation unique. But, in my observation, far more are searching because the Enlightenment philosophy of the infinite perfectibility of humanity, and the promise of complete this-worldly satisfaction, has collapsed for them. I have expatiated on a broad range of topics, but the primary purpose of this study is to portray the highs and lows of this challenge to modernity. I have also aspired to as generous a depiction of baby boomers' spiritual searches as is compatible with critical judgment, because I believe that the experiences of the divine reported to me are genuine, and because I personally accept Rabbi Heschel's observation: "Forfeit your sense of awe, let your conceit diminish your ability to revere, and the universe becomes a marketplace for you."[1]

I have been selective in the profile of baby boomers I interviewed – avoiding those blessed individuals who have an unwavering faith in the religion into which they were born, or those who slipped back into the mainstream after decades of withdrawal from institutionalized religion, in favour of those who were unsure, displeased with received forms, rebellious, and desirous of applying pressure to the established ways. Some readers will deny the paradigmatic character of this type of seeker, but, in my estimation, the choice had the merit of focusing on baby boomers who were consciously weighing the pros and cons of varied spiritual options and who thus enjoyed a heightened capacity to articulate and justify their choices. The baby boomers I spent time with, moreover, were mostly professionals who were university-educated and in social positions where their viewpoints mattered beyond themselves and an intimate circle of acquaintances. In addition, while their numbers were few, I concluded that insofar as many of these individuals were discerning analysts of the *Zeitgeist,* their self-consciousness – as "moderns" working out a relation to tradition, and as "baby boomers" with generationally defined expectations and needs – made them a representative cross-section of most baby boomers on spiritual walkabout. And, if one believes, as I do, in the transformative power of a few, then sheer numbers are less significant than knowledge and access to the levers of power. By my reckoning, little time will pass before the urgency and discourse of these baby boomers' spiritual searches permeates most of Canadian society.

There are many things I would have liked to write about and did not – the situation of Quebec Roman Catholics still negotiating their take on religion four decades after the Quiet Revolution, the gradual growth in number of conversions to Islam, the Lubavitcher Hasidic community in Outremont, Quebec, the magnet synagogues in Toronto and Thornhill, the seeker-sensitive movement in the Christian Reform Church, the Roman Catholic and Anglican Cursillo retreats, the growth of interest in Sufism and ecstatic dancing, the emerging tensions in Canada between "English" and "Southern" Baptists, the "mega-church" phenomenon, and the use of new technologies to evangelize, to name just a few – but this study was intended less as a sociological survey, and more as a philosophical commentary on phenomena I judged paradigmatic for baby boomers' spiritual searches in general. I am, of course, sensitive to the shortcomings with which this study is burdened. It remains for readers to judge whether a reduction in scope has led to a loss in significance.

To draw this book to a close with some provisional conclusions, I would like to provide a final smattering of pithy, if not gnomic, baby-boomer utterances. If baby boomers once insisted, "Go to the poets, not the politicians," today, for many of the same reasons, they say, "Go to the mystics, not the theologians." When a baby boomer adopts a farrago of techniques of sanctification, just as once any political instrument at hand would suffice, and says, "It's just a bag of tricks but it works," he or she exhibits a characteristic baby-boomer predisposition to prefer meaning to truth, and experience to reality. Theological doctrine or ecclesiastical authority count for nought before the bar of personal feeling. Church attendance or conformity to ritual is not a duty or obligation laid down by authority, but something which meets baby boomers' needs. The baby boomer who insists that priests, rabbis, and imams "walk the talk" is demanding the indiscriminate, universal congruence a whole generation demanded in its bid for holism. When another says, "It is easier for me to be ritualistic than doctrinal," he means that the experience is authoritative and revelatory, and is only secondarily proof of the tradition out of which it emerged. When baby boomers reserve the right to choose which doctrines they will adopt, and which range of practices they will follow – "I don't want to have to buy into the whole ball of wax" – they affirm their right to a made-to-measure, even a do-it-yourself lifestyle. If they put their faith in twelve-step processes of salvation and redemption, baby boomers have not moved far from familiar techniques of recovery and growth that accompanied values clarification in school and sensitivity sessions at the workplace, and that evince inextinguishable faith in human perfectibility and the efficacy of method.

The baby boomer who claims, "I prayed for a physical sign and was hit by the feeling of a 5,000-volt charge thrashing through my body," evinces an expectation characteristic of a whole generation – that, even in the absence of discipline and patience, it is given to us to enjoy ecstatic transformation and vision. When a baby boomer laments the fallen world of adults and is enchanted by old and forgotten ritual, explaining, "If we were still children, we wouldn't have to learn this," he or she sustains the four-decade dream of living the life of wishes. The baby boomer who lapsed because, "In church it was all just yadda-yadda-yadda," and who has turned to meditation, explaining, "Sitting in silence makes it safe to be together," merely extends to its logical conclusion a process begun with Dale Carnegie and Irving Goffman, who taught us to beware the games and pretenses played out in human speech, abetted by writers like Martin Buber and Alan Watts, who sowed the debilitating suspicion that everyday speech is manipulative, and who found in the communion of intimates and lovers the only truly authentic relationship. The baby boomer who believes, "We are dead men walking," or "It's the Wild, Wild West out there," reiterates a whole generation's despair at a world gone terribly wrong. And the baby boomer who affirms, "We have to have our feet on the ground and our head in the clouds," echoes the idealism, and the peculiar insouciance to the middle kingdom of the human world, quintessentially defining the baby boomers' search for sanctity, and signalling both the greatest opportunity and greatest danger.

It is now time to draw up a ledger of the negative and positive aspects of baby boomers' spiritual searches. On the debit side, one could say that despite the adventure of transcendence, many baby boomers continually revert to type. For many of them, the insatiable desire for novelty, for the latest thrill and "challenge beyond all challenges," for the one big answer, and for something they can believe in but which has to fit their "comfort zone," corrupts their approach to religion. They say they can be ritualistic, but not doctrinal; that they will trust a personal spiritual director, but not the establishment "men with hats"; that faith must be moving and fulfilling, but they would prefer to remain agnostic as to whether it is true. As a consequence, their spiritual searches exhibit an intense desire to engage spirituality, but that desire is free-floating. With no cultural memory, and a tendency to fear that all bonds are colonizing, most baby boomers are undertaking solo adventures in self-realization, and shunning traditional contexts of faith. Whether it is traditionalists looking for a lost heritage, or secularists promoting eternal justice without metaphysics, or New Agers designing their own gods, institutions and real-world communities have fallen out of the picture.

It may be that baby boomers' unorthodox ways are products of lingering influences from the formative stages of childhood, adolescence, and early adulthood. The romantic idealism which informed their culture and patterned their consciousness gave many baby boomers a sense in the 1960s that they were at ground zero – they had the opportunity to summon up a new creation, a world informed by authenticity, pure freedom, and infinite perfectibility. Moreover, as a generation destined to greatness, no dream, indulgence, or fantasy could do wrong. But, in this extravagant hope, baby boomers were, perhaps, set up for a great fall. So few of them anticipated tragedy or the sudden ruptures which tear all human constructs apart. They were stunned by fallibility and corruption. When these eventualities arose, some baby boomers went into a tailspin. They became gullible, and victims of auto-suggestion. When an exotic guru came along and offered a mantra or koan, and held out the promise of attunement with the rhythms of the universe, many of them simply leapt.

This proclivity to fideism is, in my observation, the direct result of many baby boomers' decisions to turn their backs on the world. At some point in their lives, diffuse anxiety coalesced into alienation from the world, leading to renunciation and even the subversive hope that the world would be visited by a destroyer-god who would scourge creation. A clue to many boomers' world-despair lies in the fantasy that there is no bloodline behind them, in the resolution to produce no children, and in the abdication of responsibility for maintaining and transmitting the tradition. Like the Old Testament prophet Jeremiah, it is as if they have decided that the consignment of truth and order through the generations must cease pending a new revelation. Freed from the world, these baby boomers approach religion and faith expecting to behave like *bricoleurs* playing with paradigms and recon-structing reality.

Hope in the supernatural contains the understandable desire to supersede the tyranny of the factual, or those contingent events whose power to disrupt our lives is a scandal to our reason. Excessive order, especially when it is experienced as imposing a mechanical necessity, invariably gives rise to the search for release – and the supernatural is an obvious corrective. But many baby boomers have undertaken their spiritual searches as if they were living in the Age of Kali – the primor-dial zero at the end of the historical cycle when humankind returns to Absolute Silence, and where communication between humans and gods no longer proceeds through everyday life. The world is out of joint and the infinite cannot fit into the finite. Rather than laughing in joy, thus affirming God's wise management of creation, baby boomers mourn, thus questioning God's judgment. Such baby boomers, ruminating on the God of creation who has on all counts absconded, can reason with Ivan Karamazov that, "If God does not exist, then everything is permitted," and what they will permit themselves is the judgment that God is inadequate to the world. They applaud Karamazov's conclusion that he "rejects the world and wishes to tear it from the hands of God, since he made it badly, with the pretension of organizing it differently and in a superior manner than its original author." Given the enormity of their burden, no wonder many baby boomers undertake their spiritual searches with such grim resoluteness.

The desire for an intense transformation is usually wanted by those who do not benefit from the present arrangement of the world: the economically and politically disadvantaged who see themselves as social outcasts and the disinherited of the earth. In the case of most baby boomers, such a perception could not be farther from the truth. Baby boomers, though lacking little in material goods, are nevertheless dispossessed. One sees this in the nearly universal, desperate longing for the Holy Spirit – not as an agent of reconciliation, but as an agent of regeneration who sends salvific signs and re-scripts creation. One sees it in the suggestive nostrum, "Be spiritual, experience the god indwelling," an apparent complement to or substitute for the politically revisionist dictum, "Think globally, act locally." In both cases, the mediated world, in which traditionally the infinite was encountered within the finite phenomena of everyday life, has fallen out.

Rudolf Bultmann, the Protestant theologian, once suggested a vivid metaphor for the idea of mediation. He wrote: Think about reality as a "three-storey universe" made up of the heavens, the earth, and the underworld. From the perspective of the whole, reality holds together the natural and the supernatural. Cosmology, anthropology (the reasoned account of what a human being is), morality, and law form a single, interlocking scale of order. But, as gradations of reality, each of the realms is also distinct. The middle ground – the earth – is where Christ is incarnate, though it cannot be the realm of absolute truth since He returned to the higher realm, heaven. "Down below" is the realm of the dead, the powers of hell, and the falsity of chaos and disorder. For us, the "earth" is the most interesting, and its tensions attract the greatest part of our striving and hopes. It is also the realm which is least stable. The middle is the point of connection and tension between a divinely ordered universe, the publicly established order of rules, and the fateful fall into chaos, with each threatening to engulf the others. It is where the factual and the mystical engage one another. In the past, cultures sanctified the place where profane and sacred, or nature and divine, met, by attempting to confer on it all the substantiality and imperishability of the divine itself: "Upon this rock I build my church" (Matt. 16:18). The great cathedrals and temples of the world, past and present – from Solomon's Temple in Jerusalem, to the Meenakshi temple in Madurai, India, to the Hagia Sophia in Istanbul, Turkey, to the Cathedral of Chartres in France – all attest to the human need to embody the experienced reality of tension toward the divine in a precarious substantiality. But today, it seems, the tension is exhausted, and all the traditional means of mediation – institutions, doctrines, icons, symbols – are as fragile as crystal.

Traditionally, with the exception of extreme renunciants, the world is where the work of regenerating the spirit took place. Situating faith in the world had the merit of subjecting mystical revelations of the divine to the light of public deliberation and debate, thus placing a check on private fantasies. When Jews say that one should not be alone, not even with God, they echo a warning issued in the Isa Upanishad: "Into deep darkness fall those who follow the immanent. Into deeper darkness fall those who follow the transcendent."[2] Credulity and madness are dangers wherever solo flights into transcendence are undertaken. Taking the "world" – and particularly the immediate milieu one inhabits – into account is also an antidote to the danger of aiming at everything and achieving nothing. Commending action that is closest to home, Augustine writes, "Since you cannot be of assistance to everyone, those especially are to be cared for who are most closely bound to you by place, time, or opportunity, as if by chance."[3] You are to pay special regard to those who, by the accidents of time, or place, or circumstance, are brought into closer connection with you. And neglect of the world may also run the risk of reducing the possibilities of reality, rather than their imaginative transformation through human virtue. The Jewish injunction *Tikun Olan* – heal and repair the world – contains the salutary insight that improvement and perfection of the world, and completing the work left undone by the Creator, is the true mark of commitment to YHWH. Search for an unmediated vision of God, beyond the fallen world, blinds many baby boomers to the sanctity around them. In his book *The Varieties of Religious Experience*, William James warns of the constricted condition of those individuals who would leave the world to the devil while saving their own soul. By whatever standard the abandonment of the world is parsed, baby boomers have evidently forgotten some significant traditional insights. As with all antinomianism, many of the baby boomers' apprehensions entail a reduction of the possibilities in reality, rather than their imaginative transformation through human virtue. Possessing too much knowledge and certainty, to the point that they became world-weary, baby boomers may have precipitantly closed down the self-exploration and continual self-transcendence which constitutes the adventure of life. For these baby boomers, the situation is rather like that lamented by G.K. Chesterton when he spoke of those individuals in whom there is so little love for the world that they are no longer willing to set fire to it.

Being homeless, baby boomers' spiritual searches are often undertaken in that spirit of self-righteousness that says, "Now, only spirituality matters." If once there was a danger that the "political" threatened to engulf all dimensions of human life, now we have to fear that the "spiritual," as unworldliness, becomes everything. However, one should not be surprised that this is the turn that baby boomers' minds have taken, for it is a perfect illustration of the phenomenon of the return of the repressed. All through their youth, baby boomers beat the tattoo, "We're special; what we feel is significant and true." For a while, this solipsism was channelled toward the world. Today, it reappears as the aesthetic impulse in baby boomers' religion.

What I mean by "aesthetic impulse" is the baby boomers' act of suspending disbelief in modern science's definition of ways of being and knowing, and producing through an act of will and imagination a secondary, enchanted world which *imitates* in some way what is desirable in the ancient metaphysic. The willing suspension of disbelief admits that the facts of the Bible, or the Koran, or the Torah cannot be empirical and historical, but interprets them symbolically and allegorically. The "facts" of the Bible are not facts in the usual sense, but part of a *Heilgeschichte* – a mythical, spiritual narrative – whose truth is experienced in its transforming power. Here is modernity's contrapuntal melody – sung in poetry by Goethe, advanced in theology by Schleiermacher – that seeks to capture in the feelings of awe and wonder a romantic sense of the eternal in a moment of time, in hope against hope.[4]

The complications arising from this solution are neatly addressed by J.R.R. Tolkien in his review of Andrew Lang's fairy books.[5] Lang proposed that the enchantment of fairy tales lay in their power to animate a "willing suspension of disbelief," permitting a reader to experience the tale as beautiful, fulfilling, and moving. But Tolkien pointed out that a suspended disbelief is always a substitute for the real thing. Suspending disbelief takes one outside the spell or magic of what is real. The spell is broken, the magic failed, Tolkien wrote, once one is "looking at the little abortive Secondary World from outside." Moreover, Tolkien added, Lang's depiction betrayed the tired, shabby, or sentimental state of mind of adults musing on what childhood ought to be like, and in search of fantasy, escape, or consolation – not actual children, who read fairy tales as true and real – revealing significant details of their own lives. Lang, Tolkien contended, confused "possibility" (the wish to believe) with "desirability" (wanting to know). The challenge, Tolkien proposed, was to learn to read again as children do, and to move from an aesthetic, sentimental association to a reading where the only significant question is, "Is it true?"

Tolkien's point is apposite to our discussion of faith as a willing suspension of scientific disbelief. If science has the monopoly on reason and reality, and yet can only explicate the uniform, materialist, deterministic mechanics of the natural order, then faith – which dares ask and answer questions about the ultimate ends of existence – becomes like a fairy tale. It is a way of subverting the known, mechanical order by the fantastical and the magical. Faith, then, is equivalent to charms, spells, and enchantments which reverse natural laws and causation.

But, for several reasons, this is not a satisfactory state for either reason or faith. For one, it merely confirms that reason and reality are restricted to hard, cold, physical and chemical fact (and unable to confirm our experiences of beauty, holistic harmony, and simple goodness), while opposing faith as mere sentimental association.[6] Reality is no longer one – comprehending all existence, from the things below the earth, through to the human world, up to the heavens – but is divided into the separate spheres of real, exterior mechanism and ideal and imagined interior sentiment, with no known or felt third principle capable of bridging them. Next, the bifurcation of reality is matched by the self-division of the person, who now wavers from one dimension of existence to the other, only half-heartedly capable of true allegiance to either. Needing to live a unified life, where wisdom and beauty are one, humans end up living the lie of one sphere or the other, or perpetually vacillating between the two. Finally, the willing suspension of disbelief cannot, in fact, produce an independent realm of human value, for it is inevitably conditioned by – even entangled with – the principle it opposes. The enchanted realm of faith is but the mirror image of the attenuated world it negates, and, lacking the concrete actuality of the exterior world, it is a mere ghost of the real and true, forever vulnerable to being discounted as bad faith.

Goethe brooded: "*Werd ich zum Augenblicke sagen, 'Verweile doch! Du bist so schön'*" – If only the moment in time, experienced momentarily as the taste of eternity, would not pass away. The believer's experiences cannot help but be nostalgic and melancholic, a "brooding joy," as Hegel termed the core of sentimentalized romanticism. And the diversity of faith traditions – now appearing as so many subjective "as if's" (as if there were heaven, as if sin could be redeemed, as if the cruel march of time could be extinguished and we could be like gods) – while they may be beautiful, moving, and even fulfilling, do not really matter, and have no lasting impact, in the overall scheme of things.

Indeed, as I travelled around the country conversing with baby boomers on spiritual walkabout, I kept experiencing an acute, if disjointed, sense of *déjà vu*. I vaguely recalled having passed through this spiritual landscape before, though the source eluded me. It finally hit me while bouncing down a dirt road in a broken, sputtering vehicle, amid the desiccated landscape of the prairies in search of an apocryphal prairie feud between God-fearing Christians and Satanists (which turned out to be nothing more malignant than a handful of baby boomers in the Bible belt praying ardently over the lost souls of another handful of baby boomers dabbling in aboriginal spirituality). I was in the world of Cervantes, in the make-believe kingdom of Don Quixote.

In that great novel, written at the boundary between the ancient and modern age, in which readers are still permitted to laugh at the absurdity, if inevitability, of modern life, Canada's baby boomers should see themselves. The memorable scenes of Don Quixote tilting at windmills, adopting a barber's basin as a knight's helmet, laying siege to armies of goats, and mistaking a rustic inn inhabited by rascals for a castle promising adventure and romance, speak to the death of ancient codes of honour, and the last gasp of a Christendom mired in magic and superstition, replaced by the modern world of testable fact, rational self-interest, and commerce. But the loss of Don Quixote's wits is as much an allegory of the fate of faith in the modern world.

Enthused by fanciful tales of chivalry, Don Quixote embarks on the life of knight-errantry, prepared to confront peril and danger, right wrongs, redress grievances, remove abuses, and do honour to Dulcinea del Tobosa, the ugly peasant girl he has glamourized as a noble Lady, and the light by which he will see. He is accompanied by the simple, prosaic Sancho, who cares only for his stomach and safety, but dreams of ruling his own dominion. As they confront seeming infamy and vice, Don Quixote re-enacts imaginary scenes recollected from his books, but, instead of fulfillment and achieved goodness, he precipitates one catastrophe after another, and finds himself hounded by unexpected accidents that happen at every step of the way. The world has changed – it is no longer a vast network of interconnected ranks and orders, united by reciprocal exchanges and codes of honour, but a miserable place where nothing is to be found without some mixture of wickedness and roguery.

The quest for adventure, nevertheless, becomes an adventure of transcendence. Four key "theophanies" befall Don Quixote – in caves, dreams, forests, and sky – but the consequences, played out amid the arid secularism of his world, are inconsequential. Quixote's faith is neither dogmatic theology, nor faith as doctrine promulgated by ecclesiastical authority, nor a tradition of devotional worship. It is instead fanciful sentiment inspired by books of chivalrous romance. Living in a mind-state enchanted with purpose, Don Quixote does not realize that, like the ancient forms of religion, his ideals constantly escape him, wreaking unexpected results and exposing themselves as hollowed out and indulgent. The drama of the novel is, at one level, the human story: ideals and disappointments, presumption and despair, joys and sorrows, a daily struggle for order and meaning – all aspects of participation in the reality of being. But the symbols have lost their conferring power, and no longer unify experience and reality. Romance has had to substitute for a metaphysic. Don Quixote finds he has ideals and faith without the real opportunity to realize them, and the consequence is experience where the real is continually confused with the fabulous.

Now, it is true, and here baby boomers may take heart, that all is not bitterness and sorrow, dust and ashes. Lady Dulcinea, though only an imagined object of devotion, nonetheless produces results: "Since I became a knight errant," Don Quixote testifies, "I have been valiant, courteous, liberal, well-bred, generous, polite, bold, gentle and patient, and an endurer of toils, imprisonments, and enchantments." And when he justifies his mission, pointing out that, "If there were no knight errants, all our actions would be in vain, for it is irrational and futile to devote single-mindedly all one's energies to that which will perish," Don Quixote, like the child who divulges that "the emperor wears no clothes," exhibits a fool's wisdom in exposing modernity's Achilles heel.

Don Quixote is modernity's fool and idiot. He appears in literature from Shakespeare to Dostoyevsky, and we both rightly mock and nostalgically admire him. Don Quixote, the romantic, and Sancho, the prosaic, represent the poles of modern life, where human existence is torn between the prosaic and fantastic, mechanical necessity and enchantment, and where faith is shown to have a "quixotic" fate. Baby boomers on spiritual walkabout believe their mission is a serious one, but it may all just be play.[7]

The most troubling feature of baby boomers' spiritual searches is their tendency to think aesthetically and psychologically, but not meta-physically. However gratifying it is to see a return to a "mytho-poetic" perspective on life, it is still only art. Nietzsche may have opined that, "It is only as aesthetic phenomenon that we and the world are eternally justified," believing that creativity alone is the source of truth and real-ity, but there is a limit to how much reality will accommodate to artis-tic will. The need to eat, sleep, and labour, the inevitability of disease and death, the inescapable fact that the weak will suffer injustice at the hands of the strong, and the daily need to struggle for order and mean-ing cannot be rescinded by beautiful, moving, and fulfilling images, even when such images offer consolation and sometimes generate effects that make it appear as if these existential predicaments can be transcended. As the political philosopher Eric Voegelin writes, "Men can allow the world content to grow to such proportion that the world and God disappear behind it, but they cannot eliminate the problem-atic of their own existence."[8]

Religion is not merely a perspective on life, or an antidote to the harshness of life, but an analysis of reality. Baby boomers are often "pietists" believing that personal experience and feeling are meaningful, or they find assurance in a "good story," or they gauge the possibility of undertaking religious practices by their transformative power. But they make the error of believing that what subjectively affects them (as sublime, reassuring, or inspiring) is an index of truth and reality. This "aestheticization" of faith may be appealing because it offers a powerful means of "connecting" to religion – much faster than the painstaking setting out of reasonable arguments, or the longer road of spiritual disciplines – but it does not alter the fact that choice, feeling, or intense belief are no proof of a faith's concrete actuality. As we know, individuals choose to believe all sorts of foolish notions, injurious to themselves and others, and feel any number of emotions, often simply from the perception of a situation. We may long for a god who will give us redemption or deliverance, but the longing itself does not confer reality on the object of our longing, since evidently it is possible to long for something that is not real. William James, whose book *The Varieties of Religious Experience* is heavily indebted to Schleiermacher, is an example of modern schizophrenia in the wake of the loss of a unified and knowable reality. Attempting to describe the felt reality of "varieties" of religious experience, while remaining true to the needs and thresholds of different believers, he deems it necessary to suggest repeatedly that the same experiences can be invoked by nitrous oxide, seizures, and hallucinations, sowing the deadly seeds of doubt as to whether these religious believers are in touch with anything but fantasy.

Romanticism might seem to correct the excessive materialism and reductionism of the application of science to human nature, but, in fact, by attending to the affective dimension of the neglect of those areas of reality apprehended by science, romanticism simply posits an alternative reality. The willing suspension of disbelief leaves the modern individual in a continuous vacillation between the poles of the mechanical and the sentimental. Lost is the classical idea of a hierarchically graded reality, in which eternal being is more real than transient becoming, and contemplation more revealing of truth than the senses. The Rajput warrior on the bank of the Ganges, and the Keralan family returning to strew sacred water on their fields and animals, inhabit a rich creative matrix in which the sensuous and the sublime, the rational and the emotional, and the visible and the invisible constitute a single, unified living whole. It is almost impossible to retrieve this degree of participation, and yet the modern alternatives of an inhuman reason and a superstitious unreason are hardly comforting. As Søren Kierkegaard pointed out, we are in the irreversible situation today where to know objectively is to cease to exist subjectively, to exist subjectively is to cease to know objectively.

The danger of subjectivity is compounded by human resourcefulness both in fabricating what Robert Musil called "second realities," and in inventing technology to simulate and "improve" upon reality. Many of the spiritual sites I visited were incredible. They were not simply beyond belief. They had achieved such a high level of simulation, arguably make-believe, that the complete suspension of disbelief was frighteningly viable. As "extravaganza" or "spectacle" religion proliferates, with its often seamless combination of faith and technology, one should expect even more efficient results. That is what is so problematic about "suspended disbelief" – the imaginative substitution of a second world for the reality disclosed by modern science, and known through the modern paradigm of knowledge. It demands an abandonment of inductive reason (inference from empirical facts) and deductive reason (inference from first principles), since it has yielded to science the power to supply proofs for truth. Though intensity of feeling and meaning may stand in for truth (of a shadowy kind), subjectivity is usually highly unstable, and even the alternative of "intersubjectivity," where a multiplicity of individuals confer on the meaning of things, is problematic as a test of truth – as the collective experience of meaning in the community of like-spirited contemplatives in Swami Shyam's IMI attests. A falsehood compounded many times over is still a falsehood.

Moreover, as Tolkien pointed out, often the substitute – which as an ideal is no more than the inverse of the real – is tinged with sentimentality and nostalgia and so does not truly stand in as an independent option. Consider, for example, the Shyam's vision of oneness, which is marred by so obsessive a preoccupation with overcoming duality that duality intrudes at every moment. The One is not an alternative, but just another confirmation of the duality it pretends to negate. The same dilemma saddles the dreams of pure "I-Thou" relationships and authentic "covenantal communities." These kinds of dialectics – the Rubik's cubes of academic philosophers – involve lots of spinning at standstill, but really produce nothing more than the appearance of arriving somewhere. And they engender the peculiar vacillations so characteristic of the modern age, of which baby boomers' spiritual searches gives ample evidence: From materialism they vault to supernaturalism, from technicism to transcendentalism, from scientific reason to piety, and from striving to submissiveness. These warring pairs have one further thing in common: Whether one finds oneself on the scientific or the aesthetic side of the equation, the test is certainty. But certainty is the one prize that religion is least able to deliver.

It may be that baby boomers have failed to learn the danger of getting what they hoped for. Wanting certainty, many have found how wrong it is to expect religion to have answers. At best, religion provides a more discerning formulation of questions and possibilities, rather than solutions. Religion, these baby boomers have discovered, is not simply a compilation of truth claims, but invitations to adventure. Faith – true faith – wavers in tension between longing and attainment, challenging baby boomers in search of holiness to avoid the presumption that the search can be completed, or the despair that the whole task is futile.

But, even if there are few answers, baby boomers undertaking spiritual searches are learning they are ahead of their indifferent fellow associates. One of the great errors of modernity is the belief that because we cannot know Being, we cannot know Truth. Spiritual seekers are recognizing that Truth is not a predicate of Being, nor a set of propositions derived from knowledge of Being. It is an act of living in the awareness of and attunement toward Being. That "grace," to use a Christian term – whose transformative power excites gratitude, magnanimity, and equanimity – is, as Augustine wrote, what distinguishes individuals with spiritual longings from "souls engrossed with perishable possessions, desirous of transitory power, overawed by meaningless prodigies." But, unlike some baby boomers who have bought into the postmodern idea that striving is sinful and submission is virtue, Augustine did not misconstrue the impulse which dominates human life by demanding timidity. To wonder and to pray are for him the most sublime forms of striving. He understood the way to account for both *eros* and *agape*, reconciling striving and receptivity.

On the credit side of baby boomers' spiritual searches are the signs of mature discernment that I observed in spades: the realization that humans are not autonomous and self-creating but have built-in longings and purposes; that the chastening of arrogance and pride allows an opening to a truth not compromised by human motives and expectations; that reverence and wonder are modes of knowledge; that there is a silence which is not merely the absence of sound; that ritual and ceremony in cooking, eating, and drinking are ways of hallowing life; that letting go of all the things we have desired in the world can be a prelude to a more profound sense of security; that obedience is not a denial of freedom but a liberation from the caprices of one's own self-interest, passions, and even reason; that "time out" from time – evident, for example, in the Carmelites' vow of leisure – is a means of deepening human enjoyment; and that happiness comes not from self-sufficiency and exaltation in our achievements, but from gratitude.[9]

Indeed, on a personal note, one of the most gratifying aspects of conducting the fieldwork for this study was meeting thousands of baby boomers across Canada and having the opportunity to observe how much genuine goodness exists in this country. I invariably encountered individuals who had managed to quell anger and envy, malicious talk and slanderous gossip, who had found a way of loving people more than they deserve, who did not return hate with hate but who forgave, who had the power to turn sorrow and suffering into a martyr's endurance, who were being a blessing by using their gifts and acting honourably, and who, in their actions, completed Rabbi Hillel's question, "If I am not for myself, who will be for me?" with the second question, "But if I am only for myself, what am I?" These are the baby boomers, far from the shopping malls, the corporate boardrooms, and the protest demonstrations, about whom one does not hear a great deal in the media or in Canada's universities: modest women and men who, as a consequence of faith, just feel privileged to live in a special place in the spirit of gratitude. Canada's baby boomers who have embarked on spiritual discovery are demonstrating that rescue from the endless non-finality of modernity's impulse of pursuing power and novelty is possible and desirable. And baby boomers' new experiences, in my observation, are giving pause to ringing endorsements of modernity.

Above all, baby boomers' spiritual searches restore an insight previously submerged under modernity's indefatigable optimism. Recall the Kumbh Mela to which I referred at the beginning of this book. It offered to those who were observing the pageant a vision of sanctity in wholeness where, to use Mircea Eliade's words, one could observe "the turning of simple existence into living drama."[10] Yet, sacred life along the Ganges was not all it seemed. There was great tumult the day I arrived in Haridwar – the *sannyasis* and *akharas* were in hot dispute over who had priority in bathing at the *ghat* and, indeed, one of the *shankyacharyas* had stabbed another in the chest that morning with his trident. Other prosaic elements lurked in the backdrop. The hair "offered" to the Ganges was, in fact, being sold to Delhi wig makers. A few blocks from the Ganges, a group of boys was filling the brass pots of "holy" water destined for farm fields and pregnant wives with ordinary water from the street spout. And there were evident signs that some of the ascetics' virtuosity exceeded their virtues. "Show me the money and I'll show you the motive" could be a legitimate comment on much of the "spirituality industry" – equally in Canada as in India. At times, more charlatans than genuine saints seem lined up to feed spiritual need.

But the presence of "defilement" and "impurity" amid the sacred are not marks against baby boomers' spiritual searches. They are beneficial cues for an enhanced understanding of reality. They remind us of the transience and perishability of all things – most especially human constructs – and of inescapable human fallibility. They serve as evidence of a mischief, even an evil and apostasy against life, which lies deep within human nature. The persistence of human imperfection – as St. Paul admitted ("I know the good, but to do the good I cannot") – assails modern self-confidence and its lofty ambitions of conquering the conditions of life. The realization that sin is inevitable is not evidence against religion but the occasion for a heightened human capacity for patience, tolerance, and forgiveness. Loving not only the good but the sin which brings it to presence confers the grace which braces all the other virtues – humility.

The Marxist assumption that the progress of history would exploit and finally defeat the egoism of individuals to produce a comity of interest and well-being is shown daily to be a myth. Freud precipitously predicted that, if a religion were purified of its neurotic consoling core, and if religion were limited to belief in a higher spiritual being whose nature and purposes are indiscernible, it would lose its hold on human interest.[11] Nietzsche's heralding of the "death of God" may continue to fascinate intellectuals immured in academic enclaves, but one of the most potent facts of the world at the beginning of the twenty-first century is the perseverance and growth of religious sensibility. In the final instance, neither revolutionary redemption, nor therapy, nor cynicism satisfy our deepest spiritual longings. We reckon from effect to cause, as science would have us do, and yet we find no cause for suffering. Perhaps we must conclude that human existence is not meant to be perfected by history.

In the face of Marx, Freud, and Nietzsche there is, as Hans Jonas once remarked, a transcendental mood to our age, one in which – as sociologist Peter Berger notes – there are important "signals of transcendence." The thought of Marx, Freud, and Nietzsche may contain the best thoughts of modernity, and their conclusions may be logically entailed by the premises ushered in by the modern era, but baby boomers, the generation quintessentially moulded by Marx, Freud, and Nietzsche, are saying "No." For many of these baby boomers, the promised land of modernity is, in fact, all vanity, vexation of spirit, and chasing after a wind. And yet, at the same time, they cannot shake modernity off, chastened by the scientific conclusion that, "We live amid a monstrous and meaningless accident, a cosmic eruption from nothing, that has occurred purely at random."[12]

Blaise Pascal, battling with the vexing paradoxes of modernity, once asked, "What is a man face to face with infinity?" His answer was, "A being suspended between the two abysses of Infinity and Nothingness."[13] The abyss, he noted, can be filled with ennui and diversion, and moderns are particularly adept at *divertissement* – creating endless language games and political scenarios to manage existential predicaments, while diverting reason from attunement to the true order of being. Naturalistic explanations of existence which deny the reality of transcendence but then ascribe transcendence to history, nature, and self are impugned by Pascal's charge. But can we really know there is a true order of being, a transcendent God?

Pascal's thought continues: As a consequence of the Fall, God withdrew from man and hid Himself. If there is a God, He is infinitely incomprehensible, and so we cannot know who He is. God is or is not, and reason will not present us with the right answer. In these circumstances, we have no option but to wager and believe He is. If we win, we win everything and it has paid us to believe. If we lose, we lose nothing. We cannot be certain that religion is true, but we cannot dare to say it is not possible. The laws of probability lead us to wager on the uncertain.

The baby boomers, having observed firsthand how, when God was declared dead, immanent reality was made the substitute and illusory ground of existence, are, perchance, ideally positioned to accept Pascal's wager – to mount an experiential recovery of the divine ground of being, and to reclaim transcendence. The challenge to baby boomers is whether, in risking everything for transcendence, they risk losing everything for forgetting the world they live in. The search for the indwelling god satisfies the baby boomers' taste for holism and interconnectedness – unifying, without guilt or sacrifice, the inner reality of desires, feelings, emotions, and thoughts, and enabling this spiritual core to resonate in some unexplained way with the same holism in the larger cosmos, even as the human world anomalously slips from sight. On par with today's nostrum "Think globally, act locally" in its disdain for the middle kingdom, baby boomers have produced their own profession of faith – "Be spiritual, experience the god indwelling." At its heart, the profession says to accept God but reject His world …. With one eye inward, the other up to the zenith, baby boomers are like the Laputans or inhabitants of Lagado in *Gulliver's Travels*, who have their ears tuned to hear the celestial music of the spheres, and contempt for practical geometry, yet have faith in astrology, and fear the end of the world by catastrophe. But the middle world, however inauthentic and compromised it so often is, also offers a deterrent to subjective fantasy and madness. There, by virtue of the ubiquity of human disagreement over every truth, there is a continuous need for publicly debatable evidence and commonsensical demonstration. The disappearance of the middle world leaves baby boomers in an isolated condition where, often, they are simply credulous, too willing to believe a truth promising salvation. The danger of solipsism is reinforced by many baby boomers' vow that we fall alone, and we are saved alone, and thus God does not expect corporate fellowship of us. Consonant with the baby boomers' suspicion of the "men with hats" – institutions and organizations – it must be a god who can be neither trademarked nor franchised, a god, in other words, who is uncompromised by the human world.

Baby boomers were the first generation to enjoy unmitigatedly the fruits of modernization, and refreshing liberation from centuries of dogma and taboo. And, for three decades, many baby boomers found fulfillment in the surrogates to religion which modern society offered as answers to human predicaments, and were singularly successful at these worldly enterprises. But, overcoming tradition and adopting modernity's continuous self-overcoming toward the new, baby boomers were finally left with nothing to believe in. Many baby boomers are now experiencing the truth of scripture, "What is a man profited, if he shall gain the whole world, and lose his own soul?" and "All is vanity, and vexation of spirit, and chasing after a wind." And so, as the perceptive nineteenth-century analyst of the modern world Alexis de Tocqueville predicted, a time came when individuals who had no resources outside of modern striving would seek cures for freedom's terrors.[14] The hazards in this search are the temptations to renounce liberty and find a master to tell one what to believe, or to adopt a private mysticism immune to reason's qualifications and public standards. Baby boomers graced with the experience of an epiphany, are now left with the test of how they will hallow this experience by restoring it to the world.

Nearly all faiths acknowledge the corruptibility with which we are born – "the worm that sleeps not" – and find ways of ritualizing the salutary humbling which puts paid to the dangerous hubris that causes immeasurable disorder and unhappiness. Judaism has a particularly vivid ceremony – *Sukkoth* – whose purpose offers a valuable teaching for those modern individuals who resolutely think all life can be managed and controlled. On *Sukkoth*, observant Jews commemorate the ancient Israelites' forty-year trek through the desert and their survival under adversity by leaving their own homes and building a hut in their backyards. There they must live for eight days or – at the very least – eat all their meals. The symbolic point of the exercise is to teach that ultimate protection comes only from YHWH, and that no human project can bypass reliance on Him. But the lesson is not intended to reduce humans to passivity and timidity. Another lesson comes from the requirement that the roof cannot be constructed from a man-made material, but only from YHWH's own creation – vegetation – and that it must let heavy rain through, and cause some discomfort: YHWH did not create a perfect world, He left something for

humans to do. He invites them to be partners with Him in the maintenance and renewal of creation. As a measure of how humility and realization of human imperfection may bring about positive action, one of
the many other lessons embedded in *Sukkoth* is that everyone be
responsible for one another. And, when all else fails, God gave humans
the gifts of irony and humour to withstand their own frailties and
those of others. Faith, above all, reminds us of human limits.

As I was completing this study, a baby boomer who had recently
resumed Jewish observance, and just concluded the rites of *Sukkoth*,
related a saying to me from the *Ethics of the Fathers* – germane not only
to *Sukkoth* itself, but to the tentative steps of baby boomers' spiritual
searches in general. It seemed, too, a fitting way to end this book. "It was
not granted you to complete the task," Rabbi Tarfon writes, "and yet
you are not free to desist from it either." In the adventure of transcendence, we cannot go back; we can only go forward into the unknown.

# Acknowledgements

W ords of thanks seem insufficient in expressing gratitude for the hundreds of conversations which preceded and accompanied the writing of this book. I wish to thank in particular the gracious patience of the individuals I interviewed, who endured my prying into private parts of their lives, and who opened up their homes and treasured places to a stranger. And, without the gratuitously charitable impulse of dozens of spiritual directors, I would never have been able to undertake the participant observations that form the core of this study.

Many years of rich friendship with Timothy Fuller, Barry Cooper, Tom Darby, and David Goa matured my understanding of religious consciousness, and of the complex contemporary world on which spiritual longing wishes to leave its mark. These mentors taught me a vocabulary and a habit of thought. But their advice over the years also served as an *aide-mémoire*, giving structure to the experiences of faith my parents had lovingly arranged while I was growing up.

My indefatigable and endearing researcher, Michel Charron, was a constant companion in the formation of this book. His ardent faith and openness to the polyphony of revelatory traditions translated into a discerning eye capable of recognizing shades of meaning which I, without his advice, might easily have neglected. At various times, Kristofer Liljefors, Meredith Byer-Alldridge, Samantha Copeland, Yumi Webster, and Robert Sibley made valuable research contributions. A very spirited class of students I taught at Colorado College in the spring of 1999 provided me with confirmation that the arguments I was tentatively exploring had some explanatory power. The intrepid investigative journalism skills, not to say generous spirit, of John Stackhouse made a lasting impression on me.

Above all, I owe a vast debt to my wife, Cheryl, who – apart from enduring the tiresome traits of a writer caught up in an inner world of thought – evokes in me the wonder which Plato says is the beginning of the desire to know the beautiful and the good.

PETER EMBERLEY

# Endnotes

........................................................................................................

## Faith and Modernity

1    Edward Shils, *Tradition* (Chicago: University of Chicago Press, 1981), p. 31.

2    Mircea Eliade, *Patterns in Comparative Religion*, (New York: Sheed and Ward, 1958), p. 261.

3    As cited in Huston Smith, *Forgotten Truth: The Primordial Tradition* (New York: Harper & Row, 1976), p. 17.

4    Rudolf Bultmann, *The History of the Synoptic Tradition* (New York: Harper & Row, 1968) and *Jesus and the Word* (New York: Charles Scribner's Sons, 1934).

5    Reginald Wayne Bibby, *Unknown Gods: The Ongoing Story of Religion in Canada* (Toronto: Stoddart, 1993). See also his earlier *Fragmented Gods: The Poverty and Potential of Religion in Canada* (Toronto: Irwin, 1987).

6    As reported in Bob Harvey, "Church keeps us happy: survey," *Ottawa Citizen*, September 16, 1998, p. A5.

7    As reported in Bob Harvey, "Why we're not going to church," *Ottawa Citizen*, July 19, 1998, p. B1–2.

8    As quoted in Peter Berger, *The Heretical Imperative: Contemporary Possibilities of Religious Affirmation* (New York: Anchor, 1979), p. 65.

9    Reginald Bibby, *The Bibby Report: Social Trends Canadian Style* (Toronto: Stoddart, 1995).

10    Josef Pieper, *Leisure: The Basis of Culture* (New York: Pantheon, 1952), p. 49.

11    In his thought-provoking historical study of the baby boomers, Doug Owram aptly concludes that they suffer from a "Peter Pan Complex." I have attempted to supply some of the philosophical contexts for this conclusion. Doug Owram, *Born at the Right Time: A History of the Baby-Boom Generation* (Toronto: University of Toronto Press, 1996).

12    A very fine literature, to which I am indebted for re-awakening my own

memories, offers evidence of the uniqueness of this perspective. See François Ricard, *The Lyric Generation: The Life and Times of the Baby Boomers*, translated by Donald Winkler, (Toronto: Stoddart, 1994), Doug Owram, *Born at the Right Time: A History of the Baby-Boom Generation*, (Toronto: University of Toronto Press, 1996), and Wade Clark Roofe, *A Generation of Seekers: The Spiritual Journeys of the Baby Boom Generation* (San Francisco: HarperSanFrancisco, 1993).

13    See François Ricard, who uses Milan Kundera's metaphor of the "unbearable lightness of being" to describe the same phenomenon. I explored this theme, to some extent, in my book *Values, Education and Technology: The Ideology of Dispossession* (Toronto: University of Toronto Press, 1995.)

14    Immediately, I have to acknowledge that the very enterprise I am undertaking will seem to many readers deeply problematic. First, there is the questionable practice of typifying an entire generation. Second, there is the arbitrariness of identifying some spiritual searches and experiments as paradigmatic when the obvious observable phenomenon is religious pluralism. Third, there is a danger of insisting on a grand unifying theory, and thus losing a subtle discernment of details and differences. Permit me to acknowledge these problems while formulating some justification for the use of concepts like "baby-boom generation," "spiritual searches," and "modernity" to forestall the exasperation – perhaps even solicit the forbearance – of the reader.

To be sure, unless one is being rhetorical, there is ordinarily no such thing as a homogeneous generation. Indeed, a "generation" is most often an arbitrary age cohort aggregated together to serve some didactic purpose. A writer's conclusions thus run the risk of imitating the action of Jack Horner, who "stuck in his thumb, and pulled out a plum, and said, 'what a good boy am I!'" As Edward Shils warns, "It requires a polemical ideal to create a generation out of these parallel, overlapping *trottoirs roulants* of passage through time" (as cited in Owram, *Born at the Right Time*, p. 16). While the warning is appropriate to all so-called "generations," it is particularly incongruous to portray the baby boomers as a single generation when, especially for this generation, a self-chosen unique identity was the hallmark of virtue.

Nonetheless, a few factors distinguish the age cohort born between 1946 and 1964 which, in my judgment, justify the use of the term "generation." First, the baby-boom generation was the first age cohort after the most cataclysmic events of the century, if not the millennium. Indeed, a major historical disruption, followed by the need to reassess the conditions of existence, is precisely the necessary condition the sociologist Karl Mannheim identifies as permitting researchers to treat an age cohort as a "generation" with some legitimacy. "We shall therefore speak of generation as an actuality," he wrote, "only where a concrete bond is created between members of a generation by their being exposed to the social and intellectual symptoms of a process of dynamic destabilization." Most of the young European women and men who fled from their homes to the New World of Australia, New Zealand, the United States, and Canada (the only countries where the "baby boom" occurred), and the veterans who returned less as conquerors than unwilling observers of mass destruction, brought with them little more than the terrible conviction that the Holocaust signified the culmination and collapse of the old European order and civilization. A new beginning – a new order – was imperative, and having children was one way of expressing the need to turn a corner. Not surprisingly, "baby boomers" were brought up thinking of themselves as a generation with a redemptive mission.

Second, the post-war years were marked by dramatic economic expansion, with the introduction of efficient new mass technologies, changes in corporate organization, increases in productivity, and an emerging synergy of all levels of industrial and social life. With more expendable income, there was more consumption, and, inevitably, much of the material reward came the way of the baby boomers. Whether it was television, toys, music, food, or techniques of child care and pedagogy, an emerging mass society pushed a manufactured homogeneity on the baby boomers, conferring on them commonalities of experience and expectation that gradually extinguished the meaningful differences of race, class, culture, gender, religion, and region. Generational solidarity was inevitable. So, while it is true that the baby boomers were especially urged to develop their unique selves and personalities, the effective result, paradoxically, was that many baby boomers were "different" all in the same way and all at the same time, victims of a more insidious process of social homogenization than the old order of social ranks and privileges had ever achieved.

And, third, just as the forces of production and consumption since the late 1940s privileged each phase of the life cycle of the baby boomer, so too have cultural, political, and intellectual trends nearly exclusively mirrored the preoccupations and capabilities of that generation. The major characters, plots, and themes of major books, films, and dramas in the last four decades reflect the lives of the baby boomers. The politics of health care, social security, the national debt, access to education, abortion, and euthanasia, and even the environment, gender, and race have all unfolded neatly in alignment with the needs and tastes of the baby boomers. The primary economic indicators, from productivity, to debt per capita, to the consumer index, key in to the largest bulge of the population – baby boomers. The modern sciences of dietary requirement, psychological need, and gerontology, to name only a few, all emerged as important when baby boomers found them to be so. From childhood to maturity, the baby boomers have found a nearly perfect congruence between the world and their idea of it. The baby boomers can say, with some legitimacy, "We are the world," for very little of the world – or at least the world they see – fails to mirror all that they are.

Now, to be sure, biology and socialization are not destiny, for neither can exhaust the potentiality of an individual. It is always a given, as Hannah Arendt points out, for a person to think and act independently. Appropriate to this sentiment, let me clarify that in this work, when speaking of the "baby-boom generation," I mean a family resemblance, not an undifferentiated identity. There are eight million different baby boomers in Canada, but there are also some profound commonalities found in the vast proportion of the generation. They share not merely a demographic bulge, but a mythology formed in the heady decade bookended by two charged events – the 1963 assassination of John F. Kennedy and the 1973 oil embargo.

15   Peter Berger, p. xi.

16   Still the best work on the complex relationship between the modern age and tradition is Edward Shils. However, for an equally nuanced assessment, see Hans Blumenberg, *The Legitimacy of the Modern Age*, translated by Robert M. Wallace (Cambridge: M I T Press, 1983). Another very fine analysis of the modern age is Charles Taylor, *Sources of the Self: The Making of Modern Identity* (Cambridge: Harvard University Press, 1989). I have been guided by these three writers, among others.

## Traditionalism I

1   As cited in Bob Harvey, "Graham prays for renewal of faith," *Ottawa Citizen*, June 24, 1998, p. A1.

2   *Ibid.*, p. A2.

3   *The Varieties of Religious Experience* was first published in 1902 and has remained in print ever since.

4   St. Augustine, *Confessions* (Harmondsworth: Penguin, 1968), p. 170.

5   William James, *The Varieties of Religious Experience* (New York: New American Library, 1958), p. 187.

6   The belief that true faith is experienced not by the worldly learned but by those who are like children is held equally in Western and Eastern thought. Compare

Paul's Letter to the Philippians 2:14, and the Kena Upanishad: "[The *atman*]
comes to the thought of those who know him beyond thought, not to those
who imagine he can be attained by thought: he is unknown to the learned and
known to the simple." *The Upanishads*, translated by Juan Mascaro (London:
Penguin, 1965), p. 52.

7    The Greek is *apophasis* meaning "to speak away from," while *kataphasis* means
"to speak toward (or through)." A distinction is often drawn in religious literature between the way of negation (apophatic revelation) and the way of affirmation (kataphatic revelation).

8    Charles Enman, "Graham: simple solutions," *Ottawa Citizen*, June 27, 1998,
p. A2.

9    "Spiritual tourist" is Mick Brown's apt term. See *The Spiritual Tourist: A Personal
Odyssey Through the Outer Reaches of Belief* (London: Bloomsbury, 1998).

10    Joseph Tracy, *A History of the Revival of Religion in the Time of Edwards and
Whitefield* (Edinburgh: Banner of Truth, 1997), R.L. Bushman, ed. *The Great
Awakening* (Chapel Hill: University of North Carolina Press, 1989).

11    Blaise Pascal, Pensées 89, transl. by H.F. Steward.

12    Mircea Eliade, p. 261.

13    Or, as the Valentinian Gnostics put it: "What liberates is the knowledge of who
we were, what we have become; where we were, wherein we have been thrown;
whereto we speed, wherefrom we are redeemed; what birth is, and what rebirth,"
to which the Orthodox response was, "Whosoever speculated on these four
things, it were better for him if he had not come into the world." From *Exc.
Theod.* 78.2, as cited in Hans Jonas, p. 45.

14    Michel Foucault, *Discipline and Punish* (New York: Vintage, 1979).

15    *Time* reports that its assets are midway between those of Nike and The Gap. See
"Thy Kingdom Come," *Time*, August 4, 1997, pp. 50–57. See also Brigham Y. Card,
Herbert C. Northcott, John E. Foster, Howard Palmer, George K. Jarvis, eds. *The
Mormon Presence in Canada* (Edmonton: University of Alberta Press, 1990).

16    During an interview on *On the Arts*, CBC Newsworld, September 24, 1998.

17    Of course, Mormons are not alone in anticipating the apocalypse. Fifty-seven
per cent of mainline Protestants believe that the age of the New Testament is
coming to an end, in the imminence of the last days, the Rapture – where the
faithful are miraculously removed from earth to meet Christ, safe in heaven
from the bloody Armageddon laying waste to the world – and the Second
Coming, in which the redeemed will return with their Saviour to establish His
kingdom in Israel.

18    Jaroslav Pelikan, *The Vindication of Tradition*, (New Haven: Yale University Press, 1984), p. 65.

19    Edmund Burke, *Reflections on the Revolution in France* (Indianapolis: Bobbs-Merrill, 1955), p. 110.


Traditionalism II

1    See Jean Baudrillard, *Simulacra and Simulation*. See also, Umberto Eco, *Travels in Hyperreality* (San Diego: Harcourt, Brace, Jovanovich, 1986).

2    In 1968, the Canadian Conference of Catholic Bishops stipulated that in matters of contraception, and in interpreting Pope Paul vi's encyclical *Humanae Vitae*, Catholics could follow the dictates of their conscience. The Society for Catholic Life and Culture persists in berating this decision. In 1999, three Catholic bishops – Roman Danylak, Colin Campbell, and Basil Filevich – began a new campaign to have the Canadian Conference of Catholic Bishops rescind the "Winnipeg Statement." An Angus Reid poll in 1993 showed 91 per cent of Canadian Catholics approved the use of contraceptives.

3    *First Things*, January 1997, p. 45.

4    Michael W. Cuneo, *The Smoke of Satan: Conservative and Traditionalist Dissent in Contemporary American Catholicism* (New York: Oxford University Press, 1997).

5    See André McNicoll, *Catholic Cults* (Toronto: Griffin House, 1982).

6    From "Facts and Questions About the Society of Saint Pius x," http://www.sspx.org/catholicfaqs.html. The Society's home page is: http://www.sspx.org. Viewed June 10, 1999.

7    Jean-Marie Barette, *The Prophecy of the Apostles of the After Times* (Montreal: Éditions Magnificat, 1988), p. 175.

8    *Questions and Answers on the Apostles of Infinite Love* (Montreal: Éditions Magnificat, 1989), p. 2.

9    Jean Vanier, *The Broken Body: Journey to Wholeness* (Toronto: Anglican Book Centre, 1988), p. 16.

10    *Ibid.*, pp. 11, 91.

11    *Ibid.*, p. 5.

12    *Ibid.*, p. 63.

13    *Ibid.*, p. 91.

14    *Ibid.*, pp. 93, 33.

15    *Ibid.*, p. 29.

16   *Ibid.*, pp. 98–9.

17   The two best studies of the Orthodox Church and the schism between the Latin and Greek churches are Timothy Ware, *The Orthodox Church* (London: Penguin, 1993), and Philip Sherrard, *The Greek East and the Latin West* (London: Oxford University Press, 1959). Others include John Meyendorff, *Byzantine Theology: Historical Trends and Doctrinal Themes* (New York: Fordham University Press, 1987), Jaroslav Pelikan, *The Christian Tradition: A History of the Development of Doctrine*, vol. 1 *The Emergence of the Catholic Tradition 100–600* (Chicago: University of Chicago Press, 1971), Vladimir Lossky, *The Mystical Theology of the Eastern Church* (New York: St. Vladimir's Seminary Press, 1997), Leonid Ouspensky and Vladimir Lossky, *The Meaning of Icons* (New York: St. Vladimir's Seminary Press, 1999), and Philip Sherrard, *The Sacred in Life and Art* (Ipswich: Golgonooza Press, 1990). A very fine work on Orthodox theology is that of Tomas Spidlik, *The Spirituality of the Christian East: A Systematic Handbook* (Kalamazoo, Michigan: Cistercian Publications, 1986).

18   Vladimir Lossky, *The Mystical Theology of the Eastern Church* (London: James Clark & Co., 1957), p. 87.

19   Jaroslav Pelikan, *Imago Dei: The Byzantine Apologia for Icons* (Princeton: Princeton University Press, 1990).

20   Bernard J. Cooke, *The Distancing of God: The Ambiguity of Symbol in History and Theology,* (Minneapolis: Fortress, 1990).

21   From "The Orthodox Liturgy," *The Divine Liturgies of S. John Chrysostom and S. Basil the Great and The Divine Office of the Presanctified Gifts* (Oxford: Oxford University Press, 1982), pp. 69–70.

22   Michael Prokurat, Alexander Golitzin and Michael D. Peterson, *Historical Dictionary of the Orthodox Church* (London: Scarecrow Press, 1996), p. 130. See also F.L. Cross (ed.), *Oxford Dictionary of the Christian Church* (London: Oxford University Press, 1974).

23   I am indebted to David Goa for this graceful formulation.

24   Timothy Ware, p. 217.

25   One of the best discussions of liturgy in the Orthodox Church is Archbishop Lazar Puhalo, *Understanding the Divine Liturgy* (*Scripture in the Liturgy*) (Dewdney, B.C.: Synaxis Press, 1996).

26   I am grateful to David Goa for extended conversations on the possibilities for community and religious life in the modern world.

27   William James, p. x.

28   William James, p. xx.

29    Simone Weil, "The Love of God and Affliction," in *Waiting on God* (London: Fount, 1977).

## Tweaking Modernity

1    "Is Jesus God? A conversation with United Church Moderator Reverend Bill Phipps," *Ottawa Citizen*, November 2, 1997, p. A7.

2    John Asling, "An Interview with Moderator-Elect Bill Phipps," as reported in the 36th General Council News, 1997, United Church home page, www.uccan.org/gc36/story17.htm

3    "Transcript of a presentation by the Right Reverend Bill Phipps, Moderator of the United Church of Canada, at a public forum held November 13, 1997, at Metropolitan United Church in London, Ontario," by Bill Phipps. The United Church of Canada, www.ucan.org, November 21, 1997. Access date September 19, 2001.

4    "An Interview with Bill Phipps," *Pamela Wallin Live*, Canadian Broadcasting Corporation, July 13, 1998.

5    "What does it mean to be a Christian?" *Cross-Country Check-up*, Canadian Broadcasting Corporation, December 21, 1997.

6    During the first centuries of Christianity's development, before there was an institutionalized church, there were many Christian sects debating the true nature of Jesus Christ. Some believed that Christ was divine, but not human. They were the Nestorians. Others believed that Christ was human, but not divine. They were Arians. Both dogmatic beliefs were distillates of complex theological reflections which continue to this day, and both persevered until the fourth-century Council of Chalcedon legislated that both views were heretical and that Christ was, at one and the same time, human and divine. The problem with the final formulation is that it can derail into two dangerous conclusions: that humans are divine, or that God's nature is limited to human need. While the Nestorian dogma seeks to forestall the first conclusion by deflating human presumption, the Arian dogma is an attempt to avoid the second conclusion and sustain the uncompromised divinity and utter transcendence of God. Phipps's "Arian" position is arguably both a more pious (if unorthodox) and potentially more salutary take on the nature of God than the conventional line taken by the *Ottawa Citizen*. It averts the hubristic presumption that any human or institution can have a monopoly on "knowing" God (dogma), while restoring human attention to the more modest, but practicable, scope of advancing justice in the world.

     Unfortunately, this subtlety was lost in the debate that ensued after Phipps's original interview. Instead of issuing in the opportunity for a nuanced conversation about the theoretical and practical options which might compete for the attention of the reflective, believing Christian, the United Church polarized into two camps. One wanted an even more radical, this-worldly idea of justice, thereby revealing – in my view – an extravagant faith in the human power to destroy evil. The other, like the Community of Concern, appealed to a restoration of tradition, though – rather like the dogmatist at the *Citizen* – that appeal to *tradition* seemed more like a call for *traditionalism*, which Jaroslav Pelikan once rightly rebuked as the dead faith of the living, rather than the living faith of the dead.

7 "Ratzinger Explains Changes," *The B.C. Catholic*, July 20–26, 1998, p. 9. The third proposition of the *professio fidei*, which discloses how comprehensive the "firm acceptance" must be, reads, "I adhere with religious submission of will and intellect to the teachings which either the Roman Pontiff or the College of Bishops enunciate when they exercise their authentic magisterium, even if they do not intend to proclaim these teachings by a definitive act."

8 Friedrich Nietzsche, *Twilight of the Idols* (Harmondsworth: Penguin, 1968), p. 40.

9 Mircea Eliade, p. 50.

10 Saint Augustine, *On Christian Doctrine* (New York: Liberal Arts, 1958).

11 Friedrich Nietzsche, *The Use and Abuse of History for Life*, translated by Adrian Collins (Indianapolis: Bobbs-Merrill, 1977), p. 41.

12 Rudolf Bultmann, *Theology of the New Testament*, 1951, *Primitive Christianity in its Contemporary Setting*, 1963.

13 Northrop Frye, *The Double Vision: Language and Meaning in Religion* (Toronto: University of Toronto Press, 1991), p. 18.

14 One of the best introductions to recent scholarly work is Marcus J. Borg, *Jesus in Contemporary Scholarship* (Valley Forge, Pennsylvania: Trinity Press International, 1994). A more technical study is William E. Arnal and Michel Desjardins (eds.), *Whose Historical Jesus?* (Waterloo: Wilfrid Laurier University Press, 1997).

15 See Burton L. Mack, *The Lost Gospel: The Book of Q and Christian Origins* (San Francisco: Harper, 1993), pp. 17, 230.

16 John P. Meir, *A Marginal Jew: Rethinking the Historical Jesus* (New York: Anchor, 2001), p. 84. See also John Dominic Crossan, *Jesus: A Revolutionary Biography* (San Francisco: HarperSanFrancisco, 1995), in which he writes that Jesus was an illiterate Jew near the bottom of the social order who agitated against "the standard political normalcies of power and privilege, hierarchy and oppression, debt foreclosure and land appropriation, imperial exploitation and colonial collaboration" (p. 136).

17    For Orthodox Jews, being holy is the ontological reality of increased participation in divine holiness.

18    From an email exchange between Crossan, Borg, and Johnson, February 27, 1996, posted on the Web.

19    Svend Robinson subsequently did an about-face and tabled a petition affirming the Lord's supremacy, capitulating to constituents in his riding opposed to the Humanist Association's position.

20    As reported in Bob Harvey, "Anti-God petition mocked in Commons: Bid to remove deity from Charter fizzles," *Ottawa Citizen,* June 9, 1999, p. A4.

21    As reported in Bob Harvey, "Canada becoming God-less," *Ottawa Citizen,* June 6, 1999, p. A1.

22    *Ottawa Citizen,* June 12, 1999, p. A4

23    "Ask the Experts," *Ottawa Citizen,* July 24, 1999, p. E11.

24    Alexis de Tocqueville, *Democracy in America* (New York: Vintage, 1990), Part II, ch. 5.

25    Or, as Rabbi Hillel observes in the Talmud: "What is hateful to you, do not do to your neighbour. That is the entire Law; all the rest is commentary" (Shabbath 31a).

26    Peter Berger, *The Homeless Mind: Modernization and Consciousness* (New York: Random House, 1973).

27    An infinitely more nuanced approach, and one which in my mind answers the question, "Why should Canada's baby boomers care about religion and the history of Christianity?" was taken by Alexis de Tocqueville:

> There is hardly any human action, however private it may be, which does not result from some very general conception men have of God, of His relations with the human race, of the nature of their soul, and of their duties to their fellows. Nothing can prevent such ideas from being the common spring from which all else originates. It is therefore of immense importance to men to have fixed ideas about God, their souls, and their duties toward their Creator and their fellows, for doubt about these first principles would leave all their actions to chance and condemn them, more or less, to anarchy and impotence.
>
> When a people's religion is destroyed, doubt invades the highest faculties of the mind and half paralyses all the rest. Each man gets into the way of having nothing but confused and changing notions about the matters of greatest importance to himself and his fellows. Opinions are ill-defended or abandoned, and in despair of solving unaided the greatest problems of human destiny, men ignobly give up thinking about them. Such a state

inevitably enervates the soul, and relaxing the springs of the will, prepares a people for bondage. When there is no authority in religion or politics, men are soon frightened by the limitless independence with which they are faced. They are worried and worn out by the constant restlessness of everything. With everything on the move in the realm of the mind, they want the material order at least to be firm and stable, and as they cannot accept their ancient beliefs again, they hand themselves over to a master.

The soul has needs which must be satisfied. Whatever pains are taken to distract it from itself, it soon grows bored, restless, and anxious amid the pleasures of the senses. If ever the thoughts of the great majority came to be concentrated solely on the search for material blessings, one can anticipate that there would be a colossal reaction in the souls of men. They would distractedly launch out into the world of spirits for fear of being held too tightly bound by the body's fetters. It is therefore no cause for astonishment that in a society thinking about nothing but the world a few individuals should want to look at nothing but heaven. I should be surprised if, among a people uniquely preoccupied with prosperity, mysticism did not soon make progress. (Alexis de Tocqueville, *Democracy in America*, Part 11, chapter 5.)

28 As cited in the *Ottawa Citizen*, Monday, March 11, 1999, p. A3.

29 *Ibid.*

30 "We apologize [to homosexuals] for any sense of rejection that has occurred … we pledge that we will continue to reflect, pray, and work for your full inclusion in the life of the Church." As reported in Letters to the Editor, *Ottawa Citizen*, August 13, 1998, p. A16.

31 "Love your enemies, do good to them which hate you, bless them that curse you, and pray for them which despitefully use you. And unto him that smiteth thee on the one cheek, offer also the other; and him that taketh away thy cloak, forbid not to take thy coat also" (Luke 6:27–29).

32 Only in 1992 did Pope John Paul 11 admit that the Church was wrong in condemning Galileo in 1633 for saying the earth moves around the sun, and he conceded in 1996 that Darwin's theory of evolution may be more than just a hypothesis.

33 Michael Ingham, *Mansions of the Spirit: The Gospel in a Multi-Faith World* (Toronto: Anglican Book Centre, 1997).

34 See "Why Jesus wasn't mentioned in the Swissair service," Lois M. Wilson, senator and former Moderator of the United Church, *Globe and Mail*, Friday, January 22, 1999, p. A17.

35  A discussion paper prepared by the National Task Group on United Church–Jewish Relations, February 1998. See also www.jcrelations.com

36  An account was aired in "Voluntary Simplicity," CBC, *Ideas*, June 22, 1998.

37  Catholics of Vision: Canada, *A Message to the Canadian Catholic Bishops*, August 28, 1997, http://astro.temple.edu/~arcc/english2.htm. They were demanding that the Church grant primacy of conscience in all moral decision-making to individuals, open all Church ministries to the gifts of the faithful, reverse the censuring of Hans Küng, Andre Guindon, Leonardo Boff, and other critics of the Church, permit dioceses to select their own bishop, increase ecumenical and interfaith action on behalf of social justice, non-violence, and preservation of the earth, and accede freedom from discrimination based on sexual orientation.

38  Bahá'í International Community Office of Public Information, *The Prosperity of Humankind* (Thornhill: National Spiritual Assembly of the Bahá'ís of Canada, 1995), p. 18.

39  *Ibid.*, p. 13.

40  *Ibid.*, p. 17.

41  *Ibid.*, pp. 3, 14, 18–19.

42  The Canadian Bahá'í Community Submission to the Royal Commission on Aboriginal Peoples, 1993, p. 8.

43  See "How the 'Real World' at Last Became a Myth: History of an Error," in *Twilight of the Idols*, translated by R.J. Hollingdale (London: Penguin, 1992), pp. 50–51.

44  "God is dead; but given the way of men, there may still be caves for thousands of years in which his shadow will be shown. And we – we still have to vanquish his shadow, too." Friedrich Nietzsche, *The Gay Science*, translated by Walter Kaufmann (New York: Vintage, 1974) Book III, aphorism 108, p. 167.

## Fusion Faith

1  Thomas Altizer and William Hamilton, *Radical Theology and the Death of God* (Indianapolis: Bobbs-Merrill, 1966), p. 11.

2  A body signal, I confess, I did not understand, though some Christian believers raise their hands to the heavens to signal that the Holy Spirit is moving in them.

3  Gershom G. Scholem, *Major Trends in Jewish Mysticism* (London: Thames & Hudson, 1955), p. 4.

4  "Paradox is the main tool of the mystic. It deliberately confounds logic. It appeals to wisdom's sense of ambiguity, to truth's inner simplicity. The power of paradox lies not in its rational persuasiveness but in its spiritual illumination."

Michael Ingham, *Mansions of the Spirit: The Gospel in a Multi-Faith World* (Toronto: Anglican Book Centre, 1997), p. 108. Nicholas of Cusa's words are exemplary: "The place wherein Thou dost abide is girt round with the coincidence of contradictories .... 'Tis beyond the coincidence of contradictories Thou mayest be seen and nowhere this side therefore." Nicholas of Cusa, "The Vision of God," as cited in F.C. Happold, *Mysticism: A Study and An Anthology* (London: Penguin, 1990), p. 336.

5   James Redfield, *The Celestine Prophecy: An Adventure* (New York: Warner, 1993), p. 223.

6   *Ibid.*, p. 156.

7   *Ibid.*, p. 98.

8   William James, p. 281.

9   Jerry Spears, *A Course in Miracles*, 2nd Edition (New York: Viking, 1996), p. 213.

10   Jerry Spears, *A Course in Miracles in Five Minutes* (San Diego: Associates Publishers, 1994), p. 21.

11   *Ibid.*, p. 21.

12   Jerry Spears, *A Course in Miracles*, p. 214 and "Manual for Teachers," p. 91.

13   *Ibid.*, "Workbook," p. 119.

14   *Ibid.*, "Manual for Teachers," p. 81.

15   *Ibid.*, p. 11.

16   *Ibid.*, "Manual," p. 90.

17   *Ibid.*, p. xiii.

18   Matthew Fox, *Creation Spirituality: Liberating Gifts for the Peoples of the Earth* (New York: HarperCollins, 1991), p. 9.

19   *Ibid.*, p. 10.

20   "The light I see is not spatial, but it is far, far brighter than a cloud that carries the sun ... and I call it the reflection of the living Light ... and I see, hear, and know all at once, and as if in an instant I learn what I know... And the words in this vision are not like words uttered by the mouth of man, but like a shimmering flame, or a cloud floating in a clear sky."

21   E.R. Dodds, *The Greeks and the Irrational* (Berkeley: University of California Press, 1951), p. 219.

22   St. Paul, "Letter to the Hebrews," Hebrews 11:1.

23   In the kabbalah, the ten energies are: *keter* (the divine crown), *holhmah* (wisdom), *binah* (understanding), *hesed* (mercy), *din* (justice), *tiferet* (beauty), *nezah* (eternity), *hod* (glory), *yesod* (foundation), and *ein sof* (the unknowable infinite).

24   Thich Nhat Hanh, *Living Buddha, Living Christ* (New York: Riverhead, 1995), p. xvi.

25　See Sherry Ruth Anderson and Patricia Hopkins, *The Feminine Face of God* (New York: Bantam Books, 1992); Rosemary Radofr Ruether, *Gaia and God: An Ecofeminist Theology of Earth Healing* (San Francisco: HarperSanFrancisco, 1994); Elizabeth Dodson Gray, *Sacred Dimensions of Women's Experience* (New York: Roundtable, 1988); Judith Plaskow and Carol Christ, eds. *Weaving the Visions, New Patterns in Feminist Spirituality* (San Francisco: Harper & Row, 1989); Celeste Schroeder, *In the Womb of God* (Chicago: Triumph, 1995); Naomi Goldenberg, *The Changing of the Gods* (Boston: Beacon, 1979); and Jean Shinoda Bolen, *Goddesses in Everywoman* (New York: Harper & Row, 1984).

26　Elizabeth A. Johnson, *She Who Is: The Mystery of God in Feminist Theological Discourse* (New York: Crossroad, 1998), p. 21.

27　*Ibid.*, p. 18.

28　*Ibid.*, p. 52.

29　*Ibid.*, p. 239.

30　*Ibid.*, p. 65.

31　*Ibid.*, p. 192.

32　Robert Bly, *Iron John: A Book About Men* (New York: Vintage, 1992), p. ix.

33　Robert Moore and Douglas Gillette, *King, Warrior, Magician, Lover: Rediscovering the Archetypes of the Mature Masculine* (San Francisco: HarperSanFrancisco, 1990).

34　Karl Jaspers, *Origin and Goal of History*, (New Haven: 1953).

35　Abraham Maslow, *Religions, Values and Peak Experiences* (New York: Viking, rep. 1994).

36　See Herbert Marcuse, *Eros and Civilization* (New York: Beacon, 1955).

37　Bill Clinton, the quintessential baby boomer, was described by Camille Paglia as one who is notorious for doing four things at once – watching television, reading, eating, and talking on the telephone. "He wants to suck everything up," she wrote, "have it all, cram life with every sensation and emotion … He's always behind; no day is long enough."

38　Martin Buber, "What Is Man?" in *Between Man and Man*, translated by Ronald Gregor Smith (London: Routledge & Kegan Paul, 1947) p. 202.

Turning East

1　As cited in F.C. Happold, *Mysticism: A Study and An Anthology*, (London: Penguin, 1990), p. 75.

2　Meister Eckhart, "Sermon 1," as cited in F.C. Happold, p. 278.

3    Swami Shyam, *Meet Your True Self Through Meditation* (Kullu: I M I, 1994), p. 171.

4    Ray K. Resels and Kevin Harmer (eds.), *Vision of Oneness: Talks and Discourses of Swami Shyam* (Kullu: I M I, 1996), p. 138.

5    *The Contributions of Swami Shyam to the Development of Society* (Kullu: I M I, 1998), p. 19.

6    Robert. W. Eaton, *Genesis Dawn: I Meet Myself* (Kullu: Himalchal Pradesh, self-published, 1991), p. 115.

7    Carl Jung (with Tung-Pin Lu, Richard Wilhelm, Cary F. Baynes, Hua Liu), *Commentary on The Secret of the Golden Flower: A Chinese Book of Life* (New York: Harcourt Brace, 1988), p. 31.

8    Nicholas of Cusa, p. 336.

9    As cited in F.C. Happold, p. 63.

10   *Ibid.*, p. 361.

11   *Ibid.*, p. 61.

12   *Ibid.*, p. 147.

13   *Ibid.*, p. 49.

14   Georg Feuerstein, *The Yoga Sūtra of Patañjali: A New Translation and Commentary* (Rochester, V T: Inner Traditions International, 1989), p. 11.

15   J. Krishnamurti, *The Flame of Attention* (San Francisco: Harper & Row, 1984), p. 21.

16   Ibid., pp. 24–25.

17   *Ibid.*, p. 41.

18   *Ibid.*, p. 70.

19   *Ibid.*, p. 60.

20   *Ibid.*, p. 65.

21   *Ibid.*, pp. 69–71, *in passim.*

22   *Ibid.*, p. 83.

23   *Ibid.*, p. 57.

24   *Ibid.*, p. 112.

25   However, his love may have been more venal than appearances suggested. See John Stackhouse, "Sex and the 'celibate' Swami," the *Globe and Mail*, March 3, 2001, pp. A10–11.

26   Kaushitake Upanishad, in *The Upanishads*, translated by Juan Mascaro, (London: Penguin, 1965), p. 105.

27   Alexis de Tocqueville, Part I I, ch. 12, p. 535.

28   Alexis de Tocqueville, Part I I, ch. 7, pp. 451–2.

29   See William Dalrymple, *From the Holy Mountain* (London: Flamingo, 1997).

30    This is a summary of a portion of Hans Jonas, *The Gnostic Religion: The Message of the Alien God and the Beginnings of Christianity,* 2nd edition, (Boston: Beacon, 1958).

31    I am highly indebted to the analysis of gnosticism in Hans Jonas, pp. 101–289.

32    See Peter Brown, *The Body and Society: Men, Women, and Sexual Renunciation in Early Christianity* (New York: Columbia University Press, 1988).

33    Abraham Maslow's comments are apposite: "The search for the exotic, the strange, the unusual, the uncommon has often taken the form of pilgrimages, of turning away from the world, the 'Journey to the East,' to another country or to a different religion. The great lesson from the true mystics ... that the sacred is in the ordinary, that it is to be found in one's daily life, in one's neighbours, friends, and family, in one's backyard, and that travel may be a *flight* from confronting the sacred – this lesson can be easily lost. To be looking elsewhere for miracles is to me a sure sign of ignorance that *everything* is miraculous." From *Religious Values and Peak Experiences*, pp. x–xi.

34    Northrop Frye, *The Double Vision: Language and Meaning in Religion* (Toronto: University of Toronto Press, 1991), p. 56.

## Conclusion

1    As cited in Matthew Fox, *Creation Spirituality: Liberating Gifts for the Peoples of the Earth* (San Francisco: HarperSanFrancisco, 1991), p. 30.

2    *The Upanishads,* translated by Juan Mascaro (London: Penguin, 1965), p. 49.

3    Augustine, *On Christian Doctrine,* translated by D.W. Robertson, Jr. (Indianapolis: Bobbs-Merrill, 1958), pp. 23–4.

4    As Schleiermacher writes, "In the midst of finitude to be one with the Infinite and in every moment to be eternal." *On Religion: Speeches to its Cultured Despisers* (New York: Harper, 1958), p. 101.

5    J.R.R Tolkien, "On Fairy Stories," *Tree and Leaf* (London: George Allen and Unwin, 1964), pp. 9–73.

6    See G.K. Chesterton, *Orthodoxy,* ch. 4, "The Ethics of Elfland." Friedrich Nietzsche's views on the impotence of facts also seems relevant: "A historical phenomenon, completely understood and reduced to an item of knowledge, is, in relation to the man who knows it, dead; for he has found out this madness, its injustice, its blind passion, and especially the earthly and darkened horizon that was the source of its power for history. This power has now become, for him who has recognized it, powerless; not yet, perhaps, for him who is alive." *The Use*

*and Abuse of History*, translated by Adrian Collins ( New York: Liberal Arts Press, 1957), p. 11.

7   In theology, the romantic turn would be most fully elaborated by the 18th-century theologian Friedrich Schleiermacher, whose account of the holy can still be considered the definitive statement on modern religious sensibility, having influenced the major religious writers of modernity – Jonathan Edwards, Rudolf Otto, Joachim Wach, William James, and Rudolf Bultmann, all in their own way heirs to his pietistic individualism and experientialism. Abandoning metaphysical proofs for the existence of God, Schleiermacher focused his analysis of religion exclusively on "the phenomenon of piety in human nature." He distinguishes piety from "knowing" and "doing," in favour of "feeling" or "immediate self-consciousness" of the divine, and places religious experience firmly within the realm of human subjectivity and personal experience. Schleiermacher's innovation has the merit of putting spirituality outside the reach of modern skeptical reason which abjured acknowledging any phenomena outside of mechanistic and instrumental objective reality. For Schleiermacher, our moods of contraction and expansion, dread and submission, and peace and freedom are subjectively real, and they inspire true inward feelings of the divine. The unities and relationships of which philosophical reason and nature deny us knowledge, poetic sentiment and mysticism allow us to experience.

8   Eric Voegelin, *Political Religions*. Translated by T.J. DiNapoli and E.S. Easterly III. (Lewiston, NY: E. Mellen Press, 1986), p. 59.

9   G.K. Chesterton, *Orthodoxy* (London: Bradford and Dickens, 1908), p. 82.

10  Mircea Eliade, p. 261.

11  *Ibid.*, p. 89.

12  Paul Davies, *God and the New Physics* (Harmondsworth: Penguin, 1983), p. 177.

13  Blaise Pascal, *Pensées*, translated by H.F. Steward (London: Routledge & Kegan Paul, 1950).

14  See Peter Marin, *Freedom and its Discontents: Reflections on Four Decades of Moral Experience* (South Royalton, VT: Steerforth Press, 1998).

# Permissions

# Index

Adams, Michael, 49
Age of Kali, 250
alchemy, 51, 213
Alpha Program, 14, 179–83
altars, 68,163, 198
androgyny, 187
angels, 8, 150–1
Anglican Church, 46, 79–81, 183, 187
Anglican Prayerbook Society, 9, 79–81,
    137
Anselm, 93
anti-Christianity, 33, 133–5
anti-modernism, 38–41, 141–2
anti-worldliness, 15, 34–6, 38–41, 60–2,
    77–8, 95, 153–5, 224, 236–44, 264
apology-industry, 131–2
apophatic revelation, 35, 218–9, 232–3
apocalypticism, 27, 30, 32, 35, 63,
    73–4,116–7, 121–2, 145, 153, 161
Apostles of Infinite Love, 72–5
Arianism, 84, 87, 106–7, 276–7
Aquinas, Thomas, 11, 86, 234–5
Arendt, Hannah, 5
Aristotle, 86
asceticism, 5, 239

ashram, 204, 232, 240
Athanasius, 106
*atman*, 220, 232
Augustine, 34, 84, 86, 103, 104, 108, 119,
    235, 252, 260, 272, 277, 284
authenticity, 79, 110

Baba Haridass, 8, 64, 191–3
babyboomers, 10–11, 14–21, 31, 48–9,
    60–1, 74–5, 79, 96–7, 141–3, 153, 160,
    171–2, 196–202, 243–4, 246, 248–6,
    270–2
Bahá'í, 143–5
Baudelaire, Charles, 37
Baudrillard, Jean, 66
beatitude, 231
Berger, Peter, 21–2, 112, 129, 197, 263, 269,
    278
Bibby, Reginald, 10, 12, 22, 269
*Black Elk Speaks*, 51, 94
Bloom, Harold, 56
Bly, Robert, 190–1, 282
Bonaventure, 142, 167–8
Book of Job, 219
Borg, Marcus J., 116, 120, 277

breath, 51, 189, 221
Buber, Martin, 173, 201, 282
Buddhism, 8, 174–5
Bulka, Reuven, 124–5, 128–9
Bultmann, Rudolf, 6, 110–11, 251, 269, 277
Burke, Edmund, 65, 374

caesaropapism, 74
Calvin, John, 33
Campus Crusade for Christ, 80
*Canadian Charter of Rights and Free-doms*, 123–7
Canadian Conference of Catholic Bishops, 274
Catholics of Vision, 142
*Celestine Prophecy*, 153–6, 177
celibacy, 69, 81, 206, 217
Cervantes, Miguel de, 255–7
channelling, 150, 157
chanting, 89
charity, 46, 60, 69, 72, 79, 104, 108, 120, 134, 140, 155
Chesterton, G.K., 253
Clinton, Bill, 282
community, 102, 108, 201
compassion, 100, 129, 189
conservative Christianity, 41–2, 90
conversion, 26, 86
Council of Florence, 122
Council of Nicea, 87, 106
Council of Trent, 67
counterculture, 20, 36–7
counter-Reformation, 67
Course in Miracles, 156–61
covenant, 242
covenantal community, 56, 89, 173, 196, 201, 260
creation spirituality, 161

Crossan, John Dominic, 117
Cuneo, Michael, 69
Curle, Clint, 124, 129

*darshan*, 47
data, 10–12, 22–3, 28
Day, Stockwell, 34
Debord, Guy, 48
*deosis*, 82, 86, 88, 90, 168
Dionysius the Areopagite, 219, 232
discernment, 97, 169
disestablishment, 140–1
doceticism, 84, 169
Donatist, 196, 235
Don Quixote, 255–7
drumming, 9, 50–1, 191
Dylan, Bob, 39

early Christianity, 5, 13–14, 49, 178–9, 196–7, 276–7
Eastern Orthodoxy, 8–9, 81–92, 168–9, 275
ecological spirituality, 90, 190
ecumenicism, 68, 71, 80, 135–41
Eliade, Mircea, 4, 55, 107, 185–6, 262, 269
Eliot, T.S., 133–4
endowment ceremony, 58–9
Enlightenment, 246
eschatology, 116, 121–2
evangelism, 31, 33, 35, 61
evil, 98, 104, 127, 165
existentialism, 110–11

faith, 135, 172, 238–9, 266
Farrakhan, Louis, 190
fideism, 110, 172, 250
fifty monkeys, 159, 215, 244
*filioque* clause, 86–88
Fiorenza, Elisabeth Schussler, 117

forgiveness, 127, 157, 159, 131
Foucault, Michel, 59, 212, 273
Fox, Matthew, 161, 284
freedom, 37, 97
Freud, Sigmund, 36, 97–8, 262–3
Frye, Northrop, 111, 277, 284
functionalism, 120, 160

Gaia, 188
general will, 125–7
glossolalia, 45, 128, 151
gnosticism, 59, 74–9, 88, 90, 122, 149,
    153–6, 158–9, 177, 196, 238–44, 273
golem, 169
gospels, 111–115
Graham, Billy, 9, 26–32, 41, 181
gratitude, 51, 52, 55, 91, 97, 104, 261
Great Jubilee Project, 146
Gregorian calendar, 82
Grenville, Andrew, 11
guru, 210, 228, 250

happiness, 18
Havel, Vaclav, 127
"healthy-minded" soul, 34, 156
Hebrew, 176
Hegel, G.W.F., 134
Heidegger, Martin, 110, 188–9, 224
Henderson, Paul, 24, 26, 41
Heppner, Ben, 26
heresies, 196–7
Hildegard von Bingen, 186, 233
Hindu temple, 47
Hinduism, 216–7, 233
historicism, 122–3
holiness, 44–5, 70, 71, 85, 88, 104, 167,
    197, 260
Hume, David, 224

humility, 104
Holocaust, 17, 138–9
Holy Spirit, 28, 44, 46–48, 83, 87, 89, 90,
    180, 183, 187, 251
Humanist Association, 123, 129
Hutchcraft, Ron, 25

icons, 83–5, 168
iconodulism, 168
incarnation, 84, 88, 90, 168–9
Info-Cult, 71
Ingham, Michael, 134, 184
interFaith dialogue, 136–40
Inter-Varsity Christian Fellowship, 80

Jacob's ladder, 2, 88
James, William, 34, 47, 92–3, 156–7, 170,
    253, 258, 272
Jaspers, Karl, 197, 282
Jeremiah, 250
Jesus Prayer, 91
Jesus Seminar 6–7, 105, 112–23, 127
Job, 219
John of the Cross, 197, 218–20, 232–3
Johnson, Elizabeth A., 188, 282
Jonas, Hans, 263, 273, 284
Judaism, 33, 55, 104–5, 112, 138–40, 160,
    167–9, 175–7, 206–7, 217–8, 231, 234,
    239, 242, 250, 252, 265–6, 278, 284
Jude, 198
Julian calendar, 82
justice, 102, 104, 112, 120

Kabbalah, 175–7
Kant, Immanuel, 234
kataphatic revelation, 157
kratophany, 3
*kerygma*, 111

Kerenyi, Karl, 166

Kierkegaard, Søren, 259

Kopke, Brian, 124, 129

Kosinski, Jerzy, 76

Krishna, 167

Krishnamurti, 221–2, 283

Kumbh Mela, 1–5, 261–2

labyrinth, 183–7

Lambeth Conference, 184

Lang, Andrew, 254

Lasch, Christopher, 48

Latter Day Saints (Mormons), 56–63, 273

laughter, 44, 229–30, 250–1

Lefebvre, Marcel, 71–2

leisure, 14, 59, 261

love, 97, 102, 120, 157, 227, 235, 242, 260

Luther, Martin, 32, 197

Machiavelli, Nicola, 131

Mack, Burton L., 116, 277

Mahayana Buddhists, 109

mantra, 216–7

Marcuse, Herbert, 200, 282

Maslow, Abraham, 200, 282, 284

meditation, 191

men's spirituality, 24–6, 36, 190–5

Montanists, 46

Marx, Karl, 6, 36, 95, 96–8, 262–3

Michelangelo, 230–2

miracles, 103, 157–160

misplaced concreteness, 198

modernity, 5–7, 11, 13, 16, 19, 21–2, 31–3, 55–6, 68–9, 90, 96–7, 109, 114, 118, 152, 166, 201, 240–1, 244, 246, 260

Mosaic, 136

Musil, Robert, 259

mystery, 85, 102–3, 108, 128–9, 171, 190

mysticism, 89, 152, 207, 233, 240

Nasmith, Peter, 130

national anthem, 129

Native Spirituality, 49–56

New Age, 8, 13, 148, 152, 166, 173–4

Nicholas of Cusa, 218, 281

Nietzsche, Friedrich, 36, 96–8, 107, 110, 135, 146–7, 159–60, 188, 224, 257, 263, 277, 280, 284

Nutting, Brosi, 130

oath-swearing, 130–1

obedience, 6, 20, 69–70, 81, 167, 189, 261

Opus Dei, 9, 69–71

Organ, Gerry, 25

Otto, Rudolf, 3, 46

Owram, Doug, 269–70

Pagels, Elaine, 178

paradox, 280–1

Parker, Shane, 124

Pascal, Blaise, 19, 46–7, 263–4, 273, 285

Patanjali, 221

Pathwork, 161–2

Pelikan, Jaroslav, 64

Pentecost, 48

person, 230–1, 238

Phipps, Bill, 99–108, 127–8, 131, 139, 146, 276

Pieper, Josef, 14, 164, 269

pietism, 89, 258

pipe-ceremony, 51–2, 55

Pius XI, 35

Plato, 107, 235, 242

plainchant, 168

play, 17, 48, 96, 198

Popper, Karl, 6

Poundmaker Lodge, 49–51

powwow, 51–3, 56

pragmatism, 48, 120, 160

prayer, 25–6, 91, 96, 260

pre-lapsarianism, 48, 152, 174

primordialism, 20, 48–9, 78, 97, 152, 161, 173

Promise Keepers, 9, 24–6, 137

proofs of God, 87, 93–4

Protestant Reformation, 32, 33, 107

puja, 1, 2, 168

Rabbi Tarfon, 266

Rajneesh, 109

Ratzinger, Joseph, 106–7, 277

re-birth, 50

Redfield, James, 153–6, 177, 281

Reconstructionist Jews, 110

retreats, 14

Roberts, Paul William, 178

Robinson, Svend, 123, 129, 277

Rocky Horror Picture Show, 47

Roman Catholicism, 32–3, 46, 66–72, 75, 78–9, 84–5, 89, 91, 139

romanticism, 4, 36, 173, 258, 285

Rushdoony, R.J., 32

sacramentalism, 2, 4, 33, 83–4, 88, 137, 167, 218, 233, 242–3, 251–2

saints, 85, 120

samadhi, 232

sanctification, 46, 86, 169, 201, 248

Sartre, Jean-Paul, 37

satsang, 204–5, 211, 227

Schleiermacher, Friedrich, 253–4, 258, 284–5

Scholem, Gerschom, 152, 280

Schweitzer, Albert, 113

Segal, Eliezer, 138–40

self-divinization, 156, 160

Shia Muslims, 109

Shils, Edward, 4, 269

"sick-souled religion," 34–5, 47, 156

Sikhs, 109

silence, 34, 149, 164, 221, 236, 238, 240, 249–50, 261

simulacrum, 66

Social Gospel, 105

Sophia theology, 188–9

speech, 236

Spiritfest, 148–53

spiritual disciplines, 92, 152

Stackhouse, John, 203, 208, 216, 230, 268

Strauss, David Friedrich, 113

Sukkoth, 168, 265–6

Sufism, 168, 233

Sunni Muslims, 109

Supreme Court of Canada, 130

sweatlodge, 49–51, 56, 170

Sweet, David, 25

Swift, Jonathan, 87, 234, 264

Teresa of Avila, 45, 197, 205

Tertullian, 46, 197

theology, 11, 21, 87, 92–3, 97, 101, 103, 114, 116–7, 121, 139, 179, 248

Theravada Buddhist, 109

Theseus and the Minotaur, 185

theurgy, 65, 169–70

Thich Nhat Hanh, 183, 281

Tibetan Buddhism, 174–5

Tillich, Paul, 199

Tocqueville, Alexis de, 124–6, 129, 237–8, 265, 278–9

Tolkien, J.R.R., 155, 198, 254–5, 259

Toronto Blessing, 14, 42–9

Toronto Christian Airport Fellowship, 42–9

totalitarianism, 156

Tower of Babel, 142–3, 236

tradition, 33, 41–2, 72, 91–2, 94, 98, 145, 179, 198

traditionalism, 61, 63–5, 69, 79–80, 89, 91, 94–6, 97

Transcendental Meditation, 207

tribalism, 49, 62, 95, 193

Tridentine Mass, 9, 66–8, 71–2

Tutu, Archbishop Desmond, 127

United Church Community of Concern, 9, 99, 277

Vanier, Jean 75–9, 240, 274–5

Vatican ii, 68–9

Vedantic Hinduism, 8, 217–8, 220–1

virtue, 35, 101, 104–5

Voegelin, Eric, 257, 285

voluntary simplicity, 141, 166

Wallin, Pamela, 102

Weil, Simone, 96, 142, 276

Wesley, John, 44, 171

Wiccans, 10, 187

women's spirituality, 12, 117, 144, 187–90, 193–5

workplace, 37–8

worship, 81, 86

yoga, 220–1